The Education of a Waldorf Teacher

The Education of a Waldorf Teacher

Memoirs and Reflections of

Keith Francis

iUniverse, Inc.
New York Lincoln Shanghai

The Education of a Waldorf Teacher

All Rights Reserved © 2004 by Keith C Francis

No part of this book may be reproduced or transmitted in any form or by any means, graphic, electronic, or mechanical, including photocopying, recording, taping, or by any information storage retrieval system, without the written permission of the publisher.

iUniverse, Inc.

For information address:
iUniverse, Inc.
2021 Pine Lake Road, Suite 100
Lincoln, NE 68512
www.iuniverse.com

ISBN: 0-595-30960-7

Printed in the United States of America

In loving memory of

Hubert N. Siggee
A. C. ("Bill") Paget
A. L. C. Smith
Ronny Easterbrook
Jim Kemp
A. W. ("Fishy") Walton
John Bradley
John Pryce-Jones
D. G. Williams
J. A. Ratcliffe
Harry Dawes
"Tarzan" Smith

and many others who carry some responsibility for the way my mind turned out…

…but you mustn't blame them if you don't like the result.

Contents

Author's Note xi

Chapter 1   Introduction 1
    (i) Whales, Bishops and Oysters. 1
    (ii) J-nibs and Blots 3

Chapter 2   Prehistory 5
    (i) War. 5
    (ii) Eleven-plus. 7
    (iii) Vision 8
    (iv) Choirboy 9
    (v) The Crypt. 11
    (vi) The Lab. 13
    (vii) Tarzan 14
    (viii) Masters 19
    (ix) Ashleworth 20
    (x) Light Blue. 22
    (xi) Positivism 25
    (xii) Aero-elasticity. 28
    (xiii) Poetry 32
    (xiv) Elasticity 35

Chapter 3   Becoming a Teacher, Part 1 37
    (i) Intelligence 37
    (ii) What's in a Name?. 39
    (iii) A Right-Thinking Person 41
    (iv) Student Aid 42

viii   The Education of a Waldorf Teacher

    (v) Resignation 43
    (vi) Rustication 44
    (vii) Transportation 46
    (viii) Schicksals 48

CHAPTER 4   Becoming a Teacher: Part 2 50
    (i) Pedagogy 50
    (ii) Institutionalized 51
    (iii) Farmed Out 52
    (iv) "By Schisms Rent Asunder…" 53
    (v) Manhattan 55
    (vi) Solo 56
    (vii) Enlightenment 58
    (viii) On being Wayward 60

CHAPTER 5   Becoming a Teacher: Part 3 64
    (i) Manhattan Again 64
    (ii) Geology, Occult Science and Other Digressions 66

CHAPTER 6   Becoming a Fixture 76
    (i) Pomp and Circumstance 76
    (ii) Innocence 80
    (iii) Experience 81
    (iv) MIA 85
    (v) Keeping the Peace 89

CHAPTER 7   The First Time I Left the Rudolf Steiner School . 94
    (i) Respublica, Demokratia or what? 95
    (ii) Consensus and Decision 98
    (iii) Leadership 101
    (iv) Footnotes 105

CHAPTER 8   From Harmony, From Heavenly Harmony 107
    (i) Allegro Energico 107
    (ii) Cantate Angelis Puerisque 111
    (iii) Musica Ficta 112
    (iv) Allegro Allergico 113

(v) Adagio Lamentoso 115
(vi) Come Prima or As I was saying.......................... 117

Chapter 9   Finance 118
(i) Less is Less or Who Steals My Purse Steals Trash. 118
(ii) The System... 119
(iii) Sunshine 121

Chapter 10   Being a Teacher, Part 1 123
(i) Tests and Such 123
(ii) IQ—I Question 126
(iii) The Curse of the Waldorf Schools........................ 130
(iv) Tell Me What To Do and I'll Do It........................ 134
(v) Oh, Those Intellectuals.................................. 136

Chapter 11   Being a Teacher, Part 2 141
(i) High School Teachers Wanted... 141
(ii) ...Especially in the Sciences 142
(iii) Patience and Fortitude Required......................... 144
(iv) Previous Experience Unnecessary......................... 147
(v) Imitation, Discipleship and What? 149
(vi) An Endangered Species 150
(vii) So What about the Main Lesson? 154
(viii) Less is Less—Fortunately............................... 158
(ix) It's Not Just Masochism 164
(x) Gödel, Russell and Emerson 166
(xi) Tailpiece 176

Chapter 12   A Christian School? 177
(i) Let Your Light so Shine.................................. 177
(ii) Esoteric Christianity and the College of Teachers.................. 181

Chapter 13   Epilogue 189
(i) Frankie and Johnny..................................... 189
(ii) Prognosis 192
(iii) Requiescant... 193

Endnotes... 197

Author's Note

This volume was conceived in a moment of flaming enthusiasm but it has had a long and difficult gestation. The great problem has been how to express what I have learnt in my forty years of teaching, without causing excessive offence to those who have, usually unwittingly, been my instructors, or to their friends and relatives. Colleagues who were kind and self-sacrificing enough to read earlier draughts of this volume advised me to change names, places and times or even to recast the whole thing as a *roman à clef*. Having no wish to turn my old friends and sparring partners into characters in a novel, I tried complying with the former suggestion, omitting almost all references to actual times, changing the names of places except when it served no purpose to do so, rechristening all the people who participated in my education as a Waldorf teacher and omitting several of the more depressing episodes. I realized that I had thus removed part of the appeal of a biography without substituting the possible advantages of a novelistic approach and that the result was what my mother would have called "neither he, she, nor the old woman". It also became clear that no amount of subtlety would prevent the older members of the Movement from figuring out who the principal characters really were, so, in short, I abandoned that idea and took the pruning shears to the original narrative.

◆ ◆ ◆

Anthroposophists generally agree that there is a great deal to be learnt from the study of biography, but we are usually reluctant to dig into the nitty-gritty of actual events involving real, living and breathing people or those who have fairly recently left that category. There are good reasons for this, some altruistic and some less so, such as the boomerang effect. For reasons which may become clear to the reader I don't worry very much about the latter, but I really don't want to cause distress to anyone over matters that may appear personal, so I have left out large chunks of the original narrative.

Although this approach seemed necessary it has had the unfortunate effect of defeating to some extent the original purpose of the book, which was educational and cautionary rather than biographical. The question, however, had become one of publishing either nothing or something, so I decided to adopt the half-a-loaf policy. I do not claim that this has rendered the book entirely inoffensive, only that the more serious of its remaining offences have for the most part been shifted from the realm of objective history—by which I mean blow-by-blow accounts of actual events—to more speculative anthroposophical and pedagogical regions. I'd have preferred it to be the other way around. A story is a story is a story, and people can learn what they will from it.

I have left the original introductory and editorial material intact, even though some of what it refers to has disappeared, since I'd like readers at least to get the flavor of what I was trying to do.

◆ ◆ ◆

Waldorf education as practised bears a somewhat limited resemblance to the education envisaged by Rudolf Steiner, and teachers and administrators are sometimes motivated in ways that have little to do with anthroposophy or Waldorf pedagogy. I claim no originality in making these observations, and I mention them only because I do not want anyone to be misled by the title of this volume. This is not a book about teacher training. There is no need for me to add to the number of excellent books which expound Rudolf Steiner's vision of an education based on the spiritual scientific knowledge of human development; but there is much to be learnt from the study of the many things which happen when the lofty ideals of Waldorf education incarnate imperfectly through the efforts of actual human beings and which tend to be left in obscurity by books and training courses.

Waldorf education is a form of practical anthroposophy based on a set of insights, and not a prescribed method. The fact that these insights are confirmed every day does not mean that all the applications of them will be equally successful. The converse applies too. When we experience problems it doesn't mean that there must be something wrong with Steiner's vision of the developing child. It may be, however, that even with an ideal group of teachers working under ideal conditions it would be impossible to meet all his expectations, and I don't believe that any school ever has. The first Waldorf School had formidable growing pains and internal dissensions, and Steiner died while it was still in the midst of them. Very few human institutions run smoothly for more than a year or two at a time and even angels have their disagreements. Learning about all the good things that may be expected to happen in a Waldorf School is a relatively easy matter. Coping with the way things actually turn out is more difficult.

◆   ◆   ◆

For the sake of readers who worry about things like uniformity of spelling I should explain that I always use the preferred spelling, and that I take that phrase to mean "the spelling that I prefer." Most of the unorthodox spellings are the ones that I learnt (*sic*) as a child in England at a time when we never dreamt (*sic*) that there could be different versions of our language.

K. C. F. 2003

1

Introduction

(i)

Whales, Bishops and Oysters

I am tempted to say, "Call me Ishmael." Having devoted the greater part of my life to anthroposophical work in general and to Waldorf education in particular I have become familiar with the sight of anthroposophical Ahabs pursuing Waldorfian white whales. I don't necessarily exclude myself from the Ahab category. Like the sailors of the Pequod we are all in the same boat but only a few of us can be at the helm. Unlike those unfortunate people, most of us survive somehow or other, but whether we are captains, helmsmen or just able-bodied seamen none of us comes through unscathed. You may be inclined to say "unchanged" but I'll stick to "unscathed". The real question is how to deal with your scathes.

One form of consolation that I have heard of comes from a certain Bishop of London who, lying[1] upon his deathbed, remarked that the one important thing that he had realized in his old age was that nothing really matters. Now that I am working my way through the tragi-comical region of life known as old age, where joy is tempered by experience and sorrow has a way of stealing in elusively but no less devastatingly, I can see what the old boy was driving at, although I don't altogether agree with him.

In the good old days of one's youth there was no shame in striking out on a rising fastball. There was always another game and next time around you might hit the same pitch out of the ballpark. Now if you reach first base at all it will probably be by way of a walk, but most likely you will strike out gently on a slow curve. Those youngsters may be lacking in ideals, pertinacity and all the other good qualities that you possessed when you were their age, and their natural conservatism may put your teeth on edge when you remember how you wanted, and still want, to change the world; but they sure have quick reactions. Well, old people have plenty of time to think. Maybe a quick reaction isn't needed. It's nice to have plenty of time and not to be scheduled out of existence by job and family. The trouble with old age is that it may be the best time of your life, but, as C. S. Lewis remarked, it doesn't last. Time may be plentiful on an hour to hour, day to day and even month to month basis, but somewhere up there is the terminus, and there are things that you would very much like to get done before the train pulls into the station and you switch to a different form of locomotion. It's hard to say that nothing really matters when there seems to be so much to do and so little time. I ask myself, however, whether the things that matter so much to me really matter very much to anyone else.

I have learnt a lot in the course of my life and it may be that I know things that no one else has found out, but although there are many different views of what happens when we reach the terminus I have never heard it said by anyone that we take our knowledge of this world with us anywhere when we depart. Maybe that is why some of us have a pressing desire to preserve it and make it available to others before it is too late. But the kind of knowledge that makes the memoirs of elderly people popular is not the kind that I am talking about. Eminent persons fighting their battles over again, or the obscure butlers and secretaries of the rich and famous revealing what they have overheard in the corridors and bedrooms of power, have a good shot at the best-seller list. What I have learnt about life, pedagogy, art, science, music, gardening, running and all the other things in which I have from time to time taken a passionate interest is what anyone with open eyes, ears and mind could learn. People who are interested find these things out for themselves, and one of the things that I try not to take too seriously is the fact that most people aren't particularly interested. You can read about such things in books, but if you do it is with the realization that things in books, like the things people tell you, are not necessarily true. Out of all that I have gone through there is just one thing that I want to emphasize, and that is that a great many people take themselves far too seriously, especially if they are anthroposophists. That is why I think that the Bishop had a point. Undoubtedly some things do matter, but we don't always know which ones they are, and they are probably neither the ones that seem most important at any particular time nor the ones in which we take the most pride and which give us the greatest pleasure to recount. I have arrived at the time of life at which there is a tendency to become excessively preoccupied with the past and I think that the Bishop supplied an antidote to this ailment. Whatever else the human condition may be, it is, like old age, both tragic and comical. Those of us with a melancholic tendency are more likely to spend our old age belaboring ourselves for inadequacies stretching back over more than half a century than to enjoy our last years dwelling on past achievements, and in either case the importance of seeing the funny side of things cannot be overestimated. Humor, as we say in our serious moments, is deeply therapeutic. So let's try not to take our scathes too seriously; when one of those old irritants gets a bit too annoying, just give it a good scratch by telling a story and having a hearty laugh over it. That may not be the best reason for writing these memoirs, but it is certainly a contributing factor. We are told, after all, that when an oyster produces a pearl it is merely to deal with an irritation.

It is quite possible that you will find some of these reminiscences and observations offensive, but, you know, it's just human beings behaving. These are the kinds of things that we do. If we take them too seriously it may be because we take ourselves too seriously. No offence is intended—none in the world.

◆　　　◆　　　◆

People have sometimes accused me of being cynical about the people and the institutions that you will meet if you persist in reading these pages. Cynics believe that even when people do good things they have selfish ulterior motives. My position is the exact opposite of cynicism. I think that when people do really dumb things they are usually acting out of the purest possible motives. I have done enough dumb things to be considered an expert.

(ii)

J-nibs and Blots

Most people have never seen or heard of the J-nib, that artifact of a bygone age with which millions of schoolchildren scratched the life out of billions of innocent sheets of paper. When I was a child each desk had a countersunk hole in the far right corner, an exact fit for an inkwell shaped rather like a plain Comet ice cream cone, except that the hole in the top was only just big enough to accommodate a pen. Ball-point pens had not yet been invented and village children were not expected to possess fountain pens, or, in fact, any kind of pen. The instruments with which we were to dig into both the paper and the teacher's nerves looked like small watercolor brushes, but with the ubiquitous J-nib instead of bristles. The inkwells were designed to make spillage almost impossible, so the fact that desks, floors, fingers and faces always became covered with ink says something for the resourcefulness of the English child. A few equally resourceful teachers, tired of throwing chalk and blackboard dusters at recalcitrant children, found that an inkwell made a useful missile. Some of the ink made it onto the page, sometimes in the form of writing and frequently in the form of blots. In either case another commodity was needed, namely blotting paper. Having written one's sentence one carefully blotted it. The desks of well-regulated adults were always equipped with fancy blotters, but in the classroom rectangles of pink blotting paper were given out with the pens and the paper. Cheap blotting paper, unskillfully used, was apt to cause the very calamity that it was intended to obviate, and the smeared and bleary-looking handwriting often had to be repeated.

No matter how careful we were—and most of us were not very careful—large drops of ink would descend on the page and become the means of one of life's simple and innocent pleasures. None of us had ever heard of Rorschach and his test, but we watched the blots spread out on the upper surface of the blotting paper with breathless concentration, and I can't confidently assert that all the untoward ink drops that found their way onto the paper did so fortuitously. Theoretically, I suppose, a sessile drop of ink spreading into an isotropic medium might be expected to produce a perfectly circular form, but the pink blotting paper provided invisible pathways and unexpected obstacles, so that the blot appeared to take on a protozoan life of its own. Now that blotting paper is a thing of the past, and even the sophisticated fountain pen, with its gold nib and patented hydraulic system, has a strong retro feeling about it, children seem to be left with only video games and the Internet to amuse them, and I have to give this long introduction so that I can explain that the form of these historical musings resembles that of a developing inkblot. I hope that's clear now.

2

Prehistory

I was thirty years old before my education as a Waldorf teacher began. These little tales will give you an idea of where some of the earlier blots came from.

(i)

War

"There's going to be a war", said my father one day in 1938. I was four years old and I didn't know what a war was, but my stomach turned over anyway. My father was a sawmill manager in a little village in Hampshire and he evidently didn't think we would be near enough to the action, so he took a new job in a south-coast town called Poole where our neighbors included a motor torpedo boat factory, a small port and a flying boat base. When the real war, as opposed to the "phony war", started in 1940 there were no air raid shelters, so every night when the sirens sounded my brother, my mother and I got under the living room table, while my father went off with his rescue party. The big bombs weren't intended for our somewhat rural neighborhood but a circle centered on our house with a radius of one mile would have passed neatly through each of the three main targets so we received quite a lot of accidentals. We also received more than our share of incendiary bombs. We lived in a semidetached house and one day our neighbors were going upstairs when Mrs. Thingummy said to Mr. Thingummy, "Could we always see through the roof here", and Mr. Thingummy went up to see what had happened and found an unexploded incendiary bomb in the attic. A lot of these bombs were made by forced labor in France and the workers sometimes contrived to leave something essential out of the mechanism. They also included little notes such as, "Vive la Résistance" or "Sale Bosche". Incendiary bombs were reasonably quiet, even the ones that actually went off. Most of the noise came from the heavy thuds of large anti-aircraft guns and the even more terrifying popping of the high speed Bofors guns. Luckily for us the nearest heavy bomb landed a few hundred yards away. Later in my life, when I was a Waldorf teacher and worried about what kinds of things the children were taking into their sleep, I used to remember those nights under the table.

One day we looked out and saw that an air raid shelter had been built on the village green. The construction was very simple. A wide deep trench had been dug and a very large steel tube, big enough for people to stand in, had been placed in it. The tube had then been covered with all the earth from the trench and the project had been finished off quite artistically by putting the original turves on top. A few nights previously Mr. Churchill had stated in his most characteristic tones, "We will show the enemy that we can take it." That night when the sirens sounded, instead of getting under the living room table we got dressed, stumbled though pitch darkness to the village green and descended into the dim light of the shelter. It was rather like being in a submarine, only I always imagined that submarines were rather quiet. Here the ground was shaking and the din of the bombs and anti-aircraft guns was only slightly muffled. We sat down opposite a little old lady and she looked at us and said, with tears in her quavering voice, "We can take it."

The submarine didn't hold enough people so the authorities built several brick and concrete blockhouses, known as Anderson shelters, in the Rectory grounds opposite our house. These were much darker and more dismal than the submarine and after one rather horrifying experience we decided that we would rather stay under the table at home. One night as we set off for the shelters my father called to my mother, "Have you got Keith?" My mother, being rather deaf, thought he had said, "I've got Keith." I, meanwhile, in trying to get out of the pitch black living room had walked into the angle between the door and the wall and couldn't find my way out. It was a bad night and amid the noise and the confusion of hurrying people my parents didn't notice that I was missing until they reached the shelters. My father came back and found me but it took a long time. I was still behind the door and had taken up the position known to our elementary school gym teacher as "as small as possible." One reason why I remember this event so vividly is that the experience felt just like dreams that I had already had and was to have many times again.

A little later someone, presumably Mr. Herbert Morrison, had a much better idea. The Morrison shelter was made out of heavy sheet metal and castings, and functioned as a very large living room table with detachable wire mesh sides. We kept some bottles of water in it and were confident that we would be able to survive under it for days until the rescue party came to dig us out from under the ruins of our house. The most important thing about the Morrison shelter, however, was that it made an excellent ping-pong table.

By the time the war had reached the point dubbed "The End of the Beginning" by Mr. Churchill, I was old enough to follow the progress of the armies on the maps that appeared every day in the papers, and the fear of waking up to the sound of jack-boots on the village street had begun to recede. When the spring rolled around in 1944 I had stopped hunting for shrapnel in the streets and, although London, Coventry and Southampton lay in ruins, life in our village must have looked almost normal to anyone who did not have the task of finding food and clothing for a growing family. In May of that year, at the age of ten, I was sent off on my bicycle to take the eleven-plus exam.

(ii)

Eleven-plus

In the 1940's and '50's most educators seem to have thought that intelligence is a unitary characteristic of the human being that can be effectively measured and legitimately used to determine the course of a person's life. Intelligence was supposed to be partly inherited and partly the result of conditioning, but in what proportion was a matter of debate. The gut feeling was generally that it was mostly a matter of heredity. It was this situation that made the notorious eleven-plus exam possible. This was administered in the spring to all elementary school children who had reached the age of eleven during the current school year. Elementary school teachers were allowed to send slightly younger children if they thought fit, or if they felt that they would prefer not to see a certain child again the following year. I'm not sure why they sent me.

In most school districts the top fifteen percent or so were admitted to grammar schools and placed in A, B and C streams according to what was believed to be their intelligence. The rest were divided between technical schools and secondary modern schools. The eleven plus was a momentous event in the life of the child since, with few exceptions, grammar school provided the only path to higher education or, failing that, to respectable clerical work in banks, insurance companies and solicitors' offices. "No one 'fails' the eleven-plus", government officials proudly proclaimed. "The test simply places you in the kind of school most suited to your age, attainments and aptitude." The facts of life, however, spoke otherwise, most loudly at the poorly equipped, understaffed and overcrowded secondary modern schools.

Not many children from our village were admitted to Poole Grammar School, hereinafter referred to as PGS, so those who were, and who went off to school every day in their conspicuous green and yellow blazers, were subjected to a great deal of inverted snobbery in the form of taunting and catcalls. Having indulged in some of this behavior in earlier years I was somewhat nonplussed—or should I say "eleven-plussed"?—to discover a few weeks after the test that I was *en route* to the grammar school and would have to change my tune.

I wasn't very happy at PGS. For one thing, we had to share the building with a school from Southampton, which meant that we worked very odd hours and weren't allowed to keep anything in our desks. Every morning we had to try to remember what lessons we would have and pack all the necessary books and equipment in our satchels. I was very forgetful and the teachers always seemed to be angry. In retrospect it seems to me that I encountered most of the bad things that are popularly associated with English school life. Schoolboys, as has often been observed, can be very cruel. Fate had somehow designed a few of my classmates as obvious victims, *gauche* and slow-witted, and they suffered inordinately not only at the hands of the bullies and their hangers on, but also under the lash of sarcasm from the masters. I was not victimized in this way but although I can't claim any moral superiority I did find the situation very distressing. I was, in fact, scared most of the time. I found the work very difficult, the masters unyielding and the social life of the class mystifying.

(iii)

Vision

One day in a chemistry lesson the boy next to me put down his glasses on the workbench. I picked them up, looked through them at the blackboard and had an experience somewhat analogous to that of St. Paul when the scales fell from his eyes. It turned out that I was quite shortsighted and that I had spent the first twelve years of my life not being able to see properly. I remember that the pictures at the local cinema always looked blurred and that I had to copy my chemistry notes from the boy next to me instead of from the blackboard, but I don't remember how I explained this to myself. The lab was a problem since a boy in the middle of the room was about fifty feet from the board. I think that I knew that other people could see better than I could, and one day I plucked up the courage to ask the chemistry master if I could sit in the front row, but I seem to have been under the impression that the way it was was simply the way it was. My mother used to say that our family motto was "We shall contrive", meaning that we could always find a way of co-existing with prevailing conditions.

A few weeks after my discovery I was fitted with glasses and suddenly became a much better student. Nobody seemed to be very pleased, however. People were generally rather annoyed with me for not having said anything sooner. My parents couldn't really afford to buy glasses for me, and I lived in constant fear of losing them.

(iv)

Choirboy

One day in July of 1945 a schoolboy wandered out of his home on Blandford Road, turned down Albert Avenue, still pock-marked by a string of incendiary bombs, avoided Victoria Crescent, where the slightly more well-to-do lived, crossed the railway lines on which small tank engines shunted undistinguished goods waggons, and entered the public park. The greatest attraction of the park was that it bordered Poole Harbour, and, now that the flying boats and other signs of war had gone, the beach and the water and the views of Purbeck and Brownsea were sources of endless delight. On this particular day, however, there was an unexpected and even more intense experience awaiting the boy. As he crossed the lines he heard music and saw that there was a crowd of people round the bandstand. Worming his way through the crowd he saw bright red and yellow uniforms and gleaming golden instruments, whose sounds filled his whole being with ecstasy. His face broke into a smile so uncontrollably broad that his cheeks began to ache and he wondered if people would stare at him; but he was standing close to the great grunting tubas and the smile wouldn't go away.

◆   ◆   ◆

Towards the end of the war our parish acquired a new vicar, the Reverend J. A. Kingham. Mr. Kingham was very zealous and visited almost everyone in the village to explain his vision of the future and all the good works in which we should expect to assist. We all listened respectfully and my father, as he escorted the new broom to the front door, quoted the old rhyme:

Patience and perseverance[2]
Made a Bishop of His Reverence.

Later we heard His Reverence's description of my father, *via* the grapevine: "He is a good man but he makes jokes about the church."

One of the good works accomplished by Mr. Kingham was the reinvigoration of the church choir. I became a choirboy and received the modest stipend of 4/- (four shillings) every three months. A dollar a quarter doesn't sound like much these days, but to me it was a small fortune. More important, however, was the part played by the choir in my musical education. One momentous event took place when I was ten years old.

I was standing in the living room of our home with a copy of Stainer's *Crucifixion* in my hand and it occurred to me that I ought to be able to sing my part straight from the music without having to hear it played on the organ. So I worked at it, using the hymnbook and the psalter as well, and soon became a good sight-reader. I also discovered that I could improvise harmony fluently. If you think that I exaggerate in calling these events momentous it may be because you underestimate the potential importance of music in a child's life. I may have been something of a "natural" but I believe that many children would be able to do these things if they grew up in a culture that valued the experience of music for its own sake and not merely as a pleasant background, a commercial product or a pedagogical tool.

As a ten-year-old choirboy I enjoyed Stainer's *Crucifixion* and Handel's *Messiah* equally, and was very annoyed to hear that Stainer was not regarded as a very good composer. Thanks to the BBC, however, I was hearing quite a lot of music and Chopin soon became my favorite composer. The excitement of *Fling wide the gates* and the *Hallelujah Chorus* was nothing to the physically palpable *sehnsucht* of the Chopin *Nocturnes*. Novello, who published vocal scores of all the major oratorios, used an ornate cover with the names Beethoven, Brahms, Mendelssohn, Bach, Mozart, Elgar and so on, printed in large capital letters and surrounded by curlicues. Since Chopin had not bothered to give the world any choral masterpieces he was not represented, but I did not realize that that was the reason, so I printed CHOPIN in large block capitals right in the middle of the cover of my copy of the *Crucifixion*. I managed it without blots, but the Vicar, who was also the choirmaster, was not pleased. I was demoted to the second row in the hope that no one in the congregation would notice. Over the next two or three years I developed a certain disdain for Stainer. I still loved Chopin but, like me, he had to move into the second row, and Beethoven, Tchaikovsky and Rachmaninov became the front-runners. Apart from the church choir, the local brass band and the annual performance of the *Messiah* at the Winter Gardens in Bournemouth, my only source of music was the BBC, and I must say they did me proud. I scanned the *Radio Times* every week in the hope of finding a performance of Beethoven's Fifth Symphony, Tchaikovsky's Fifth or Rachmaninov's Second Piano Concerto. It is not possible to convey the intensity of the feelings aroused in me by these works. While waiting for them to reappear I listened to everything else and endured agonies of frustration when the rest of the family rebelled and insisted on switching to *Bing Sings* or *Music While You Work* on the only radio we possessed. I got away with quite a bit, however. Sir Adrian Boult, the conductor of the BBC Symphony Orchestra, became my idol and in the course of a few years I became familiar with most of the standard repertoire from Bach to Richard Strauss. Boult conducted a great deal of more modern stuff, including, for instance, the British premiere of *Wozzeck*, but at that stage I still resented the activities of composers who, as we used to express things in those distant times, did not use a good Christian key signature. When I was fifteen my aunt gave us a gramophone that was already an antique—this was in 1949, the very beginning of the LP era. Naturally the gramophone played only 78's and it played those at a somewhat variable speed. It had to be wound up every five minutes, so I listened to my Beethoven and Tchaikovsky symphonies one side at a time. By then we had moved a long way from Mr. Kingham's orbit.

(v)

The Crypt

When the war was over, my father soon decided that he had had enough of the south coast and he took a job in a small West Country village near the city of Gloucester. Gloucester, at that time the lowest bridge point on the Severn, and dominated by its great cathedral, was in the process of transformation from a market town to an industrial sprawl. We lived in the town and I went to the Crypt School, an ancient foundation that had been taken over by the government but still retained traces of its former upper-crust status. Like my previous school, the Crypt accepted boys at the age of eleven, streamed them according to ability and prepared the cream of the crop for university entrance. The cream of the cream was sent off every December to take entrance scholarship exams at Cambridge or Oxford, and to be awarded a scholarship or even granted common entrance at one of those seats of learning was regarded as the ultimate prize by pupils and teachers alike. Meanwhile the weeding-out process had continued. Many boys left at sixteen after taking the school certificate and quite a lot more left at eighteen without managing to gain admittance to any kind of university.

In spite of the fact that the Crypt and my previous school were supposed to be doing exactly the same job under exactly the same conditions, the contrast could hardly have been greater. Exchanging the green and yellow of PGS for the primrose and claret of the Crypt turned out to be one of the most important events of my life.

My years at the Crypt may not have been not the happiest of my life, but they were the most carefree. I had become very good at my work and it is hard to imagine that I could have had a better group of teachers wherever I had been. I was in a friendly and harmonious class and England seemed to be the best place in the world. It was clear to me that all was not well either in the world as a whole or at the Crypt School, but somehow I had the good fortune to be protected from the conflicts of the world at large and from the internal struggles of my school. I was in the A-stream and so were all my close friends and most of my acquaintances. We worked and played together, talked about interesting things and committed no blatantly egregious sins. If the system had been organized with the express purpose of giving us the finest possible opportunity to learn and flourish it could not have succeeded better. For the benefit of Waldorf teachers who may suspect that we were pale and over-intellectualized, I must add that we were relaxed, rosy and healthy. We had plenty of physical exercise, a great deal of which we organized ourselves, and most of us sang in the school choir. No doubt it is to be deplored that we had no eurythmy and little art, but as a group we tended to be interested in everything and we filled in some of the gaps for ourselves. Now all of this was as wonderful as it sounds, but I was not totally unaware that it was achieved at considerable cost. Clearly the B- and C-streamers were not having anything like such a good time, and neither were the masters who taught them. The B-streamers seemed for the most part to be reasonable and likeable people, although somewhat lacking in conversation, but the C-streamers were, on the whole, sullen, scary, unkempt, uncouth and ungrammatical, and it was a relief to see them leave at the age of fifteen. If you gather from all this that there was something severely wrong with my values you may well be right. But I wish to plead that it may be too much to demand of a teenager that he should have perceived that while these observations were accurate, they reflected more the effects of the system than the innate qualities of the individuals. I was under the illusion, shared by a large part of the population, that the eleven plus test measured something real and clearly defined. Intelligence, we thought, was distributed unevenly. My friends and I were the lucky ones, but the C-streamers had been behind the door when it was given out. As for the unfortunate students at Linden Road Secondary Modern School I can only say that my imagination retreated—and still does—under the stress of trying to picture what went on in their classrooms. My quickest bicycle route to the Crypt took me right past Linden Road School, but I soon learnt to give it and its inhabitants a wide berth. We may have felt superior to them but they hated us with a passion.

(vi)

The Lab

Wandering around the Crypt on my first day I encountered a room that seemed to be oddly shaped, in that its width was greater than its length. I was very young, a mere thirteen, and I was allowed only as far as the door, where I stood and sniffed the delicate mixture of aromas, the lingering mementos of past experiments. I had no idea what was in the air at the time, but hindsight, or hind-scent, suggests the mousy smell of acetamide vying with the more aggressive pungency of sulphur dioxide and the inevitable trace of hydrogen sulphide from a leaky Kipps apparatus. I was standing in a long corridor. Behind me was a door leading to a large concrete playground and if I had looked through the windows on the far side of the room I should have seen a playing field and the lower slopes of Robinswood Hill. In spite of these attractions my attention was gripped by the contents of the room—two very large workbenches at right angles to the corridor, with sinks, gas taps and shelves of bottles with ground glass stoppers, and shelves all round the room loaded with more bottles. In front of the windows was a narrow bench with a dozen chemical balances in glass cases. Sticking my head in as far as I dared I read some of the labels of the bottles on the benches; sulphuric acid, nitric acid, hydrochloric acid, yellow ammonium sulphide, .880 ammonia. My heart leapt as high as any poet's, and the attractive force of all the wonderful chemicals and imagination-tickling pieces of apparatus dragged me willy-nilly across the threshold.

"What's your name and what do you want?"

The questions came from a large youth several years my senior who was boiling something in a retort.

"Francis, 3A", I said, too unnerved to answer the second one. I didn't really want anything; I was just looking, but that was too hard to explain.

"If you're not in the Sixth Form you're not allowed in here. It's dangerous and there isn't much space."

"Oh, I'm sorry. I'm new here."

I turned away.

"You like chemistry?" he asked.

"Yes", I said over my shoulder. I was too shy too tell him that I spent hours reading chemistry books and messing about with chemicals.

"That's good. You'll have it in the junior lab with Tarzan."

He turned back to his experiment and I resumed my walk along the corridor. I had read some of the Edgar Rice Burroughs stories and my mind simply refused to struggle with the implications of my informant's last remark.

The building was a double-decker at least three hundred feet long, and on the ground floor it housed a geography room, two chemistry labs, two physics labs, a biology lab, several classrooms, and the music, woodwork and art rooms. My confusion over the dimensions of the senior chemistry lab was due to my unconscious assumption that the long side of any classroom must be the one parallel to the corridor. Somehow the senior lab had got shortchanged in that direction. The junior lab was rectangular in the usual sense and had satisfactory quantities of chemicals, balances, benches and sinks, but somehow it lacked atmosphere. I tried to imagine what Tarzan would be like.

(vii)

Tarzan

At PGS I had been scared of most of the teachers. In those days they were known as masters and they seemed very formidable in their black academic gowns. No one, however, could possibly have been scared of Tarzan, in spite of his height and girth. He knew a lot of chemistry, he was a thoroughly nice, well-meaning person, and he let the boys run rings round him. I can't claim to have been any better than the others, but most of them were not particularly interested in chemistry, whereas I and my new friend Hoppy were devoted to it. Hoppy's parents were Plymouth Brethren, so he wasn't allowed to go to plays and movies or listen to the radio, but he did have permission to do experiments in the kitchen and he possessed a great treasure—a copy of Mellor's *Modern Inorganic Chemistry*. I also had a treasure—*Theoretical and Inorganic Chemistry* by Philbrick and Holmyard. The names mean absolutely nothing to the modern reader, even if that reader happens to be interested in chemistry, but in the 1940's these books were like bibles. Now they are like the more disregarded sections of the Old Testament—full of an ancient wisdom that nobody is interested in any more.

You might wonder what a couple of thirteen-year-olds were doing with these quite advanced textbooks. I never learnt the history of Hoppy's fascination with chemistry, but my book was a relic of my older brother's transient affair with the discipline. When he was fourteen and I was ten he bought a chemistry set and started doing little experiments and ordering chemicals and apparatus by mail from a company called A. N. Beck and Son. He had test tubes, beakers, conical flasks, glass and rubber tubing, and small brown bottles containing things like granulated zinc, copper sulphate and dilute hydrochloric acid. His enthusiasm was for a while so great that he ordered two textbooks, the aforementioned Philbrick and Holmyard and a book of practical chemistry by two gentlemen called Meerendonk and Crewe. I was transfixed and when, after a few months he moved on to fresh woods and pastures new, I inherited his scientific establishment, including the books. You might expect that I would have been more interested in the practical one, but somehow its authors' presentations lacked pizzazz and I was not too young to enjoy Holmyard's spicy literary style. (It was mostly Holmyard, Philbrick having been responsible for bringing later editions up to date.) My experimental work could have used a little of M and C's expertise but Holmyard had grabbed me. The second half of the book was a detailed survey of the elements and their compounds, which I absorbed like a sponge. The first half started with a fascinating historical introduction and continued with two hundred and fifty pages of theoretical chemistry, a much tougher proposition. My learning technique for this section was to start at the beginning and read until I got to a place where I really couldn't understand what the author was talking about. Then I would put the book aside, wait a few weeks and start again, getting a few pages further with each repetition. By the time I arrived at the Crypt I was not only familiar with the chemistry of elements that most people had never heard of, but also had more than a hundred pages of the theoretical section under my belt. I soon found that I knew everything that Tarzan wanted to teach us, and then some. Meanwhile Hoppy had immersed himself in Mellor and reached more or less the same position. I later discovered that Mellor was just as spicy as Holmyard and included such titbits as the use of sulphur dioxide by Odysseus to fumigate his home after the slaughter of the suitors.

Tarzan used to do a lot of demonstration experiments and Hoppy and I watched him like a pair of amicable cats studying a mouse.

◆   ◆   ◆

"Boys, come to the front", says Tarzan in his usual mild tones.
Nobody moves.
"Boys, *please*, come to the front."
There is an element of entreaty in his voice and most of the boys, being in fact rather good-natured, begin to stir a little. We bring our lab stools with us and eventually we are clustered around the demonstration bench. Nobody is wearing goggles, lab coats or aprons. Hoppy and I get into the front row because we want a close-up view of everything.

We have been studying oxygen and today Tarzan is showing us how to prepare it by heating a mixture of potassium chlorate and manganese dioxide. The mixture is in a large combustion tube clamped over a Bunsen burner and fitted with a glass delivery tube. Tarzan is going to collect the oxygen in gas jars, so the other end of the delivery tube is under the water in a pneumatic trough. The gas jars are like heavy, cylindrical glass tumblers with ground glass rims, and each one has a ground glass disc that fits on top. Tarzan fills several of the jars with water and covers each one with a disc. He takes one of them, inverts it over the end of the delivery tube and removes the disc, so that any bubbles coming from the tube will rise into the gas jar. After filling several jars with oxygen he intends to demonstrate some of its properties. Tarzan's technique is pretty good except when he is being distracted by the antics of small boys. He lights the burner and for a few minutes there is respectful attention. He warms the combustion tube gently at first and then gradually opens the air hole of the Bunsen burner until the flame begins to roar just a little. The temperature in the tube is perhaps 400ºC and bubbles of oxygen begin to rise into the gas jar. Tarzan fills the jar, slides the disc under it, removes it from the trough and stands it upright on the bench. Things go quite well at first. He fills a few more jars and turns off the burner. With thirty boys crowded around the demonstration bench not everyone can see very well. Those who want to see begin to jostle a bit, and those who don't find other ways of amusing themselves. Fidgeting and conversation are on the increase but Tarzan is used to that and keeps on teaching. A glowing wooden splinter is rekindled by the oxygen in one jar and in another red-hot charcoal in a deflagrating spoon bursts into brilliant crackling flame. In spite of our premature sophistication Hoppy and I enjoy the proceedings, and so do most of the other boys. But the background noise continues to grow and while Tarzan is explaining things a boy falls off his stool and the exposition is drowned in a gale of laughter. We all know that MacDonald fell off his stool deliberately, but somehow Tarzan doesn't. While he is trying to get the class settled down Hoppy and I notice that as the combustion tube is cooling down it is drawing water from the trough up the delivery tube. Will the water be sucked all the way back into the combustion tube, and if it does will the tube still be hot enough for the quick change in temperature to crack it? We are not really bad boys but we watch with awful anticipatory glee. The commotion dies down a little and when Tarzan gets his attention away from the back row his eye falls on Hoppy and me, and surprised, perhaps, by the fixity of our attention, he follows our gaze and sees what is happening. The water has almost reached the downturn in the delivery tube where it fits into the hot combustion tube. Tarzan hesitates, unable to think of any way of averting disaster. Suddenly I relent and start to say, "Light the burner again, Sir", but before the sentence is half finished the water flows into the combustion tube, there is a violent flurry of activity and an ominous crack, and the bottom half of the tube breaks off and falls to the bench. The class is quiet. We are not goody-goodies but we don't like to hit a man when he is down.

Tarzan looks at Hoppy and me; we know that he knows that we knew, but he doesn't say anything. I still feel guilty.

◆   ◆   ◆

We handled chemicals and apparatus very casually in those days, and I suppose it is a wonder that none of us joined the ranks of those who lost their health or even their lives in pursuit of the Egyptian art. Dulong lost an eye and two fingers in the process of discovering nitrogen trichloride and Ballard nearly died after being discovered by fluorine; Bunsen became seriously ill while working on the cacodyl radical and later refused to allow any work on organic chemistry to take place in his laboratory; Humphry Davy nearly killed himself investigating the effects of breathing various newly discovered gases; but we sat within a couple of feet of a large flask in which Tarzan was distilling common salt with concentrated sulphuric acid and releasing the extremely noxious hydrogen chloride gas, and we watched at close range while he showed how copper is attacked by concentrated nitric or sulphuric acid, and we breathed quantities of oxides of sulphur and nitrogen, and none of us suffered any immediate harm. When Tarzan broke a thermometer we enjoyed pushing the little globules of mercury around with our fingers. I have lost touch with all my old classmates, and I don't know how many of them have sickened and died prematurely because of chemical poisoning. I am 70 now, and disgustingly healthy, but who knows how much better I should be without those doses of poison, or when all the lingering traces of past poisonings will somehow gather together and kill me. I still nurse the hope that, like Mithridates, the ancient king of Pontus, I have gained some measure of protection. As Housman recounts the story at the end of the penultimate poem of *A Shropshire Lad*:

> There was a king reigned in the East:
> There when kings will sit to feast,
> They get their fill before they think
> Of poisoned meat and poisoned drink.
> He gathered all that springs to birth
> From the many venomed earth;
> First a little, thence to more,
> He sampled all her killing store;
> And easy, smiling, seasoned sound,
> Sate the king when healths went round.
> They put arsenic in his meat
> And stared aghast to see him eat;
> They poured strychnine in his cup
> And shook to see him drink it up:
> They shook, they stared as white's their shirt:
> Them it was their poison hurt.
> —I tell the tale that I heard told.
> Mithridates, he died old.

Housman's poem is not really about poisons but about the advantages of pessimism. "Luck's a chance", as he says, "but trouble's sure." Anthroposophists are not supposed to be pessimistic, but we are not supposed to be irrationally exuberant either. In my more sombre moments I often think of another Housman poem:

> I to my perils
> > Of cheat and charmer
> > Come clad in armour
> > > By stars benign.
> > Hope lies to mortals
> > > And most believe her,
> > > But man's deceiver
> > > > Was never mine.
>
> > The thoughts of others
> > > Were light and fleeting,
> > > Of lovers' meeting
> > > > Or luck or fame.
> > Mine were of trouble,
> > > And mine were steady,
> > > So I was ready
> > > > When trouble came.[3]

(viii)

Masters

In the course of my forty years in the teaching profession I visited many classrooms and encountered hundreds of teachers. Thinking back through five decades to my boyhood I realize how few of them could stand comparison with my teachers at the Crypt. Apart from Tarzan there was only one teacher who had disciplinary difficulties and he had been moved into the area where it was considered that he could do the least harm—religious education. This is not mere rose-hued romanticizing. Teaching is not only a matter of knowing one's subject and being able to expound it fluently while maintaining an orderly classroom. These things are par for the course and many teachers are below par. The names mean nothing to anyone who reads this, but Messrs. Easterbrook, Pryce-Jones, Walton, Dawes, Paget, Smith, Bradley, Kemp and Siggee were anything but anonymous sources of standard instruction in French, English, Latin, music, mathematics, chemistry and physics. Par was not a consideration for them—they shot birdies and eagles all the time. They had humor, funds of miscellaneous knowledge and a genius for fitting their explanations to the processes of their students' minds. In their relationships with the students there was warmth without familiarity on either side, and, unlike many of today's teachers, they all spoke excellent English. It is only fair to say that one can hardly blame today's teachers for this when so many of our public figures[4], television and radio personalities, writers, reporters and college professors are unaware of the inner logic of language and use words as if they had no particular meanings. As a boy I learnt to love the bones and muscles of the English language. We were taught all the rules, but the process was managed in such a way that in the course of time it became unnecessary to think about them. Speaking and writing good English did not become automatic, but it did become as natural as walking. "Everyone teaches English", as our headmaster, Colin Ewen, remarked. It is as well not to become complacent, however; anyone can slip on a banana peel.

(ix)

Ashleworth

In the spring of 1950, when I was sixteen, we moved from Gloucester to the village of Ashleworth and lived in a house right in the middle of the sawmill that my father managed. My bedroom looked out on a vista of cranes, heavy woodworking machinery and piles of huge logs. In the distance, beyond the sawmill, was a small round hill with a little clump of trees at the top. There was something mysterious and enticing about this hill quite apart from its resemblance to a woman's breast. The locals called it Berry Hill, which I found later to be a corruption of Barrow Hill. I don't believe that it was really a barrow, but it had an atmosphere that stayed with me, and fifty years on it still stands there plain to my imagination.

Next door to us was a factory building containing smaller saws and various machines for making specialized products for carpenters and undertakers. In a way our house was the opposite of the one where we had lived in wartime. At Ashleworth the din was tremendous and incessant from eight o'clock in the morning until half past five in the afternoon, but at any time during the night you could have heard a pin drop. It was almost ten miles from the Crypt and in another school district. I desperately wanted to stay at the Crypt, and the headmaster pulled some strings to make this possible, but I soon discovered that the only way I could get to school was by bicycle. So every school day for the next two and a half years, whatever the weather, I bicycled twenty miles over some very steep hills, and in the process became a very successful middle distance and cross-country runner.

In retrospect it seems to me that the events of the following couple of years would provide ample evidence for anyone who wished to show that the study of one's life history reveals the workings of karma. It has to be admitted, however, that the same events might be used as evidence of the workings of an orthodox benevolent God, a capricious puppeteer or an undirected universe.

After successfully taking the School Certificate exams when I was fifteen, I had entered what is known as the sixth form, where preparation for university entrance becomes really serious. Although I had thoroughly enjoyed my studies of French, Latin, history, geography and English I had never had any doubt that I would specialize in the sciences, and with eight periods a week each of chemistry, physics and mathematics I had a wonderful time. This was all in preparation for the advanced and scholarship levels of the General Certificate of Education, which I was due to take at seventeen, and the subsequent process of getting into the best possible university. After a year or so of this regime, however, I went through one of those passages of teenagery that are popularly supposed to be connected with hormone levels, and decided that I had had enough of education and that as soon as I had taken the GCE I would leave and get a job and have some money in my pocket. Nobody in my family had ever been to university—in fact nobody that I know of had ever been educated beyond the age of sixteen—and I had no real idea of what a university was like or what it might mean for the future. So I went to a factory in Gloucester which made insulating materials for all kinds of electrical products by compressing thin laminae of wood with artificial resins. They needed a lab assistant and I got the job easily enough, although they said that I was terribly over-qualified. I was due to start in the September after I took the GCE. About six months before the GCE I had more or less stopped working. I didn't copy up any science notes and did my homework as skimpily as possible. I took the exams in my three subjects and when the school year ended I had a stormy interview with the headmaster. He had plans for my future and was furious that I was leaving. His last words to me were, "Get out!"

One morning, two or three weeks later, my mother came into my bedroom with a letter in her hand. It was the middle of August and I was to start at the insulation company in another three weeks.

"Look at this", she said, "You've won a scholarship", and she read a couple of sentences of official language.

I didn't believe it at first.

"That's just a form letter that they send out to everybody", I said, defensively. I didn't want a scholarship.

"No", she insisted. "You read it."

I read it, and my heart sank. It seemed that I had accidentally won a State Scholarship, which would pay all my expenses—tuition, books, board, lodging, clothing, travel—for my undergraduate years at any approved institution of higher learning. It was the end of my hopes of becoming a man-about-Gloucester. I was trapped and I knew there was no way of getting out of it.

(x)

Light Blue

The headmaster and all my other teachers seemed quite pleased to see me back. The next stage was to persuade some appropriate institution of higher learning to accept me. For reasons which I do not understand now, and which I was not very clear about at the time, I decided that there was only one place where I wanted to go and that was Cambridge. I think it had something to do with the Boat Race and my preference for light blue. In the England I grew up in there was only one Boat Race. It was between crews from Cambridge and Oxford and it took place every year in the early spring over a four-and-a-half mile course from Putney to Mortlake on the Thames. People who had never had anything to do with either University rooted passionately for one side or the other. The BBC broadcast the race every year, and millions of people gathered round their wireless sets and for twenty minutes listened with a degree of concentration rarely available for the more important things of life. My family came from East Anglia and I was born about twenty miles from Cambridge, but I never consciously connected this with our strong commitment to the Light Blues. My Auntie Edie, who had given us the old gramophone, lived in Oxford and I had not found the place attractive. Rightly or wrongly I had seen it as a large industrial city with a university embedded in it, whereas I had an image of Cambridge as a university with a town attached to it. Getting into Cambridge or Oxford was a couple of degrees of magnitude harder than winning a State Scholarship, so I had to get down to work again, the first task being to copy up the six-month's-worth of physics and chemistry notes that I had neglected while my hormones were rearranging themselves.

The university consisted of eighteen or so colleges which were in many ways autonomous, but which were united under the aegis of a central council. As an undergraduate you slept, ate and had most of your social life at your own college, which provided you with a tutor *in loco parentis* and a Director of Studies. Most of the academic work, however, was the concern of the university as a whole. For the business of admissions the colleges had arranged themselves into small groups, administering entrance scholarship examinations in December and, in a few cases, March. The headmaster of the Crypt had been an undergraduate at Sidney Sussex, one of the smaller and less fashionable colleges. It was also one of the newer colleges, having been founded in 1596 by Lady Frances Sidney, the Dowager Marchioness of Sussex, whose greatest distinction was, if I have got my genealogies sorted out correctly, to have been the aunt of Sir Philip Sidney. The foundation cost her £5,000, so it was quite a bargain. If I had known at the time that the deplorable Oliver Cromwell had been a student at Sidney I might have acted differently, but I liked the name and I confess to thinking that applying there would be a good way of getting back into the headmaster's good books and ensuring the maximum of support. I found out later that in thinking this way I had done him an injustice. Every student who applied anywhere received the maximum possible support.

The only way for anyone in my position to ensure acceptance was to win an entrance scholarship. It wasn't a matter of money. For people who had already won State Scholarships the entrance scholarships were purely honorific. But there were far more State Scholarships than there were available places at Cambridge and Oxford so applicants had to be able to show something on the entrance exam papers that went considerably beyond anything that they had done before. The task of reviewing the combined curricula in chemistry, physics and math being obviously impossible, I saw that the only realistic approach was to study as many old exam papers as I could and try to reduce the field a bit. Knowing the contents of *Philbrick and Holmyard* from cover to cover I wasn't too worried about the chemistry, and I knew that success on the math papers depended on the ability to use a combination of standard methods and mathematical instincts to solve whatever weird problems the examiners happened to throw at you. Physics was more difficult, requiring a great deal of phenomenological knowledge and considerable fluency in the algebra, trigonometry and calculus used to develop that knowledge in mathematical terms. I put a great deal of effort into selecting the topics that seemed most likely to appear on the papers and making sure that I could answer any questions on those topics. In spite of all this single-minded devotion it took me three shots, one of them at a less demanding group of "March" colleges, before I finally won my scholarship to Sidney.

The entrance scholarship exams included two three-hour papers in each subject—in my case, chemistry, physics and math—practical exams in chemistry and physics, and a three-hour General Paper that required the writing of two essays on subjects that had nothing to do with science. I found out later that one of the most important factors in winning the scholarship had been my essay on the music of Vaughan Williams. I think that the greatest asset anyone can have in this kind of endeavor, and perhaps for life as a whole, is a strong impulse to know, understand and enjoy things for their own sake and not for any profit that may accrue. My encyclopaedic knowledge of chemistry and music, so important in my gaining admission to Cambridge, came about through inner passion[5] not external expediency. My passion for cricket involved me in a discipline which is no less mysterious than eurythmy and enriched my life in ways that would take a whole essay to explain. Later on when the demands of life allowed less time for the indulgence of such enthusiams I never lost the desire to learn and to avoid having to take someone else's word for things that I could find out for myself. Now that I am old and I meet people who want to be teachers and who don't seem to know anything much about anything in particular, I puzzle about all this knowledge that I have, knowledge which has made my life richer in all sorts of ways and which is shortly going to disappear. Is it important? Does it really matter? Probably not. Knowledge can be passed on but passion is a different matter. It can be awakened only if it is already there in some germinal form, and this is a matter of karma.

◆ ◆ ◆

Having won my entrance scholarship in December I was blessedly able to spend the rest of the school year studying harmony and counterpoint with Harry Elgar Dawes. Harry had a reputation for laziness, but I realized that his purpose in avoiding general school duties was not to spend his afternoons with his feet up in the music room but to devote as much time as possible to studying and preparing music. He was an accomplished composer and an excellent conductor. By the time I left Harry admitted that I was pretty fluent at four-part Palestrina-style contrapuntal writing, but he objected to my habit of never staying in the same key for more than a couple of measures at a time and was quite bemused by a quadruple psalm chant that I wrote that passed through a complete enharmonic cycle. When I wasn't doing music I was generally to be found in the physics lab designing weird experiments on viscosity, a physical property that has always fascinated me, or playing bridge with my three best friends in the physics supply room.

◆ ◆ ◆

I never lost my enthusiasm for chemistry even when it came to occupy a much smaller part of my consciousness, but I found high school and college chemistry very easy, so I quixotically decided that I had better specialize in physics, even though it meant that I had to work much harder. Chemistry was, after all, rapidly becoming a branch of applied physics—nobody really wanted to mess about with chemicals any more. Space, time, the interior of the atom and the mysterious nucleus all fascinated me. At the Crypt I had learnt about electronic structure, orbits, energy levels, bonds and the rudimentary ideas of the solid state that were then current. I knew how to deduce such things as the gas laws and the viscosity of a fluid from the kinetic theory. But at Cambridge I encountered the latest versions of relativity theory, quantum theory and statistical mechanics and I was bowled over by them. The Bohr atom which I had thought of as the greatest marvel of modern science, and which had seemed to be unlimited in its explanatory potential, suddenly appeared as a crude toy. I forgot that it had been the product of a century of intense thought and labor, that it continued to be of great value, particularly in understanding chemical combination, and that since it had got so much right and its inadequacies had suggested such fruitful paths of further exploration, it deserved reverence rather than disdain. My fellow anthroposophists, who tend to be disdainful of modern science in all its forms, may find this hard to understand, so let me point out that anyone who disdains modern science disdains the modern human being. The science that we have is a product of the way we are, and the way we are manifests itself in whatever human niche we happen to occupy. Anyone who thinks that anthroposophical activities are somehow exempt from the effects of the fallen human condition is seriously deluded.

(xi)

Positivism

Science students at Cambridge generally had lectures and lab classes from nine in the morning until one in the afternoon six days a week. There were tutorials, meetings and additional lab classes on some afternoons, and there were plenty of assignments. In spite of all this we somehow had time to play cricket, soccer or rugby three afternoons a week, to go punting on the river, sing in the college choir, go to plays and concerts and to sit around the coffee table for hours on end. Sometimes we slept a little. Since the university was divided into men's colleges and women's colleges, there being very few of the latter, many of the men decided that it was quite possible to put their sex lives on hold for nine weeks at a time and make up for it in the vacations. This situation had a tendency to lead to fewer distractions and more earnest conversations about the Meaning of Life. The other side of the coin is that many secretaries, nurses and shop assistants had a far better time than they might have anticipated in most other cities.

We did, however, work very hard, and it may seem odd that so many of the details of what I studied at Cambridge are lost, whereas the fruits of my labors at the Crypt and all the self-education I have undertaken as an adult are very much with me. Several plausible explanations spring to mind, but none of them seem compelling enough to be worth mentioning here. What I did bring away with me was a mind schooled in the art of disputation and a positivistic outlook on knowledge. I should hasten to say that I don't mean "disputation" in its modern sense of irritable argumentation. There is—or was—something in the atmosphere at Cambridge that allowed the civil discussion of reasonable disagreements to become something in the nature of an art form. The talk may have become heated but the fundamental object was to get at the truth, not to score debating points. We were having "Goethean conversations" and "dialogical discussions" long before these terms were thought up by anthroposophists.

Perhaps the point about positivism can be made clear by the following example. If you are allergic to scientific discussions you may find this difficult, but I urge you to give it a try, since the point that it makes goes beyond the details that are needed to make it. As a student at the Crypt I thought that an electric current was a stream of electrons flowing along a wire from the negative to the positive. I thought that this was perfectly clear, that everyone knew it and that I knew exactly what an electron was. I had also learnt how to measure currents, how to use Ohm's Law to make calculations about currents, electromotive forces and resistances, and how to extend these methods to cover capacitors, inductors and radio tubes. At Cambridge I realized that my notion of the electron was almost as metaphysical as my notion of God, and that the only things that physicists deal with are magnitudes—numbers of amps, volts, ohms and so on. Our picture of what goes on in a wire when a current flows through it has been in a state of continuous change ever since the electron was invented in the 1890's, and, in fact for more than a century before that, but 2 has always been twice 1. We know that the current is 1 amp if the pointer of the ammeter stops on 1. If it stops on 2 the current is 2 amps. We have theoretical reasons for the decision about where to put the 1 and the 2 on the ammeter scale, but they must be expressible in terms of something that you can, in principle, do with an actual piece of apparatus. The phrase "in principle" used to crop up quite frequently. Images of atoms and electrons are fine up to a point, but they are subordinate to the mathematical expression of relations between measurable quantities.[6] Since the only essential aspect of an electric current is its magnitude it is perfectly natural to use expressions like "measure the current" or "a current of two amps", so I was quite startled about forty years ago when I opened an American textbook and came upon the phrase "the intensity of the current." "Intensity" is a poor choice since physicists habitually use it to mean a rate of flow of something per unit area. "Magnitude" or "measure" would have been better, but if you use the phrase "magnitude of the current" you are guilty of redundancy, since the only useful component of meaning attached to "current" *is* magnitude—unless you don't happen to be a positivist. For the positivist, when the notion of magnitude is removed from the notion of current there is virtually nothing left. The non-positivist who refers to the "magnitude of the current" has a very difficult problem when he is asked to explain what he means by "current".

The basic question asked by the positivist is, "What do you actually observe?" You don't observe a stream of metaphysical electrons moving through metaphysical interstices in a lattice of metaphysical ions. You observe a pointer on an instrument. People started asking this fundamental question in the nineteenth century and when it was asked about space, time and light it was largely responsible for Newton's having to move over and make way for Einstein. It may also ring a loud bell in the ears of anyone who is interested in Goethean science. As Rudolf Steiner put it: "The theory must be limited to the perceptible and must seek connections within this."[7]

The bell becomes louder when you realize that in the 1920's Steiner linked the phenomenological approach and the subsequent mathematization of experience with the path of spiritual knowledge. Statements like the following came—and still come—as a bit of a shock to some of the members of the anthroposophical society:

"The first step [in spiritual scientific knowledge] would be the familiar grasping of the real outer world. The second would be the mathematical penetration of the outer world, after we have first learnt inwardly to construct the purely mathematical aspect. The third would be the entirely inner experience, like the mathematical experience but with the character of spiritual reality."[8]

Ideas like this were in the air at that time. The Vienna Circle, a group including the philosophers Rudolf Carnap and Moritz Rosenthal, was building on the work of the previous generation of mathematicians and philosophers in an effort to introduce mathematical methodology and precision into philosophy and to dismiss traditional metaphysics as nonsensical—very much as Steiner wished to supersede vague traditional ideas of mysticism. I mention these things now so that the reader will understand why it was that, at a later stage in my life, *The Philosophy of Freedom* appealed to me so much more strongly than other books by Steiner that I encountered at the same time. I should also mention that although physics is still fundamentally positivistic, for workers at the frontier the motto is really "anything goes"—anything, that is to say, however fanciful, that has some chance of providing a clue, an insight or an idea of what the next experiment should be. The way eminent physicists sometimes talk, especially through their journalistic interpreters, might lead you to think that positivism is dead, and some make it clear that they would like to dance on its grave, since they believe that it is a hindrance to theoretical advances.[9] As a general philosophy, positivism ran into considerable difficulties and has been out of fashion for the past fifty years. Such seems to be the fate of general philosophies.

(xii)

Aero-elasticity

When I graduated from Cambridge in 1956 I had what was technically known as a "good honors degree", which meant that it was something better than third class honors[10], that it might possibly justify starting a research assignment that would lead to a Ph. D., and would, if I became a teacher, bring a considerable financial reward. I had, however, reached a position somewhat similar to the one I had come to at the Crypt a few years previously. I was sick and tired of education. At the same time I had absolutely no idea what I wanted to do with the rest of my life. I soon found that being twenty-two years old and having a degree in physics put me at a great advantage over many other people. All kinds of companies were lining up to obtain the services of young scientists, and physicists from Cambridge seemed to have quite a pull. I had interviews with three aircraft companies and two firms working on nuclear reactors, and I ended up with the Bristol Aircraft Company, where I was told that I would be working in a top-secret design office in the guided weapons section. Because it was top-secret they couldn't tell me exactly what I would be doing, but this seemed appropriate for someone who didn't know what he wanted to do. I chose BAC because I liked that part of the country, the place seemed clean and well organized and the pay was decent. The intensity of the competition for recent graduates may have had something to do with the fact that I received a raise before I even started.

When I walked into the design office for the first time in September 1956 something inside me turned over and I knew that I had made a terrible mistake. In my innocence I had pictured something more like a lab with a missile somewhat resembling a torpedo suspended in the middle. I and my white-coated colleagues would be fussing around it, doing interesting things with instruments and notebooks. The reality was a huge room furnished with very large tables and nothing visibly scientific at all. People sat four or six to a table, each supplied with a calculating machine of the old-fashioned mechanical kind and reams of paper. The staff of eighty was divided into sections—guidance (electronic, not moral), aerodynamics, thrust, weights, stress, aeroelasticity, thermo-aeroelasticity (which I was assigned to) and, I believe, several others that I do not now remember. Somewhere there was someone who was supposed to be in charge of the project as a whole, but I never met him. You may be wondering, as I was at the time, what the project as a whole was.

Possibly there are a few people who remember that in the late 1950's the British deployed an air defence system based on a ground to air missile called "Bloodhound". Bloodhound was designed and built by BAC, where it was known by its secret code name of Red Duster, and like all such systems it was obsolescent by the time it became operational. BAC was entrusted with the task of designing the replacement for Red Duster before Red Duster went into service. When I arrived on the scene Red Duster had got to the stage of being able to intercept slow low-flying aircraft, and its replacement, to be known as Blue Envoy, had barely made it to the drawing board. I was informed that I would be working on Blue Envoy in the thermo-aeroelasticity section. I then had to be told what thermo-aeroelasticity was.

When a plane or a missile travels faster than sound it is heated by the air rushing past it. The rise in temperature depends on the speed and is easy to calculate. The change in temperature affects the mechanical properties of the materials of the missile with the general result that everything becomes less rigid, increasing the distorting effects of aerodynamic forces. Since the outside of the missile gets hot while the inside is still cool and temperature changes spread unevenly through the structure, thermal expansion is also a problem. Our missile had no wings but it did have something known as an elevon, a cross between an elevator and an aileron. Aerodynamic forces on the elevon caused slight distortions in its form, which caused slight changes in the flight path, which changed the aerodynamic forces slightly, which changed the form of the elevon, which changed the flight path, which…A set of cyclical relationships like this causes a series of changes that may die down to nothing or may multiply into violent instability. Between them the Aerodynamics Section and the Aeroelasticity Section were supposed to keep track of these possibilities, which they did using mathematical processes of iteration—meaning repetitive calculations following the variables as the changes got smaller and smaller. If the changes got bigger and bigger the situation was unstable and something serious would have to be done to the initial conditions. Our job in the thermo-aeroelasticity section was to predict the effect of temperature changes on the whole structure and particularly on the elevon. All the structures were geometrically irregular and mathematically nightmarish, and the only way we could think of to deal with the situation was to take an object like the elevon, divide it into very small bits, calculate what was happening to each bit and add up the result. We would spend many hours setting up a calculation of this sort and then send it down to the Computing Section.

The Computing Section consisted of a couple of supervisors, a huge machine called the Digital Electronic Universal Computing Engine, or DEUCE, and a staff of about twenty young women, known, of course, in those days as "girls" except when they were referred to as "computers". ("I hear Charlie is going out with a girl called Mary." "Who's Mary?" "She's a computer from downstairs." One of my colleagues actually married a computer.) The DEUCE took up a whole room and was considerably less powerful than an inexpensive PC of the present day. Since it included an immense array of radio tubes it was down more of the time than it was up. The job of the young women was to convert our huge arrays of numbers into holes in sets of punched cards. A typical calculation would take at least a week to get to the DEUCE and at least another week to get back to us, even if the DEUCE happened to be up. The average cycle was about three weeks. Often, by the time we got our calculations back, an engineer in some other section had decided that changes were necessary in the part of the missile we were working on, so that the initial conditions were different and the whole calculation had to be repeated. Sometimes it had to be repeated simply because the engineer who had set it up had made a mistake in the first line. In view of the emphasis that had been placed on the high priority, top-secret nature of the whole operation I was amazed at its lackadaisical inefficiency. Although I had absolutely no experience in the field I was entrusted with several crucial calculations without having been given more than a vague idea of the methods I was to use or how what I was doing fitted into the project as a whole. Communication between sections was very poor and the director of the whole operation was hardly ever seen. The organizational problems were beautifully illustrated by something that happened to the Weights Section.

One morning I arrived at work to find that the usual happy-go-lucky atmosphere had been replaced by one of doom and gloom. The leader of Weights had been reduced to the ranks and some of his underlings had been given the sack. Naturally we wanted to know why, but it took some time for the explanation to filter down to the junior engineers.

Two of the most important statistics for an airplane or a missile are its total weight and the position of its centre of gravity. The latter is crucial since its precise relation to the thrust of the air on the wings or elevons and fuselage determines whether or not flight is stable. Decisions by engineers in different sections always had a tendency to increase the weight and to move the center of gravity around, and it was the task of the Weights Section to keep track of these items. Their biggest difficulty was that in a missile in which everything keeps moving around at the whims of sections who never talk to each other, there is no fixed point, or *datum* from which to measure anything. Officially the main bulkhead acted as *datum*, rather like the origin of a system of axes, but this was simply a matter of convention since at any moment the structural engineers might decide to move the bulkhead in relation to everything else or, worse, in relation to *some* of the other bits and pieces. Students of high school algebra will probably remember wrestling with very confusing problems about changing axes. If you move the origin three units to the right is the new co-ordinate $x_1 = x + 3$, or is it $x - 3$? So although the position of the centre of gravity, given as a distance from the main bulkhead, sounded very precise, its usefulness depended on being quite sure that the said bulkhead was still where you thought it was. It turned out that on the previous afternoon someone had put everything together and had woken up to the fact that the centre of gravity was now 23 inches in front of the nose! It didn't take a Euclid to figure out that this was absurd, but what nobody was quite sure of was how long this absurdity had been in operation. Fortunately the position of the centre of gravity was not something that concerned the thermo-aeroelasticity section directly, but the aerodynamicists were deeply concerned and had to repeat a great many of their calculations.

My swan song was a calculation on the effects of heat flowing into the main bulkhead, which was of such a complicated and irregular shape that I despaired of getting more than a very rough approximation to what might actually happen. The rate at which the temperature inside the missile would rise depended on the thickness of its steel sheathing. Before I could start the calculation the engineers in another section had to make up their minds whether they were going to use "36 thou." or "48 thou." "Thou." is short for thousandths of an inch. Finally they settled on 36. I set up a huge calculation and sent it to the young ladies downstairs. During the three weeks that elapsed before it reappeared I made up my mind that I didn't want to spend even a few years of my life designing missiles. The work was boring and stultifying and I couldn't believe that it was really going anywhere. Having been at BAC for seven months I sent in my resignation, which required two weeks' notice. My calculation came back and a few days later I heard that the engineers had changed their minds about the skin thickness and it would be 48 thou. Someone would have to repeat the whole calculation, but it wouldn't be me! It didn't turn out that way, however. The day before I walked out of the office for the last time I heard that Blue Envoy had been "put in abeyance"—in other words, placed on the shelf where, I'm sure, it remained until someone decided that it was time to consign it to the shredder.

When I was a teenager I thought that flying must be very exciting and wonderful, but after my experience at BAC I found that I really preferred to stay on *terra firma*. I remember thinking that somewhere in the same complex of offices and factories a team of engineers had designed the Britannia, Bristol's most successful commercial plane, and I hoped that they had kept track of things better than we did.[11]

You may be wondering what all this has to do with Waldorf education, but that's something I'll let you figure out for yourself.

(xiii)

Poetry

While I was working at Bristol I heard a BBC program about George Butterworth, a very talented English composer who was killed in the Battle of the Somme in 1916 at the age of thirty-one, and I listened to his *Shropshire Lad* song cycle. My relationship to my work and to my bachelor digs—the feeling that I was a stranger passing through on my way to some unknown destination—along with a growing preoccupation with the passage of time—I began to feel old at twenty-four—and immersion in the exquisitely painful beauty of the English countryside, put me into a mood that made me extremely susceptible to the stoic melancholy of Butterworth's music and Housman's poems. The way Housman characterized life went beyond the merely melancholy to the utterly pessimistic, and that was the way I experienced it. It requires either a highly developed spiritual vision or a great deal of simple faith to see beyond the tragedy of being human, and I had neither. Feeling as surely doomed as any soldier who ever goes into battle, I emulated the many young men of the First World War who bought their copies of *A Shropshire Lad* and carried them wherever they went. Tattered, torn and yellowed with age mine still has a place of honor in my study, as does my old record of John Cameron and Gerald Moore performing Butterworth's songs. I have a nice new copy of Housman's collected poems, but it is the old one that I turn to when I feel the need to revisit that world.

> Be still, my soul, be still; the arms you bear are brittle,
>   Earth and high heaven are fixt of old and founded strong.
> Think rather,—call to thought, if now you grieve a little,
>   The days when we had rest, O soul, for they were long.
>
> Men loved unkindness then, but lightless in the quarry
>   I slept and saw not; tears fell down, I did not mourn;
> Sweat ran and blood sprang out and I was never sorry;
>   Then it was well with me, in days ere I was born.
>
> Now, and I muse for why and never find the reason,
>   I pace the earth, and drink the air, and feel the sun.
> Be still my soul, be still; it is but for a season:
>   Let us endure an hour and see injustice done.
>
> Ay, look: high heaven and earth ail from the prime foundation;
>   All thoughts to rive the heart are here, and all are vain:
> Horror and scorn and hate and fear and indignation—
>   Oh why did I wake? When shall I sleep again?

Housman provided inspiration for many composers, including relative unknowns like Arthur Somervell, Graham Peel, Armstrong Gibbs and Ivor Gurney, as well as those who are more likely to be familiar to serious music lovers—Moeran, Ireland, Bax and Vaughan Williams. It was through such musical connections that I became involved with other poets, especially Hardy and Whitman, but I also fell under the spell of Robert Graves, and I have no idea how that happened.

Graves's poetry is usually quite unassuming. It lacks the sententiousness of some of his contemporaries and the pretensions to modernism of others, but it can be very disturbing and very humorous. (If you don't know his work try *Warning to Children* and *Welsh Incident.*) His opinions about poetry and poets, as expressed in *The Crowning Privilege*, appealed to me very strongly, and I was soon deeply immersed in *The White Goddess,* "An Historical Grammar of Poetic Myth" which has about the same relationship to anthroposophy as the doctrine of free love has to Victorian morality. I'd better remind the reader that at that time I had never heard of anthroposophy. One literary eminence described *The White Goddess* as one of the three most unreadable books ever written, but I read it several times in the course of a few months. The story of an ancient matriarchal society subject to the insatiable demands of a moon goddess, and its transformation into a male-dominated society with prosaic values of reason and logic, took hold of me in ways that I didn't understand at all. I had mixed feelings about the White Goddess but I could see that she had what it took and I felt some contempt for the relatively wan male figures who took her place.

In the introduction to *The White Goddess* Graves described himself as "the fox who has lost his brush", meaning the individual who no longer acknowledges or responds to the demands, conventions and expectations of society. Graves's brushlessness was a great deal more far-reaching than mine but it does seem to me that I have spent a great deal of my life trying to acquire a brush, looking for a setting in which I could say, "Yes, these are my values and beliefs; these are the ways in which I perceive the world", and that although my search did not go altogether unrewarded it was to a large extent a waste of time and effort. It would be wonderfully calming and reassuring to find a group to which one could make such a commitment, and people sometimes think that they have discovered it in the Anthroposophical Society, but this desire for the comforts of like-mindedness is not what anthroposophy is all about. The sensation of being a stranger, of never quite belonging, is part of the consciousness-soul experience, something not to be suppressed or anaesthetized, but to be worked with as the expression of a potential organ of perception and the beginning of something new.

There is clearly a great deal more to be said in this connection, although not necessarily by me. I think I've said enough to help the reader to understand why I have always been happiest when left to find my way on my own, and I feel very lucky to have joined the Waldorf Movement in the days before newcomers were automatically saddled with mentors, advisers, visitors and such, people who usually have enough to do already, without taking on supervisory duties, and who have their own problems to deal with. There is a lot to be said for the philosophy of D. G. Williams, the headmaster of the Crypt in my early days there: "Find good people and let them teach."

(xiv)

Elasticity

At some point during this winter of discontent I had decided that I wanted to try my hand at teaching. Science teachers were in very short supply and I found out that if I could get myself accepted into a teacher training programme the government would very kindly continue my State Scholarship. I spent a day in Cambridge and found that my old college was willing to take me back for a year so that I could study at the Cambridge Institute of Education. Needing something to do for a few months before the next school year started, I took a temporary position teaching chemistry at Bristol Grammar School. I can't say that I felt a great sense of vocation, but I did feel that as a teacher I should be doing something both more important and more congenial than working as an only partially engaged cog in a missile design office. One thing I thought which turned out to be true was that as a teacher I was unlikely to be bored.

◆　　◆　　◆

It was pleasant to spend another year—or, rather, two thirds of a year—at Cambridge, but the only part of the experience that contributed significantly to my education was the one third of the year that I spent doing teaching practice at Sir Thomas Rich's School in Gloucester. Tommy's, as the school was known, was very much like the Crypt, having some excellent masters from whom I learnt a great deal about what it means to be a teacher. It was while I was at Tommy's that I found out something potentially awkward about my relationship to teaching, which was that putting a lesson plan on paper was a task that I cordially detested and found all possible means of avoiding. Every so often I had to do it to satisfy the requirements of my supervisor, but it seemed to me to be an awful waste of time. If you knew exactly what you intended to teach and how you proposed to do it, and, at the same time you knew that at any moment something unforeseen might happen in the classroom that would mean a change of manner or direction, what was the point of spending precious time writing it all down? Would I find throughout my teaching career that someone was hovering over me, demanding carefully written-out lesson plans? Arnold Hurd, my mentor at Tommy's, assured me that experienced and competent teachers didn't bother with such things and that once my training was over it was unlikely that anybody would ever ask me for one. In Arnold's view teacher training courses were largely a waste of time and going over lesson plans was a way of filling up the instructors' time with something that had the appearance of being useful. Arnold was the head of the physics department at Tommy's, and a great teacher.

While I was at Tommy's I heard that the Crypt needed a physics teacher for the following year. Not everyone would relish the thought of returning to his old stamping ground and becoming a colleague of his former teachers, but I didn't hesitate. There were people at the Crypt whom I knew and admired, there were excellent facilities for my work, the school was right in the middle of a tract of countryside that I loved passionately and, last but not least, I should be able to continue to play for my old cricket team.

3

Becoming a Teacher, Part 1

No prudent writer would justify the form and content of his memoirs in terms of irritation and inkblots, thereby giving critics ready-made vehicles for their disapproval. Prudence, however, is a virtue that can easily be overworked.

(i)

Intelligence

In spite of all the reactionary texts and opinions that are still to be encountered, I'll take it that my readers—if any—agree that intelligence is not a unitary characteristic of the human being that can be effectively quantified and legitimately used to determine the course of a person's life. People have many different kinds of abilities, and geneticists have assured us that the connection between individual characteristics and genetic make-up is more tenuous for the human being than for any other species. None of this corresponds with what I was taught at Cambridge in the course of studying for my Certificate in Education. People talked about intelligence in a way that was reminiscent of the way in which physicists spoke about heat in the early nineteenth century. We can't see it, but we know that it's there and we can measure it. Later on the physicists realized that they had been treating a complex situation in a unitary way and getting the wrong results. The process of putting things right—or somewhere near right—took several decades and was not accomplished without controversy. It takes a physicist, however, to get steamed up about thermodynamics and the quantum theory, whereas most people are apt to be deeply hurt when told that they are not intelligent enough to expect anything but a life of manual labor. Intelligence was a much hotter topic but it took a very long time to see that class and position were based much more on inheritance than on heredity—that the effects of your genetic make-up were open to question but there was not much doubt about the advantages of being well provided for as a child and inheriting a healthy bank balance as an adult. I am not talking about millions—just enough to help pay off the mortgage. It is observable that the children of wealthy parents are not always well provided for, but years were to elapse before we started hearing about the problems of poor little rich kids. That, in any case, is another story—we had very few rich kids of any kind at the Crypt.

The teachers at the Cambridge Institute of Education subscribed to the view that intelligence is partly inherited and partly the result of conditioning. Cyril Burt's fake research on identical twins was still in all the textbooks and the message that I received was that whatever anyone might say for social or political reasons it was really a matter of genes. It seemed to be clearly observable that intelligent parents had intelligent children, and it was not yet clear that this observation rested on several unexamined assumptions, one of which was that we had a realistically applicable meaning for the word "intelligent." In a positivistically inclined university we ought to have put the matter in terms of what we *actually* observed: most of the children who did well enough on the eleven plus test to make it into the A-stream at grammar school had parents who were skilled workers or professionals of some sort and who lived in what we thought of as better class localities. Not so many A-streamers came from the families of unskilled factory workers or farm laborers. We ought to have noted that it is a very big jump from these observations to the conclusion that intelligence is passed on genetically.

We might also have noted that very few of the A-streamers were members of the aristocracy, but this was not surprising since aristocrats were not numerous in the vicinity of a school like the Crypt. It is perhaps more surprising that I met very few of the sons of the rich and famous at Cambridge. In the absence of a statistical study I can offer only the impression, discussed at length over the coffee table, that wealth and position were still very helpful in getting into the university, but that those who gained entrance through such advantages were unlikely to pursue stressful academic programmes such as the physical sciences and mathematics which my friends and I were wrestling with, and which we were expected to complete a year early so that we could be doing postgraduate work in our final undergraduate year. The sons of peers, tycoons and film stars, we thought, were apt to take the maximum of time over the minimum of work and end up with ordinary, not honors, degrees. Having rather low opinions of the intellectual capacities of peers, tycoons and film stars we concluded that we were seeing a restratification of society, and that what would count most in the future would be intelligence as we then thought we understood it. The beneficiaries would be the children of the middle class and the skilled working class. There is no doubt that this assessment fitted some of the facts, but it still incorporated unwarrantable assumptions about the nature of intelligence. To put the matter crudely, as we saw it, people who have good jobs and nice houses must have got them by being intelligent. This intelligence is passed on genetically, so their children do well in the eleven-plus and end up with good jobs and nice houses. QED. An older and wiser friend at Cambridge once reproved me with the remark, "Blessed is the man who earns his living by the sweat of his brow." This was in 1956, when, as my English master used to put it, "man" still embraced "woman." Fortunately I was later to spend enough time in the company of people who paid their bills with physical labor to realize that intelligence, however one understood it, was not in any way restricted to the white-collar genetic pool.

While I was at Cambridge I developed a philosophy of government the main principle of which was that those who were able should take responsibility for those who weren't. In other words, the emerging meritocracy should do what the old aristocracy was supposed to have done in its palmy days but largely didn't. *Noblesse oblige* would be replaced by *intelligence oblige*. I thought that my educational experiences had made it reasonably clear who would fall into each category but I was not too stupid to realize that dividing the whole population along these lines would be rather more difficult than splitting up the eleven-plus group with a one-hour intelligence test. It even occurred to me that there might well be millions of people who did not wish to place themselves in the care of their designated intellectual superiors. Nevertheless, it was an idea about which I was apt to hold forth with great enthusiasm.

(ii)

What's in a Name?

In 1958, when I joined the faculty of the Crypt School, my official designation was "Second Physics Master." If I had gone to teach at an elementary school instead of a grammar school I should probably have been referred to as a teacher instead of a master. When I took private students I was a tutor, but later in my life, when I taught at the SUNY College of Optometry in New York City, I was an instructor. Had I become famous it would probably have been as an educator, whereas in humbler circumstances I should have been a docent and in spiritual circles a guru. This welter of vaguely understood nomenclature arises from some genuine insights into the different roles of those from whom it is our desire or duty to learn something. In the academic circles in which I have revolved the differences between *teacher* and *instructor* have not, to my knowledge, been clearly stated, but the words themselves and the contexts in which they usually appear carry certain implications. There are, for instance, flying instructors and music teachers. Flying teachers and music instructors are more rarely to be encountered. The word *instructor* seems to imply that the individual is expected to impart knowledge and technique in a setting which is morally, ethically, metaphysically and emotionally neutral. Whether it is possible for anyone to achieve such a feat is another matter. I have met people who assume without, perhaps, much pondering, not merely that it is possible, but that it is the only proper form of education. I have noticed a tendency for *instructor* to replace *teacher* in job descriptions, so perhaps this opinion is gaining ground. The word *teacher* carries associations with spiritual or moral guidance which may arise out of the needs of the students or out of the nature of the subject matter. I have, however, known people called instructors who, out of the warmth and goodness of their hearts, have given their students help and guidance in a way that went far beyond the mere transmission of information; and I have met teachers whose desire to get alongside the students and explain the real meaning of life or rap with them about personal problems has pushed the ostensible purpose of the teaching relationship far into the background. I am not going to propose that somewhere there is a golden mean. An experienced, resourceful and thoughtful educator—delightfully neutral word—develops a flair for doing the right thing and knows when to be a teacher, when a tutor, when an instructor and even, perhaps, when a guru. What I *am* saying is that people who believe that any form of teaching can take place in a moral, metaphysical or emotional vacuum—the Skinner box approach, so to speak—are deluded. From personal experience I know that they can be excellent people and fine teachers, but their standpoint on this question means that they teach from *unconsciously* held positions and are easily used by those who have an agenda. It is far healthier to acknowledge where one is coming from, and, if necessary, to use a little introspection in order to find out. When I was a very young man I disagreed with my friends, parents and teachers about many things, but I was quite unconscious of the possibility that where I had come from was not altogether a good place. It was quite a long time before introspection caught up with me. In the years that have since elapsed I have had many colleagues, from teaching assistants to faculty chairpeople, who never seem to have given the matter a moment's thought. This situation makes it easy, for instance, to believe that your teaching is free from any religious implications while unconsciously promoting atheism, or to believe that you are working anthroposophically while unconsciously promoting the conventional morals of New England, old England or *Mittel-Europa* that you grew up with.

(iii)

A Right-Thinking Person

I had, in fact, acquired rather a lot of excess baggage—ideological and philosophical positions nurtured by plain old prejudices. I felt immensely proud and lucky to be English; one of the most shocking experiences I have ever endured was the discovery, at the age of ten or so, that Beethoven had been a foreigner. The experience of living through my childhood on the south coast of England in the midst of the Second World War had deep and lasting effects on my perceptions of the other nations involved. Having been brought up in the Anglican Church, I felt, a little obscurely but quite definitely, that this was the only right and proper religious milieu for any normal kind of person—and this even after I became an atheist. I became enthusiastic about socialism at the age of eleven but swung to the right in my teens. Subsequently I was dismayed but not surprised to find that politicians are not always strictly truthful. As a high school student I accepted the generally held and largely unexamined view that the universe is, in principle, explicable in terms of the atomic theory and its ramifications. I thought that coeducational schools were a bad idea and that Cambridge and Oxford were the only universities that mattered. Over my thoughts about relationships between the sexes I draw a decent veil.

Now I say, "I thought", but I was really only spasmodically aware of a somewhat nebulous set of attitudes and values which seemed irreproachably correct and shared by most of the people around me. Sitting here at the computer, fifty years on, I find the process of dredging up old mind-sets quite humiliating. People don't grow up with such prejudices in these times. They are much more aware, alert and conscious of what is going on inside them. Or are they? Perhaps this is simply another example of prejudice—the kind that Owen Barfield used to call chronological snobbery. It is, after all, hard to be aware of the things that you are not aware of. Everyone who tries to become a teacher takes a load of some sort into the classroom. Some of it is harmless enough, no doubt, but all of it, to a greater or lesser extent and in more benign or more harmful ways, affects the way we teach, even if we attempt merely to instruct. If we wish to train ourselves to find the best responses to the great variety of situations that will confront us in the classroom, out of that whole world of instructor, tutor, teacher, educator and guru, we have to look into ourselves, bring the inner world to consciousness, and start to regulate it. This is not easy, but sometimes the students help.

(iv)

Student Aid

Young men faced with embarrassing situations often don't know what to do with their hands, especially when putting them into their pockets is obviously not quite the right thing. It seems that in such circumstances I had developed the habit of putting my right forefinger on the side of my nose. At the beginning of each day there was an assembly in the school hall. At a given signal six hundred boys would rise to their feet and thirty masters would walk in at the rear, proceed up the aisle and take their places on the stage. Before reaching the stage it was necessary to pass through the school choir, who, unlike the other boys, sat facing the aisle. I found running the gauntlet of their incurious stares strangely embarrassing. One morning when I was about to pass through the choir, fifty or so of the boys, in a most impressive unison, put the first fingers of their right hands to the sides of their noses. A few weeks later Harry Dawes, the music master, asked me to help the tenors to sing in tune. I was glad to do so, since it enabled me to stare instead of being stared at. In the meantime, it occurred to me that if I was capable of being so unconscious of my physical gestures in a public setting, I might be even less conscious of my mannerisms in the classroom. As a boy I had indulged in a certain amount of relatively innocent merriment over the idiosyncrasies of my teachers and as a young man I often smiled at the quirks of my colleagues. Everyone had some kind of hobbyhorse or axe to grind. Now, at last, I was ready to begin some serious self-examination. What were my own stock reactions and knee-jerks? Were there innocent remarks or questions which automatically triggered my inner set of conventions and produced the impromptu lectures of a right-minded person? Having observed this phenomenon with many other people, including, of course, my parents, I was particularly anxious to find myself blameless. As a natural sceptic I thought that it would be humiliating to find myself loaded with unconscious assumptions. A description of what I uncovered would be extremely boring, but one example may be instructive. As I have mentioned, recalling these old habits of mind is embarrassing. I need both hands for typing, so I don't even have the solace of putting the forefinger of my right hand on the side of my nose.

When I returned to the Crypt I found that I was the Form Master—roughly the equivalent of a class adviser—of 2A, the young incoming *intelligentsia*. This little tale is particularly embarrassing but I think it had better be told. Looking at this group of fresh-faced, well scrubbed young boys in their nice new blazers I realized that it was quite possible that a few of them, through misconduct or dereliction of duty, might fall from grace sufficiently to be demoted to the B or even to the C stream, so I gave them a little lecture. The more difficult members of the less gifted classes were commonly referred to as louts, and my lecture was an exhortation on lout-hood and the advisability of avoiding it. I didn't think of it at the time, but I now believe that my speech was the direct descendant of a harangue given by Mr. Overnall, the Deputy Headmaster at Poole Grammar School, which had culminated in the dire prediction that the louts to whom he was referring would, on leaving school, "go out into the world as errand boys." It didn't take me long to see that my little performance had been out of place, ill-judged and not distinguished by the application of intelligence. I preferred not to think about it, but I'm pretty sure that the event marked the beginning of some overdue changes of perspective. Only the beginning, however; the nose incident took place a few months later.

(v)

Resignation

When I was a boy at the Crypt the teacher who made the biggest impression on me was Hubert Siggee, my physics master. Mr. Siggee never had any difficulty in keeping our attention. He was strict without being rigid, kind without being sentimental, and he knew exactly what was going on in the classroom at all points and at all times. He was a master in deed as well as in title, but not without idiosyncrasy. When he wanted us to concentrate on a difficult point he would stride around the room declaiming, "Watch and pray lest ye enter into temptation." "What are we going to put into this flask?" he would ask. Silence. "The stuff the lions drink!" After a moment we caught on. He didn't expect us to laugh or even to comment. Every so often a little sparkle, a pleasantry, would shine out, giving added life to his enthusiastic discourse. When I went back to teach I pictured myself being like Hubert Siggee but, of course, it didn't work out that way. I don't know whether his apparently effortless control of the classroom was inborn or acquired through experience, but whatever it was I didn't have it. I spent the first few months wondering how soon I could decently resign and take up some less arduous activity like mountain climbing, or even try to get back into the missile design office. Things eventually began to improve, although I really don't know why. It may have been something to do with the feeling, common among students, that a new teacher ought to be put through a difficult initiation process. Perhaps that stage was coming to an end. One does, of course, learn from experience, but I was, and am, unable to articulate what it was that I had learnt. It was a pleasure to discover that I could crack a joke without losing the class, and I soon became rather too well known for digressions and bad puns. It was just as well that being a teacher had turned out not to be such a bad life after all, since somehow I knew that it was what I was going to be doing for the foreseeable future.

(vi)

Rustication

I don't intend to describe the lengthy course of self-examination that I undertook. At the time I thought it was a great and revolutionary experience. Now that I am old I can see that it was only the beginning of a lifelong pursuit of freedom. One factor contributing to its length was my unwillingness to see that no matter how wonderful and productive my own schooldays had been, a system which nurtures ten percent of the population at the expense of the other ninety percent cannot be justified. It would have been very helpful if at that time I could have read Stephen Jay Gould's *The Mismeasure of Man*[12], but that great work, which blows the conventions of intelligence-testing to pieces, still lay twenty years in the future. There were, however, several aspects of my life that were exceedingly helpful.

As a descendant of farm workers and artisans I grew up in what are usually described as humble circumstances. My father, being a resourceful and intelligent man, ascended from the ranks of the unemployed ex-Tommies of the nineteen-twenties to skilled work in the timber trade and finally to a managerial position. My childhood friends and acquaintances included no one of wealth, position or intellectual eminence. I am fairly certain that I reached the age of ten before meeting anyone, except our local vicar, who had been to university. It is true that after being such a late reader that I had to be put into a remedial class, I developed a habit of bookishness and a surprising vocabulary that earned me the nicknames "Diction'ry" and "Parson", but I got on well enough with the local children and their parents. The children of the lower classes are supposed to grow up with some respect for those of higher station, but somewhere along the line I began to develop a characteristic scepticism towards the pronouncements of those with position and authority. If this statement is regarded as inconsistent with my later plans for a society in which most people are guided by a minority of the *intelligentsia*, I must point out that I have never advocated consistency at the expense of honesty and creativity. Art, science and life use inconsistency as a major propulsive force. During my years at Cambridge, where any statement of principle or belief was taken as a challenge to intense debate, this constructive scepticism continued to develop. I was fortunate to complete my high school education at a time when County and State Scholarships not only made it possible for me to attend one of the ancient universities but also put me in the company of a body of students much more diverse than had been usual at Cambridge in earlier years. One of the results was that I became equally at home with people of many different backgrounds. Another was that I developed a habit of trying to say exactly what I meant in the most economical terms and assuming that people would take what I said at face value and not look for innuendoes and ulterior motives. These were characteristics that were quite difficult to maintain, especially after I joined the Anthroposophical Society.

My family's move from the city of Gloucester to the village of Ashleworth had been an important event in more ways than one. One consequence was that I became friendly with many of the villagers. After I had finished at Cambridge they elected me captain of the local cricket team and Clerk to the Parish Council. In their company I drank, played cribbage and darts, and discussed the problems of the world. None of them had university degrees and less than a handful had been to grammar school. A standard intelligence test might well have floored a lot of them. But they were smart, knowledgeable and the salt of the earth, and their companionship was deeply therapeutic. I'm not sure whether or not I had been well on the way to becoming an intellectual snob, but if so they were instrumental in reversing the process.

The countryside around Gloucester was intensely beautiful, and I was deeply in love with it. I do not like to think about what I suspect must have happened to it over the past forty years, but I still dream of it and sometimes wake up in tears. I must state firmly, however, that the task of teaching academic subjects to large classes of very large boys, whose principal desire was to leave school and get a job at the earliest possible moment, was exhausting, frustrating and, at times, alarming. A senior master, on departing after having introduced me to a new class, muttered, "Watch that boy in the front row; he's apt to pull a knife." The only woman teacher on the staff at the Crypt collapsed into her chair after a strenuous session with 5C only to find that she was sitting in a pool of sulphuric acid. The classroom windows looked across the playing fields to the rich pasture of Robinswood Hill, but anyone who believes that there was much of the idyllic about the life of a teacher in the England of the 1950's is misinformed.

(vii)

Transportation

In my early days as a teacher at the Crypt I used to arrive and depart on a disreputable old motorcycle. My salary as a teacher soon enabled me to graduate to a disreputable old car. The bike and the car both had side-valve[13] engines, so I became quite good at replacing things like piston rings and cylinder-head gaskets. After three years I tired of these exercises and bought myself a new car, "new" being a relative term. It was a Hillman convertible and it was only three years old. Someone told me that, according to Sigmund Freud, when a young man buys a convertible it means that he is looking for a mistress. The first thing I encountered was anthroposophy, a circumstance which, in a manner of speaking, supports Freud's contention.

The transaction—buying a car, not encountering anthroposophy—left me somewhat impoverished, so, having reluctantly agreed to undertake a tutoring assignment, one of the first things I did in my "new" car was to drive to the top of Horsepools Hill on the road from Gloucester to Stroud and turn into a narrow lane, where I parked and emerged to find myself, like Dante, at the edge of a dark wood. Unlike Dante, I encountered a young Valkyrie standing on a tump[14] and awaiting my arrival. Having passed through a wicket gate and traversed an unkempt path we came to a clearing with a view of the distant Severn. There, in the cottage in which Beatrix Potter had written *The Tailor of Gloucester*, a woman lived with her four daughters, the eldest of whom was the Valkyrie, and all of whom either were or had been students at Wynstones School, a Waldorf School on the outskirts of Gloucester. One was a brilliant violinist, but she had decided that she wanted to be a doctor, so I was engaged to give her some science lessons. The events of the following year or so had many of the ingredients of both farce and novel, and I pass over them with no reluctance at all. Let it suffice to say that through this encounter I was introduced to some of the teachers at Wynstones and to the local Christian Community priest, Michael Tapp.

Wynstones in the early 1960's was not the school that it became in subsequent decades. Its temperament was phlegmatic-melancholic and its atmosphere reminiscent of *The Cherry Orchard*. Most people in Gloucester had never heard of it and those who had often had rather strange ideas about it. I was in the common-room at the Crypt when I received the telephone call asking me to tutor one of those bosky girls, and my end of the conversation was overheard by several of my colleagues, including A. L. C. Smith, the deputy headmaster. "Wynstones", he said. "It's a Waldorf School. They do a lot of horse riding there." The girls had arrived at the interesting view that Waldorf education was superior to all other types and that if you really wanted to learn anything you had to go elsewhere. Salaries at Wynstones were extremely low, even for an English Waldorf School, and qualified people who were willing and able to live such a financially deprived life were few and far between. After going to a few meetings at the school I realized how the girls had come by their opinions. Talks on Waldorf education dwelt mainly on the malfeasances of other educational approaches in which academic subjects were taught by conventional old-fashioned methods. I learnt that I was employed in a maleficent system and that I was teaching the wrong things in the wrong way. I learnt also that modern art, modern music, modern science and modern technology were all bad except as practised in an extraordinarily ugly concrete building called the Goetheanum, and kindred locations. I have since revised my opinion of the Goetheanum. It has its good points but I still prefer its back to its front.

Although I was a ripe old twenty-seven, Michael Tapp asked me to attend meetings of his Christian Community youth group, but after a few weeks he kicked me out. It seemed that I was asking the wrong questions and allowing my scepticism to show too much. Fortunately he didn't prescribe a bowl of hemlock. Spurred by these encounters but reticent about my newly acquired interest, I looked for Steiner's works in the County Library. My initial reading of anthroposophy was therefore determined by what happened to be on the shelves, and included *Theosophy*, *The Course of My Life*, and *The Philosophy of Freedom*. I thought *Theosophy* was a repulsive little book, arrogant in tone and dogmatic in exposition. I did not much care for the flavor of *The Course of My Life*, but it was more readable than *Theosophy*. *The Philosophy of Freedom* I found very interesting. Having thoroughly absorbed the positivistic manner of my Cambridge teachers I found Steiner's positivism of mind and spirit congenial. I still found his style difficult, but I felt that I was meeting a different character from the presumptuous pontificator of *Theosophy*.

(viii)

Schicksals

In spite of the inner obstacles something seemed to be pulling me into anthroposophy. I thought at the time, and still believe, that my attendance at some Christian Community services had something to do with it. The services were, and are, hard for me to sit through, but there is no doubt that they tap into something for which there are no mundane explanations. Perhaps the most important thing, with one exception, that happened was that after struggling with the books that I have already mentioned, I went to the library one day to see if anything different had turned up, and found *The Knowledge of Higher Worlds and Its Attainment*.[15] This, I thought, was a book that almost anyone could read without immediately wanting to throw it out of the window, and I wished that I had come across it before my encounter with *Theosophy*. Here was a gentle Rudolf Steiner, a teacher who encouraged his readers to work with humility, patience and guarded optimism. This was a combination that seemed to be rare among anthroposophists.

The exception mentioned above was my meeting my future wife, Barbara. She had encountered anthroposophy by chance six years previously when she was a junior counselor at a summer camp in New England, which was run by teachers from a number of Waldorf schools. Later on, as a student at Antioch College, she had spent several of her work periods at Waldorf schools in California, Mexico and New York, taking whatever training she could pick up along the way and meeting many of the fabled anthroposophical authorities of the time. After finishing at Antioch she had planned to attend Emerson College in the first year of its existence at Clent, England, but at the urgent request and recommendation of Werner Glas, a former Wynstones pupil and one of the aforementioned fabulous characters, she had agreed to teach second grade at the dear old place. From Barbara I learnt a great deal about the theory and practice of anthroposophy and Waldorf education. Apart from mentioning that theory and practice are often at loggerheads, an observation which any unprejudiced observer, to borrow a phrase from Steiner, can make, I don't wish to dwell on Barbara's perceptions. They were very important to me, and continue to be so, but she is entitled to present them herself in the somewhat unlikely event that she ever wishes to do so. Among the consequences of our getting to know each other, one was that in spite of what I had seen of Waldorf education in England I wanted to become a Waldorf teacher. Another was that because of what I had seen and heard of Waldorf education in England, I wanted to do it in America. I knew that the teachers at Wynstones had consigned America to the devil, along with modern art, science *et cetera*, but by this time I had figured out pretty well which of their opinions to take seriously.

4

Becoming a Teacher: Part 2

The interaction between cheap ink and cheap pink blotting paper produces a blot that appears black only to casual inspection. A closer look shows that as it spreads further from its point of departure it develops interesting shades of purple.

(i)

Pedagogy

That the budding young teacher is significantly helped by a year or two of training has never been among my most strongly held convictions. Perhaps this state of relative agnosticism has something to do with the two-thirds of a year that I whiled away at the Cambridge University Institute of Education. The other third of the year, spent at Sir Thomas Rich's School in Gloucester, under the wise and benevolent guidance of Arnold Hurd, was of inestimable benefit, as also was the term that I had worked at Bristol Grammar School standing in for an absent chemistry master. To be able to spend a few months learning from one's mistakes, without having to spend another year or so living them down, is very salutary. This is not to imply that after the first fine careless rapture I stopped making mistakes. The reason why I continued, as the poet says, to sing each song twice over was that I often got it wrong the first time.[16]

A strong belief in the value, indeed in the necessity, of self-education is not incompatible with an appreciation of what is potentially to be gained from a training course. It is merely a question of distinguishing between the essential and the conditionally desirable. The author of a well-known book on nutrition began a chapter with the words, "Which apricot, grown where?" "Which training course, taught by whom and under what circumstances?" might be a very useful question. I knew a headmaster in England who, as a result of years of experience, automatically rejected applicants who had been to training institutions. He made an exception of Cambridge because, as he said, "They don't really try to teach you anything there." There is an acute worldwide shortage of Waldorf teachers. People sometimes remark that this is especially the case in the high schools but my experience has been that although lots of people want to be class teachers, *good* ones are just as hard to find as good high school teachers. What makes the situation different in the high school is that requirements are more easily quantified and communicated and incompetence is more quickly and inescapably identified. Some people can prove in theory that this is not so, but I'm talking about what actually happens. Waldorf training institutions, as I experienced them in the days when I was deeply involved in the search for teachers, had difficulty in attracting promising applicants and often ended up with classes loaded with flower children who had somehow got the idea that the Waldorf classroom is a kind of Garden of Eden where they could render what they understand as being due to God, ignore Caesar completely and remain in blissful ignorance of the serpent. Caesar, however, gets more and more insistent as the children get older and it becomes clear that teachers are having difficulty in teaching subjects that they don't understand very well themselves. It's probably better not to go into the question of the serpent. Perhaps things have changed since 1996.

Plunging fully clothed into the deep end of Waldorf education may or may not be the quickest and most thorough way for anyone to get a grip on the question of what it means to be a teacher, but it short-circuits a great deal of the humbug that seems to be so hard to keep out of teacher training courses, and enables the neophyte's colleagues to make a more reliable prognosis than the understandably over-optimistic reports of a training institution are apt to yield. This mode of entry also has the advantage of screening out most of the flower children. My entry into Waldorf education was quite a muddle, and I'm still not sure whether or not I can claim to have been trained.

(ii)

Institutionalized

Having decided to cross the Atlantic I wrote to the Waldorf School of Garden City, the Rudolf Steiner School in Manhattan, and Highland Hall in California. At this time (1964) there were only eight Waldorf Schools in the whole of North America. The Garden City school was starting a new venture, the Waldorf Institute, which would offer a year's training in Waldorf Education and would eventually reward successful students with a master's degree. After some correspondence with John Gardner, nominally the Faculty Chairman but, *de facto*, the Principal of the Garden City School, I was quite surprised to find myself offered a fellowship for a year at the Institute, with a stipend of $4,000. This seemed to me to be a large sum of money. It was more than my annual salary at the Crypt, even though I was, by that time, an experienced teacher with a special responsibility allowance. While this was going on I was also in touch with Henry Barnes, whose position in Manhattan was similar to John Gardner's at Garden City, although more subtly registered. Henry actually had to go through the process of being re-elected every year. It turned out that the Manhattan school needed a physics teacher, and I was offered the job, sight unseen, at a salary slightly greater than the aforementioned stipend. I can't remember who wrote to me from Highland Hall, but I do remember that the response was repressive and discouraging. Barbara, meanwhile, had undertaken to spend a year at the Waldorf School in Reutlingen, Germany, teaching English and learning German, so we appeared to be heading in opposite directions. Naturally we discussed my situation at some length. Eventually, in my innocence, I decided that it would be a good idea to accept John Gardner's offer. I thought the training would be useful, that it would give me time to look around before making a long-term commitment and, I blush to say, I rather liked the idea of being a Fellow. It did not occur to me to wonder where the $4,000 was coming from. If I had known I might have made a different decision.

After a while we discovered that someone at Reutlingen had pressed the wrong button and Barbara's arrangement fell through. So she accepted an invitation to take the first grade in Manhattan, and we crossed the ocean on the same plane. We have been on more or less the same plane ever since. It couldn't have turned out better if we had planned it, and before long that was what we were accused of having done.

(iii)

Farmed Out

There were six students at the Waldorf Institute. One doubled as art teacher and another as executive secretary. Four became teachers in Waldorf schools and two remained so for most of a lifetime. I think that's a pretty good average, but this, of course, was before the flower children discovered anthroposophy. We were a very congenial group, intelligent, serious-minded and full of humor, and the studies that we undertook with John Gardner and other members of the faculty were extremely rewarding. I'd like to describe some of the good times we had together, but the inkblot has other ideas. At the moment it seems to want to explore a different kind of learning experience.

After a week or two of visiting various classes, beginning a study of the basic educational courses and doing some painting and eurythmy, I was summoned to the presence of the Director of the Institute—John Gardner—and informed that my plans had been changed. It seemed that once I had signed on the dotted line at the Institute the wires had started buzzing between Garden City, Manhattan and Kimberton. I had never heard of Kimberton, but I learnt that it was a small village in Pennsylvania, about a two-hour drive from Manhattan. The Waldorf School there, which went under the name of Kimberton Farms School, had recently started a high school and someone was needed to teach physics and chemistry to the ninth and tenth grades, starting in January. I was further informed that the Manhattan School had no physics teacher and that I should be teaching eleventh and twelfth grades there in the spring. The powers that were thought that this was all a very good idea and it was put in such a way as to leave no room for discussion. It is therefore fortunate that I thought it was a good idea too. This is why my formal training in Waldorf education lasted only twelve weeks and I set off for Kimberton Farms School in the following January.

(iv)

"By Schisms Rent Asunder..."[17]

In November I was "requested" to spend a couple of days at Kimberton to be interviewed and to attend a faculty meeting. "The first thing they will want to find out about you", John Gardner told me, "is how weird you are." It seemed that the faculty at Kimberton consisted of two groups, the anthroposophists and the non-anthroposophists. The latter were in the majority, included the school principal, Mrs. Lord, and considered the former to be strange. John was rather anxious that I should appear to be a perfectly normal, regular kind of person, and I gathered that the important thing was to make a good impression on the non-anthroposophists. What the anthroposophists thought was apparently of less consequence. I remained for some time entirely unaware of the origin of this peculiar situation.

Having visited the Goetheanum and various schools in England and Germany, I had a pretty good idea of what a Waldorf School was supposed to look like. The Manhattan School occupied two converted houses, so there was not much opportunity to achieve an anthroposophical look, but the building at Garden City and the high school at Kimberton had been constructed specifically as Waldorf Schools, so why were they so unremittingly rectangular? For all its conventionality the Waldorf School at Garden City makes a very pleasant impression of color, texture and form, but the Kimberton High School had no redeeming features that I could discover, even when considered only functionally. Everything from the overall form down to the concrete blocks of which it is constructed is square. I have a very limited capacity to digest anthroposophical architecture, but in this case a few cut corners and a mushroom-style roof would have been welcome.

In the course of my time at Kimberton I met some wonderful people on both sides of the schism, but the bifurcation was real and made things difficult for everyone. Kimberton is on what was known as the Main Line, and needed to earn its bread and butter by catering to upper middle class clients who would be repelled by the appearance of anything "weird". In the minds of the faculty majority there was a considerable overlap between "weird" and "anthroposophical". This made it very hard for the minority to do what they considered to be right for the children both in and out of the classroom. My sympathies were very much with the teachers who were doing their best, in difficult conditions, to work out of anthroposophical insights, and I winced with them whenever Mrs. Lord[18] closed a discussion with the words, "Well, I don't pretend to be an initiate, but..." I can't remember how much of this I figured out in my initial visit, but it was probably very little. I had been in the USA for only a few months and there were many things that I had not yet figured out. One was that I had come to live in what may well be the most conservative place on the face of the earth, but somewhere along the line the rigid conventionality of the Garden City community was forced upon my attention. I was given a couple of early warnings.

I had arrived two weeks before the opening of school and John and Carol Gardner had very kindly allowed me to stay in their house while I looked for accommodation. One day John told me that the parents of a sixth grader had a room to let, and sent me off to investigate, first taking the precaution of telling me exactly what to say when I got there. The room was fine and I moved in, but it seemed a little bare, so the next day Barbara brought some rugs and other things to make it feel more like home. Unfortunately she made the mistake of helping me carry the things upstairs, so a few hours later I had a very uncomfortable interview with my landlady, Mrs. McCann. "But she was only up there for about two minutes", I protested. "Doesn't make any difference", she replied. "I have to worry about what the neighbors think." I decided that it would be impolitic to give my opinion of the neighbors and their thoughts. This incident was not sufficient to dispel my romantic notion of America as the land of the free, so the next day, when I turned up at school wearing sandals, I was surprised to find myself the target of a number of pointed remarks about such things as the danger of stubbing my toe. Americans used to get their impressions of England from authors like Agatha Christie and P. G. Wodehouse whose little comedies gain point by being enacted against a backdrop of stuffy conservatism. These images were then reflected back to the English strongly enough and with enough airy condescension to convince us, not necessarily that England was really like that, but that we might expect Americans to be much more free, easy and relaxed. After a while I realized that it was all an illusion, but it took time. The point of all this, if one is needed, is that eventually it dawned on me that the Garden City School was playing the same game as Kimberton Farms School, but doing it a great deal more subtly and with a much more serious commitment to the anthroposophical foundations of Waldorf education.

(v)

Manhattan

My visit to the Manhattan Rudolf Steiner School was interesting in a different way. The high school had graduated its first senior class a few years previously. Whereas I was at Kimberton for two days and now remember virtually nothing of the visit, I was in Manhattan for a few hours and have vivid memories of meeting Henry and Christie Barnes, Amos Franceschelli, Swain Pratt, Nanette Grimm, John Root and Karl Ege. The Garden City School was certainly not lacking in energy but in Manhattan there was a feeling that the school was in a state of constant vibration. No doubt this was partly due to the proximity of the subway and a great deal of heavy traffic, but it was in the atmosphere too. I liked it and, having seen three American schools, I began to feel confident that my decision to come to this country had been a good one and that given the choice I'd prefer to work in Manhattan. After various meetings and conversations I was taken upstairs to see the lab. The wonder is that after seeing it and looking at the physics apparatus and supplies I was still of the same opinion. The Crypt School had two labs for physics, two for chemistry, one for biology, various conservatories, darkrooms and preparation rooms, and a full-time professional lab assistant. For student experiments it was always possible to provide a dozen sets of apparatus and for demonstrations there was everything that the most enterprising teacher was likely to need. At Garden City there was only one lab for physics and chemistry but it was large and very well supplied. Kimberton had a large lab and a demonstration room. The lab at the Rudolf Steiner School was tiny and was used for all three sciences. I could see that chemistry and biology were in the hands of a strong-minded person, a situation which explained itself perfectly when I met Mrs. Grimm. The random collection of antiques provided for the use of physics teachers was a different matter. Expensive but incomplete instructional kits with manuals in Gothic German script jostled with old batteries, electrical instruments that would have been useful if they had not been broken, and objects with no obvious use, *mathoms* donated no doubt by parents who had been unable to figure out what they were for. By the time spring rolled around and I was trying to teach the eleventh and twelfth grades I had been able to do very little about the situation and lab classes varied from masterpieces of improvisation to monuments of frustration.

(vi)

Solo

Barbara and I were married by John Hunter at the Christian Community in Manhattan on December 20, 1964, a few days after taking part in one of the Oberufer Christmas plays. Barbara says it was the Shepherds' Play and that my opinion that we were Adam and Eve in the Paradise Play is just wishful thinking. She says that we did that later. Be that as it may, it is an inescapable fact that two weeks later I had to leave and start my stint at Kimberton. We had managed to buy ourselves a car but I had not yet acquired an American driver's license, so I was obliged to depart from Paradise by way of Pennsylvania Station. The nearest I could get to Kimberton was Paoli, which meant that someone had to turn out on cold Sunday evenings and pick me up at the station. It was a one hour round trip, so it was not surprising that Franklin Kane, my honorary chauffeur, was not usually in the best of tempers when he arrived. I wasn't either—the station was very cold and Franklin was always at least half an hour late. At that time I hadn't realized what Sunday evenings mean to Waldorf teachers.

Franklin was automatically elected to the position of ferryman because I was staying at his house, along with his wife, Betty, and the children, Andrea and George. George was a pre-toddler and I was quite fascinated to see him teething on the dog's tail. I forget the name of the dog. Franklin and Betty were very kind in an absent-minded sort of way. As committed anthroposophists and teachers they had plenty to think about, although the causes and extent of their preoccupation only gradually became clear to me.

One of the most striking features of my early years as a Waldorf teacher was that no one ever told me what to do, offered to help or sat in on my classes. The only exceptions to the last category were a few visitors who were apparently there to see how things are done in Waldorf Schools! So there I was, in a strange school in a foreign country, about to teach four main lesson courses to students I had never seen before. I had never taught a main lesson in my life. No doubt the results were a long way from ideal but things could have been very much worse. One positive aspect of the situation was that although I got very little help of a purely Waldorf nature the teachers and staff of the school were extremely kind and thoughtful in every other way. Another was that the students, although unevenly gifted in scientific insight and not uniformly diligent, were very friendly, good-natured and helpful and I never had to worry about discipline. They thought I was a little funny in some ways, as only befitted an Englishman, but it was clear to them that I knew my subject matter, and that always helps. My knowledge of Waldorf education was largely theoretical, but I had learnt more physics, chemistry and mathematics in high school than most American science majors do in college.

I had some very difficult adjustments to make, however. Compared with what is taught in Waldorf Schools, mainstream physics courses are very apt to seem more like essays in applied mathematics. Computation should certainly not be absent from physics main lessons, but the emphasis is more on descriptive work. Waldorf students, in any case, tend to be resistant to the importation of mathematical methods into courses which do not have a mathematical label. In my thirty-two years as a Waldorf teacher I met very few classes in which more than a handful of students were fluent in the most elementary math. I remember one young lady who was surprised to find that you could use the theorem of Pythagoras in physics. She thought it applied only in geometry. Having taught quite a lot of math classes I might be expected to accept some of the blame for this, but, for reasons that we may eventually come to, I don't. For the moment let it be enough to say that I managed reasonably well and that I'm not at all sure that having someone there to tell me what to do would have been much help.

One of the problems of being a visiting main lesson teacher is that when the lesson is over and you have cleaned up and done some correcting, you may find yourself at a loose end. No doubt this is a terrible thing to say. Surely there is always something useful to do, or there are people to talk to, classes to visit or "useful observations" to make. If, however, the projects you are working on are at home, nobody has time to talk and nobody is anxious to be visited, and if, furthermore, you have no desire to sit and read for four hours, the weather is too bad to make a long walk enjoyable, and you don't have a car, then you actually do have a problem. You can say a lot of bad things about computers, and many anthroposophists do, but these days I take my laptop computer wherever I go and I always have something to work on.

I find it interesting to note that the people I remember most strongly from Kimberton are seven anthroposophists. There may be mundane explanations for this, such as the fact that I continued to see some of them occasionally in later years, but it is true, nonetheless, that with the exception of Narcie-Lou Lord and Cammie Miller, in whose house I stayed during my first visit, most of the non-anthroposophists have vanished without a trace. I am sure that even if I had not stayed with Franklin and Betty Kane for three months and carried away memories of their highly individual way of running a household I should have been sufficiently impressed by their fervent commitment to everything anthroposophical and Waldorfian to retain vivid images of them. They and five of their colleagues come into this story again.

Actually they don't. The episode in which they reappear has had to be excised—not, I should hasten to add, because of any malfeasance on their part.

(vii)

Enlightenment

This all happened a very long time ago. Some of the events are clear and bright, although diminished by distance, but there are large gaps and chronological uncertainties. The following events took place, but I am not sure exactly when or in what order;

I was told that Mrs. Myrin held the purse strings for both Kimberton and Garden City and that Mr. Myrin, who was by now *hors de combat*, had been the one with the commitment to anthroposophy. Hence the house divided.

John Gardner told me that Mrs. Myrin had contributed my $4,000 stipend and therefore expected me to take the position of science teacher at Kimberton the following year.

Henry Barnes offered me a position at the Manhattan Rudolf Steiner School for the following year, and I decided to accept it.

I had a conversation with Mrs. Myrin in which I explained that I had not known that she had financed my fellowship and that although I was very grateful I did not feel that I was under any obligation to teach at Kimberton. She didn't say much but was evidently not amused.

I had another conversation with John in which I repeated what I had said to Mrs. Myrin and added that I thought such financial aid as I had received might properly be thought of as a contribution to the Waldorf Movement in general rather than as having strings attached. John laughed and told me that if I thought anyone was capable of such a purely altruistic action I was deeply mistaken. He taxed me with having known what the implications were, and having planned all along to marry Barbara and take a job in Manhattan. I concluded that John had been on the wrong end of a telephone call from Mrs. Myrin and that in spite of his laughter he wasn't amused either.

During the course of these clarifications some of the facts of Waldorf life became more obtrusively evident. Before I left England I had realized that there was something close to a consensus among the teachers at Wynstones that their school was the one place in the world where things were being done correctly according to Rudolf Steiner's wishes. It is remarkable that this was so in spite of the number of middle-European expatriates who worked there and gave a decidedly un-English flavor to the establishment, and who might have been expected to compare Wynstones unfavorably with schools in Germany or Switzerland. I also learnt that the staff at Michael Hall in Sussex thought the same thing about *their* school, although the exactly correct things being done there were often in contradiction to the exactly correct things being done at Wynstones. It did not occur to me that the same kind of scholastic chauvinism might operate in the USA until I practically had my nose rubbed in it, but that is one of the stories that I feel compelled to omit…

I can only tell you how it seemed to me afterwards. The teachers at Wynstones and at Michael Hall knew that they carried the sacred flame of Waldorf education. Some of people at Garden City had the same idea about themselves but, unlike the Wynstones people, they were fortified by the fact they had Mrs. Myrin to pay for transportation. The situation was different in Manhattan. Parents frequently detected elements of weirdness in the way in which the school operated and a magazine article referred to it as "zany". At that time, as far as the faculty was concerned, there was no doubt about the commitment to an education based on the anthroposophical knowledge of the human being, but there was no sense of being the School among schools. Some of the teachers evinced symptoms of insecurity and cast envious looks in the direction of the Garden City school, with its superabundance of space, its well-oiled financial machinery and its scrupulous attention to appearances; but people generally took a measure of pride in the feeling that they worked in a financially independent, faculty-run school. This was just as well since to the best of my knowledge and belief the school had never received a cent from the Myrin fortune and some solace was needed for the hardships inflicted by the miserable salary scale on teachers who had no other means of support. It was said, with how much truth I do not know, that Mrs. Myrin believed that money spent on a school run by a bevy of anthroposophical teachers (two strikes there) was not a sound investment. How the school was actually run is a matter of interpretation; Henry Barnes got his way most of the time but he sometimes had a tougher time doing it than John Gardner.

(viii)

On being Wayward

The original title of this book was *Memoirs of a Wayward Anthroposophist*, but I was told that this would put people off, so I changed it. I call myself an anthroposophist because I have been a student of Rudolf Steiner's work and a member of the Anthroposophical Society for over forty years. Anthroposophical work encourages us in the belief that the age of peripatetic authorities and stationary gurus is over. Being possessed of a healthy disinclination to take other people's word for it, whatever "it" was, I simply progressed further in that frame of mind. Anthroposophists generally practise what anthroposophy preaches in this regard, but only up to a point. We certainly have no difficulty in rejecting most of the world's recognized authorities, along with the orthodoxies of politics, economics, medicine, science, art, agriculture and education that they represent—except when they just happen to fit in with something that we are pushing. As a group we believe that we have access to knowledge that puts us in a superior position, and the tendency to let this feeling of superiority show is one of the most off-putting features of the anthroposophical personality. The "anthroposophical personality" is a palpable presence, not just another example of reification. Forty years ago it made it quite difficult for me to join the Society, but I gradually became used to it and realized that my real mistake was the unconscious assumption that anthroposophists ought somehow to be better than other people, whereas in fact all they are doing is to react to a conversion or *eclaircissement* in the same way as almost anyone else who has seen the light. "*They* don't believe what *we* know", as an old anthroposophist said to me. To feel pity for one's less enlightened brothers and sisters is in itself admirable, but when the feeling is adulterated with a strong dose of *de haut en bas*, the situation is not healthy.

Having disposed—at least in thought—of the regular pantheon, we might have hoped for an access of fresh air and independent thinking. Unfortunately it doesn't often work that way. Rejecting the old gods or authorities seems automatically to lead to accepting or appointing new ones. The English beheaded their king and ended up with Oliver Cromwell, who was a much worse bargain. In similar circumstances the French acquired the Emperor Napoleon, about whom it is, perhaps, better not to comment. The Russians swapped the Tsars for Joseph Stalin, who proceeded to arrange for the deaths of fifteen million of his comrades.

As anthroposophists we are enjoined to practise veneration and to silence the inner voice which is apt to be saying, "But…But…But…" There is, we believe, an element of goodness and beauty in everything. Jesus, in a story quoted by Steiner, instead of recoiling from the decaying body of a dog, pointed out the beauty of the dog's teeth. Veneration, however, has to be realistic and truthful, and is a quality of soul that is apt to be wasted when it is applied to persons. Steiner made no bones about identifying the evils of the world or what, in our current fit of preciosity, we would call the "negative influences". Anthroposophists, however, seem to adopt their gurus[19] uncritically, often simply on the strength of reputation or position. I have seen it happen often enough and it seems to be quite easy to become an anthroposophical guru. A specialized study of Steiner's work, the gift of the gab and the ability to say the right things in the right places seem to do the trick, especially if accompanied by an anthroposophical pedigree and financial independence. I have no doubt that some of the anthroposophical authorities whom I have encountered over the years have been people of genuine insight who deserve our attention. Equally there are those who are "negative influences", some of whom do it with charisma and some with bumbling sincerity. A few are self-serving charlatans. Such individuals would be of little importance if it were not for the tendency of the anthroposophical community to put them on pedestals and say, in effect, "These be your Gods, O Israel." Even for those most deserving of our admiration, such idolatries and apotheoses are out of place in the modern world. My appearance of "waywardness" is due, at least in part, to my inbuilt distaste for such gurifications and deifications, and the circumstance that the perception of incompetence, humbug and fraud is sometimes on an intuitive level that makes it very hard to communicate my misgivings even in favorable circumstances. Circumstances are, in any case, rarely favorable. People who have been drawn into the orbit of someone by whom they relish being led and guided tend either to take serious offence or to manifest symptoms of spiritual superiority when such doubts are expressed. The situation is apt to be exacerbated by the ease with which the innocent gurified can be used by the politically adroit. In my earlier years I used to protest sometimes, but on the whole it seems best to withdraw rather than to try to influence the course of subsequent events. It may take years but most people do eventually see what has been happening.

It is possible to hear and see no evil if you are willing to go around with your eyes shut and your fingers in your ears, but it is much harder to ignore a bad smell. If your fingers are already in your ears it is hard to hold your nose and, in any case, you still have to breathe. A chronically sceptical frame of mind and an inability to applaud at the right moments have many disadvantages and are apt to affect one's political status. When I am told quite casually that J. is clairvoyant or that Rudolf Steiner said such and such to an elderly eurythmist in 1924, although he never said anything of the sort to anyone else, it would be nice if the inner voice occasionally said, "Wonderful!" instead of "I doubt it."

Things said by X to Y have a knack of getting around to Z, even when Y is a visiting dignitary. One distinguished visitor from Stuttgart was told by the teachers in whose apartment he stayed that the Francises were "not really anthroposophical." Eventually it filtered through to me that I was regarded by some of my colleagues as unsound, possibly subversive, apt to speak frankly at inopportune times and definitely not a proper anthroposophist—or, to put it kindly, I was "wayward."

◆   ◆   ◆

I am sorry if anyone is offended by these dispatches from the front line, but a great deal of what may be taken as offensive is simple reporting, and my opinions, hard as they may be on the anthroposophical digestion, are the results of observation and thinking, not merely of metabolism.

5

Becoming a Teacher: Part 3

No one would want to read the story of my thirty-two years at the Manhattan Rudolf Steiner School even if I wanted to write it. Please remember that, instead of following a carefully planned itinerary of events chosen for their historical significance and edifying implications, we are guided by the inscrutable flow of dark blue ink into pink paper and the sieve of a memory with somewhat unconventional ideas about which particles are worth examining.

(i)

Manhattan Again

In those days one of the most interesting and, to me at any rate, admirable, peripatetic anthroposophical dignitaries was René Querido. I speak here only out of personal experience. It was generally acknowledged that René had had a distinguished career as a class teacher and high school teacher at Michael Hall, but he was not without his detractors. He was now visiting some of the American schools. I had attended workshops that he had given in Manhattan and had been particularly enthusiastic about his presentations on earth science, a subject which I had never taught. A few months later, after noting that there was no earth science or geography in the high school schedule at the Rudolf Steiner School, I made a little speech. I must have been quite eloquent, for the faculty quickly decided that earth science should be added to the curriculum in ninth and tenth grades. A quick decision on anything was a remarkable event. "Who's going to teach it?" I enquired. "You are", they said.

In the April following my arrival in the USA I began teaching my main lessons in Manhattan, two weeks earlier than had been planned. This happened because the high school music teacher fell ill exactly at the time when he was due to start a music history main lesson with the senior class, and someone had the bright idea that this would be a perfect time for me to begin my adventures with earth science. So now, in addition to all the handicaps that I mentioned in connection with my main lessons at Kimberton I had the problem of teaching a subject with which I was quite unfamiliar to a class which, in rather violent contrast to the Kimbertonians, was anything but docile. It included Henry Barnes's daughter, the very likeable and far from angelic Marian, and Colony Elliot, who made no secret of her opinions about people and institutions and who later achieved an admirable professionalism in the unassumingly titled but hugely demanding role of elementary school receptionist. Colony never told me her opinions of earth science and physics, but I figured them out from her preference for reading novels on her lap behind the desk. After a while it dawned on her that I always knew what she was doing. It was too easy really. She could hardly expect me to believe that her downcast eyes were the signs of a becoming modesty in the presence of a master, and her rapt concentration the result of the quality of my discourse. I wrote Clerihews for most of my colleagues at one time or another. Colony's is one of the nicer ones.

Ms. Colony Weiss
Has attended the Rudolf Steiner School twice.
The first time she was very sarcastic;
Now she's much more elastic.

I used the word "handicap" a few sentences back, but I don't want to give the impression that teaching this course was a grind. It wasn't easy, but the fact is that except for parts of my first year at the Crypt I have always enjoyed teaching, especially when I am getting my teeth into something new.

I heard the news of my accelerated translation to the status of earth science teacher while I was at Kimberton, so I scurried around looking for sources to add to my notes from René Querido's workshop and found the Larousse Encyclopaedia of the Earth, and a marvelous book, *Down to Earth*[20], by two Midwestern professors, Carey Croneis and William C. Krumbein, who knew how to write graceful English with a light touch but, since they were writing in the early nineteen-thirties, were highly sceptical about continental drift, had never heard of plate tectonics and did not know that the Piltdown man was a fake. By the time I got involved with earth science Wegener's ideas were being taken more seriously and we had learnt the truth about *Eoanthropus*, but plate tectonics was still lightless in the quarry. Earth Science, I discovered, consists of pilferings from various disciplines, including, but not restricted to, geology, palaeontology, mineralogy, evolutionary biology, seismology, physics and chemistry. I was delighted and surprised to find that I knew quite a lot of it already.

It was while I was working with this subject matter and this group of students that I became conscious of one of the chief problems of the Waldorf teacher. Whatever subject you are teaching—earth science, physics, history, music, literature and so on—there is a whole mass of exoteric knowledge and there are techniques for organizing and communicating it. The sensitive and perceptive teacher who works entirely from the exoteric can go a very long way. There is also, however, a whole mass of esoteric knowledge. For the Waldorf teacher this nearly always means anthroposophical knowledge. I won't take up the question of other esoteric sources since I have very little experience of them. The question of what to do when there is a collision between the exoteric and the esoteric is only the surface of the problem, but it has to be considered before we can penetrate the situation any further.

(ii)

Geology, Occult Science and Other Digressions

Geology, as a discipline, gradually came into existence in the late eighteenth and early nineteenth centuries out of the study of strata, the classification of rocks into igneous, sedimentary and metamorphic, and observations of the work of river systems, the air, the tides and the weather. Once it was clear that geology is largely a study of processes the question of time became important, and James Hutton's famous remark of 1785, "I can see no vestige of a beginning and no prospect of an end", has resonated for the past two centuries. Since it does not seem to have occurred to any of the geologists that there might never have been a beginning, one of the frequently asked questions was "How long?" How long must it have taken for such and such a layer of sediment to have formed, and for the salt in the sea to have reached its present concentration? If the earth was formed at a temperature comparable to that of the sun, how long must it have taken to cool to its present temperature? All these calculations resulted in answers in the millions of years. It is true that they were based on crude assumptions but it seemed that the tendency was likely to be to underestimate rather than to overestimate. It was hoped that someone would find a sample of the original crust of the earth, which would presumably be some kind of igneous rock, but studies of strata and metamorphism indicated that the oldest known rocks were sedimentary. No matter how old these rocks seemed to be they must have come from the fragmentation, transportation, deposition and consolidation of far older rocks. Lord Kelvin, whose authority among physicists was hard to challenge, calculated that the earth must have been cooling for at most forty million years, but in the latter part of the nineteenth century the biologists realized that to make sense of Darwinian evolution a much longer time was needed. Meanwhile the geologists were demanding a hundred million years for the sea salt process. Then came the discovery that, unknown to Lord Kelvin, radioactive processes in the earth's crust had been keeping the planet warm. Eventually radioactive dating shifted the time scale into the billions of years.

Anthroposophists have been known to speak derisively of the scientists' habit of extrapolation and to demonstrate its foolishness by giving silly examples, so it is as well to mention that the scientists have better reason to understand the perils of extrapolation than most of those who criticize them. I have heard it pointed out that just because Johnny grew six inches in his first year of life it doesn't mean that he'll grow fifteen feet in his first thirty years. Since we are considering extrapolations from the present into the past, it would be just a little more to the point to say that we have observed over the course of a comparatively short time that Johnny's height is staying the same. Therefore we have no reason to suppose that he wasn't always five feet seven inches tall. After being regaled with such inanities we are invited to draw some conclusion, but I've never been quite sure what it is. It can't be that all extrapolations are wrong, since some have already turned out to be right. Furthermore we could reach that conclusion only by extrapolating about extrapolations. If the conclusion is merely that extrapolation is apt to give the wrong answer all we can say is that we knew that already. But as exoteric scientists, if we want to find out about the distant past, extrapolation is all we have. As Rudolf Steiner remarked: "As long as geology invented fabulous catastrophes to account for the present state of the earth, it groped in darkness. *It was only when it began to study the processes at present at work on the earth, and from these to argue back to the past, that it gained a firm foundation.*"[21] [My italics]

The normal processes of physics and chemistry are influenced by prevailing conditions of temperature and pressure, the presence of catalysts and the chemical constitution of the immediate environment. Rates of salination and sedimentation are anything but constant. Having said that, we must add either that radioactive decay is not a normal process or that it is the one exception. Radioactive disintegrations proceed at constant rates[22] no matter what extremes of temperature and pressure are applied. The only way to change anything is by exceeding the critical mass, an event which doesn't happen in nature. If it did we wouldn't be here, and even if we were, the residues left by the resulting cataclysm would not be of the kind that are helpful to geologists. The problem of radioactive dating is figuring out whether all the evidence is still there, or whether some of it has been removed by water, air or some other agency. Since the radioactive samples are often taken from granite, a very hard and impervious rock, this is not something that geologists worry about very much. The age of the oldest known rocks is now put at about four billion years, and since these are sedimentary they must have been formed from even older rocks. The age of the universe as a whole can be estimated from its rate of expansion calculated from spectroscopic measurements of the wavelength of the light from stars.[23] Once again extrapolation results in an answer in the billions of years—fifteen billion or so the last time I heard the figures.

As a person trained in the physical sciences I find that these results have the same kind of appeal as the quark and exchange particle theories of modern physics. They are fascinating and one part of me would like them to be true. As a historian of science, however, I know that theories should never be taken unsalted. The question is how much salt to use. A moderate pinch suggests that when the theories become more refined we shall see that our figure for the age of the universe is wrong and it really ought to be thirty or ten billion years. But we can look back and see that estimates in the billions of years have been current for a century or so, and if we have cogent reasons for believing the earth to be much younger than that we are going to have to open a new salt mine and discredit a century of scientific work. Perhaps that's the way it has to be. "Ye are the salt of the earth", said Jesus. Paracelsus added salt to the principles of mercury and sulphur, forming the *tria prima* of body, soul and spirit. Steiner tells us that the heavenly city will be made of salt. To us it is the symbol of scepticism, which it resembles insofar as a certain amount of it is essential to life, but too much is bad for you.

◆ ◆ ◆

Some of my fellow anthroposophists have told me that when they have encountered contradictions between anthroposophical spiritual science and orthodox disciplines they have always been able to see eventually how the orthodox beliefs are mistaken, or how some reconciliation can be made. I have noticed that "eventually" often means "when a highly intellectual system of wishful thinking has enabled them to reach the desired conclusion." Others appear to be willing to suspend judgement indefinitely, an appealing attitude which, by allowing the suspension to last until some future incarnation, often helps people to avoid coming to unpalatable conclusions. Still others appear to have embraced a modern version of the old "double truth" heresy[24]—perfectly aware that Steiner dismissed atomic theory as an intellectual fantasy but speaking and acting for all the world as if they accepted the theories of modern physics.

    Life is difficult for the honest anthroposophist. We can't always see exactly what Steiner was driving at, we sometimes misinterpret his words, and we must allow for his having made mistakes. There have been occasions when I have said to myself, "Steiner was wrong about this", and other times when I have felt very strongly that the real problem lay not in what Steiner said or what a modern scientist, musician or historian said, but in the interpretation of Steiner's words. I have spent more than half my life trying to come to terms with the problems of understanding the relationships between Steiner's pictures of the world and those of modern science and I do not believe that it is possible either to demonstrate in mundane terms that one view is right and the other is wrong or to find any honest way of believing them both at the same time. The knowledge that Steiner gained through his journeys into the spiritual world and the application of his insights to the physical world contradict many of the results of modern physics, astronomy, physiology, archaeology and musicology. In view of these difficulties it is helpful to remember that anthroposophy is not a body of knowledge but a path of spiritual development that you can follow with Steiner's guidance. In addition to your meditative work you can study *Occult Science*, *The Light Course* or *Eurythmy as Visible Music* and take the content into your thinking without feeling compelled to say either Yea or Nay. Your own experience may well convince you of the truth of Steiner's view of human development, as it has in my case. Experience will also almost certainly reveal the healthiness and validity of the Goethean approach to science. You may come to the conclusion that there is something very unhealthy about modern scientific methods and that you can dismiss their results if it is convenient to do so, but there you may be on very shaky ground because anthroposophists usually don't know much about modern science, and much of what they hear is in the nature of pseudo-anthroposophical propaganda.[25] Those who take the trouble to study the history of science and to learn about the vast quantity of phenomenological evidence and concentrated thinking that lie behind its current body of theory are much less apt to indulge in easy dismissals. The only conclusion I can draw is that if you are a teacher, a lecturer or a voluble anthroposophical enthusiast you need to be careful, tactful and honest.

♦   ♦   ♦

I am tempted to say that Steiner's *Outline of Occult Science*[26] ought to be required reading for anyone who takes Waldorf education seriously, but I have to admit that for those who are noble, pure in thought and action and defended by virtue, and who do not have the task of teaching courses that touch on the evolution of the earth and its inhabitants, *Occult Science* may, like the weapon and the guardian, be unnecessary[27].

This does not exclude many people; the study of evolution begins with fairy stories in first grade. Steiner's picture of human evolution is in many ways the exact opposite of Darwin's. In Darwin's theory and all its progeny there is nothing purposive, and the apparently miraculous organization of even the simplest organisms is the result of statistical inevitability and the self-replicative properties of certain molecular structures. The stages of development reached by present generations of people, animals and plants have been deeply affected by conditions of earth and sky, but any appearance of purpose can be traced back to the effects of natural selection and the properties of particles produced by the Big Bang. According to Steiner, human beings were present in a remote age of the world at the very beginning of evolution, long before our present states of matter appeared. The whole process has been one of physical densification and evolving consciousness, and has proceeded under the guidance of successive levels of spiritual beings, who have gone through their own parallel stages of evolution and have appeared to humanity as gods and angels. Minerals, plants and animals are the modern representatives of beings who sacrificed their humanity at different stages of evolution. All of which being the case, there is absolutely no reason to suppose that there is any validity at all in the backward extrapolations performed by present-day scientists. The time scale has been determined by the operations of the hierarchies, not by inanimate physical processes. I have heard, but not taken part in, some heated discussions about the correct interpretation of Steiner's observations, but it is safe to say that the age of the earth in its present incarnation is to be measured at most in the hundreds of thousands of years, and there is no reason to suppose that time as we experience it operated at all in the "sleep of worlds" between planetary incarnations or in the previous incarnations of the earth.

This knowledge leaves the teacher in quite a hole. We don't teach anthroposophy in Waldorf Schools, and even if we did we wouldn't be teaching ninth or tenth graders about hierarchies and planetary incarnations. It is tempting to try to avoid getting into the question of time, but I don't think that this is either possible or desirable. I used to follow René Querido's advice and start the ninth grade earth science course by thinking about scenery, getting the students to describe a favorite spot and wondering how it got to be that way. One thing that we often did was to consider the Hudson valley and go thoroughly into the topic of peneplanation, following the river from its sources, tracing the changes in the shape of its bed as the slope changes, characterizing the flood plain and the forms of bordering hills, and noting the formation of an estuary and the effects of the tides. With this came observations of weathering, erosion, transportation and deposition and, inevitably, James Hutton and his famous remark. There are other ways to start a course. You can go into the classification of rocks. You can study volcanoes, active and extinct, and learn about intrusions, extrusions, sills and dykes, but whatever you do you always run into the question of time. There is no secret about what the geologists and astronomers think. Many students will have visited the arid monstrosity that has replaced the Hayden Planetarium in New York City, and come away without the faintest inkling that there is any doubt about the numbers.

I don't believe that it is the function of the teacher to tell the students that the scientists are wrong, but I have found that a little history goes a long way towards creating a balanced picture. Given Hutton's study of the sedimentation cycle and William Smith's work on strata, it would have been impossible for the early geologists not to feel that they were involved with immense expanses of time. We can see, however, that the assumption that the evolution of the earth can be *fully* explained in terms of such gradual processes was unwarranted. This idea, known as uniformitarianism, was developed and publicized by Charles Lyell in the 1820's and became the ruling principle of geology. In order to do so it had to overcome the opposing principle of catastrophism, that the history of the earth has been punctuated by global disasters which had from time to time wiped out whole species, changed the face of the planet and enabled us to reach our present state of evolution more quickly. Lyell was a lawyer and you can have quite a bit of fun seeing how he built a persuasive case out of fragmentary evidence. If you don't have time to do your own research you can find everything you need in the first few chapters of Emanuel Velikovsky's *Earth in Upheaval*. In doing so you don't have to buy Velikovsky's theory that the earth has suffered near misses from the planets Mars and Venus, although he piles up the evidence, both geological and literary, in highly fascinating ways.

Even more fascinating, however, is the uproar, the sheer panic in fact, caused by the publication of his theories. This episode took place at about the time when

Senator Joseph McCarthy was busy pinning the communist label on some of the best citizens this country has ever produced, and although the scientists worked on a much smaller scale than the House Un-American Activities Committee, the parallel is unmistakable. A full account of the efforts made by the scientific establishment to discredit and suppress Velikovsky's ideas was given in *The Psychologist*[28] and provides excellent material for a main lesson, provided that the teacher is sensitive to the need to avoid exaggeration and sensationalism. Teachers with a chronic desire to give the scientists a collective black eye should probably seek a cure for their own condition and look elsewhere for their inspiration. When I was at the Garden City Waldorf School I was staggered to find that Velikovsky's books were banned from the school library on the ground that some of the parents might find them offensive. As far as I am concerned Velikovsky's theories are in a category labeled, "Things I'd like to believe but can't manage to." Be that as it may, it is now commonly accepted, for instance, that the dinosaurs were wiped out by a catastrophic event, and not by stealthy environmental changes.

A knowledge of history is the best antidote for any form of scientific totalitarianism, whether of an anthroposophical or a conventional nature. Since this phrase ("scientific totalitarianism") has an unpleasant ring to it, and "conventional" includes quite a range of "doxies"[29], let me add that nearly all the "conventional" scientists I have known or know about have been nice people who meant well and were undoubtedly kind to children and animals. They were, and are, busy doing their thing, as we used to say, and their thing is giving a complete explanation of everything in the universe in purely material terms. Exactly what "material" means is as difficult to explain as exactly what "spiritual" means. To the Greeks of Homer's time matter and spirit did not exist as separate categories. For two thousand years after Homer people spoke as if they believed that all matter was ensouled. According to Owen Barfield[30] the English philosophers made their well-known contribution to the evolution of the consciousness soul by descending so far into materialism that they could be quite sure that there was no trace of spirit left. Just as "all that's not verse is prose", all that's not material is immaterial. "[English philosophy] sought for matter everywhere—in order not to confuse it with spirit." Barfield was English, so I suppose he knew what he was talking about. I am English too, and I agree with at least 50% of what Barfield said on the subject.

What history shows is that science has not progressed through the orderly combination of observation, theory and prediction described by popularizers and propagandists, but in fits and starts governed by individual insights and accidental discoveries. Every major theory, from Descartes to Dalton to Bohr and Born, and to Hoyle and Hawking, has had to be continually revised or totally discarded. Who, in the heyday of Newtonian mechanics could have forecast the outbreak of new forms of relativity a century or so later? In the early nineteenth century John Dalton confidently closed the discussion of a difficult point with the remark, "Thou knows[31] no man can split an atom." At the same time, we must recognize that a discipline that develops by way of spasmodic advances and strategic retreats is not very predictable. We had better not try to forecast its future by extrapolation from its past and present. It is probably best to take it as a working hypothesis that although the theories will continue to be modified, something like the present picture of the structures of both the atom and the universe will be with us for a long time. This is what we have to deal with, and I must confess to being somewhat disturbed by the observation that anthroposophical scientists are much closer to embracing the quantum theory than their conventional counterparts are to accepting the Akashic Record.

Meanwhile, back on the ranch...Catastrophism is more popular than it used to be. Even so it's hard to get around the evidence from radioactivity without invoking spiritual science. If you try you had better know what you're talking about. Quite a lot of books have been written by anthroposophists on topics related to earth science. It doesn't hurt to plough through some of them as long as you don't expect miracles and can tolerate rather a lot of special pleading and the selective transmission of old wives' tales. In the end you have to work things out for yourself and realize (a) that the schedule has you down for earth science, so if you teach something that's not recognizable as such by normal people you had better have an explanation handy, (b) that although casting appropriate doubts on the uniformitarian picture and time scale of geological evolution is a reasonable thing to do, it is not going to create a space that will automatically be taken over by something more spiritual, (c) that students tend to be rather sensitive to the insertion of little anthroposophical goodies, and (d) that if you love your subject and keep an open mind the students probably will too. You really can't expect much more than that.

If you feel that I have not got you out of the hole that I mentioned a few paragraphs back you are right, but you must remember that I didn't say that I would. From choice or from necessity a great many of God's creatures live in holes and bunkers. The caption of a famous cartoon from the Great War, which shows Old Bill crouching in a crater, reads, "If you can find a better (blank) hole, go to it." You can, like the hobbits, take measures to make the hole more habitable, but it is never going to be as comfortable as Bilbo's.

◆   ◆   ◆

Such dilemmas abound. A seventh-grade teacher, having followed one of Rudolf Steiner's insights and taught his students that the heart is not a pump, was confronted by a deeply distressed parent who happened to be a physician. The teacher's colleagues understood his position but made the suggestion that such an insight should not have been passed on to the children unless the teacher had been able to work with it to the point of justifying it out of his own perceptions. This sounds good in theory but it is actually a very tall order. If it were to be applied to everything that we teach it would cause a sudden and radical reduction in the size of the curriculum, which might not be such a bad thing since we obviously try to teach the children too much. Generally we have no difficulty in speaking of exoteric knowledge, even when it is not to our taste, since we can always preface it with the words, "Many scientists believe that…" or "Many historians believe that…" When we put things in those terms we are being strictly truthful and reflecting the general beliefs of the culture in which we live. If we begin a sentence with the words, "Rudolf Steiner said that…" we are invoking a single authority reporting from regions where to the best of my knowledge and belief no one within our movement has followed him. Some of what he says is confirmed by our observations in the sense-perceptible world. Some of it produces conviction on a deeply intuitive level. In my own case there are things that have never made sense and probably never will. The decision to accept Steiner's reports from the spiritual front is something that we make as individuals. Therefore if I tell the students that the heart is not a pump or that Woodrow Wilson was really a bad guy I do so on my own authority as well as Steiner's. If I don't wish to put myself in that position I can say, "Rudolf Steiner said that…", but then I am open to the question, "Why Rudolf Steiner? Why not Mme. Blavatsky or Edgar Cayce?" Or why any of them at all? The words may be Rudolf Steiner's, but the decision to use them is my own.

If you think that such questions don't matter you will be picking your way through a minefield and you will have to rely on virtue to protect you—unless you happen to be working in a community of New Agers who love to wallow in anything that sounds vaguely spiritual and saves wear and tear on the intelligence. As Waldorf teachers we are playing with a deck that is stacked against us. If we happen to win, the prize is a little apple or the tiniest nugget, not some trillion-dollar settlement that will change the face of society.

Remember that in deciding to follow Rudolf Steiner you applied the tests of common sense and inner conviction. Do not fail to apply a corresponding degree of scrutiny to what you hear from anthroposophical eminences and Waldorf dignitaries. What you are hearing may be characterized as "the anthroposophical approach" to the subject when it is in fact deeply personal and full of unexamined assumptions. No matter how much help you get along the way, what you finally decide to do is between you and the spiritual world. Our object is not to dismiss the material world but to make our modest contributions towards reuniting it with the spirit.

6

Becoming a Fixture

Ink imitates life only to a certain extent. After a while it stops expanding and its colors are fixed, whereas life continues to vibrate and to assume different complexions.

(i)

Pomp and Circumstance

If I don't write any more episodes under the heading "Becoming a Teacher" it is not because the process ever ended, but because, as I said before, thirty-two years of becoming is too much for anyone to handle. In any case, not all of it was becoming; some of it was distinctly unbecoming.

Some time after finishing my first batch of main lessons I went to a faculty meeting at the Manhattan Rudolf Steiner School. All that I can remember about the meeting is that I was startled to find that the faculty wanted me to be the next ninth grade adviser. Some plausible reasons were given, but as the discussion went on it became clear that there were no other viable candidates.

"Do you think you can do it?" asked Greta Fröhlich dubiously. It was rare for Greta to be dubious about anything.

"How would you like to do it?" I replied.

"There's your answer", said Henry Barnes. He seemed rather pleased about it.

Not long after this came the three-day circus that marked the end of the school year. As an ignorant Englishman I was completely unprepared for it. At the Crypt those of us who had achieved athletic or scholastic distinction received our rounds of applause at the appropriate times. At the end of our final year we simply left. I think it was a good system. Passages are important to individuals but accompanying them with rites that may at one time have pulsated with the spirit but have since become matters of convention is not what Waldorf Schools are about. Most of the seniors gave the impression that they would really prefer to be elsewhere. They had already done the prom and performed *The Tempest*. "The last word in modernity", they said; "Shakespeare's latest play!" Now came all the pother of caps and gowns, assemblies and speeches for three different sections of the school, the meeting with the faculty to receive Steiner's valedictory verse, and the graduation ceremony, grandly referred to as the "commencement exercises." All of this took place under the supervision of the redoubtable Miss MacArthur, who taught physical education and physiology and made it very difficult for anyone to step more than a millimetre or so out of line. Some of the seniors managed it, however, and so did I. I don't intend to tell tales about the class of '65, but here is my own little story.

I think it was Swain Pratt who invited me to the verse-giving ceremony, but he didn't use the word "ceremony". He called it a meeting with the teachers to say goodbye, and made it sound quite informal. It took place at 4 o'clock in the afternoon on a very hot and humid June day. It was so hot and sticky that the only reason why I didn't turn up in shorts was that I thought I would probably be the only one. But it certainly wasn't a day for a jacket and tie. I arrived at 3:59, by which time the seniors and about twenty-five teachers were already crammed into the tiny library. I immediately saw that all the males were wearing jackets, ties and beads. The beads were perspiration. I seemed to be the cause of a certain degree of consternation among the faculty members and some innocent merriment on the part of the seniors, one of whom—I believe it was Michael Pepper—offered me a tie. I declined with thanks and Miss MacArthur fixed me with a basilisk stare. When the discomfort of the heat, humidity and speech-making came to an end I left the room as quickly as possible, but not quite quickly enough. On the way down from the library I celebrated my freedom by putting my hands on the rails and vaulting the last ten or so steps to the ground floor, only to land in the arms of Miss MacArthur.

"And you're going to be ninth grade adviser?" she said grimly.

She said several other things as well, but they must have gone in one ear and out of the other.

The next day we had the commencement exercises. Thinking about them reminds me of a comment made by Dorit Winter a few years later about the eighth grade Christmas Play. "It smacks of *dressage*", she said. *Dressage* has never seemed to me to be a suitable occupation even for horses. I always hoped that our students would acquire *puissance*—the capacity to surmount the apparently insurmountable.

◆   ◆   ◆

At the end of the "Commencement Exercises" I was astounded to hear someone playing *Land of Hope and Glory* as the graduates walked down the aisle. The last time I had heard this music was during a BBC broadcast of what is known in England as the "Last Night of the Proms", the "Proms" being the great series of Henry Wood Promenade Concerts held every summer in the Royal Albert Hall in London. Edward Elgar's five *Pomp and Circumstance* marches fit the usual form of the patriotic march, with an opening *allegro* followed by a heartfelt *cantabile* middle section. In the middle section of No. 1, first heard in 1901, Elgar knew that he had come up with a tune "that would knock 'em all flat." At the first performance, before the great melody had acquired any words, the audience had no premonitory anxieties and were[32] simply carried away by the music. Henry Wood, the conductor, wrote: "I shall never forget the scene at the close of…the D major [march]. The people simply rose and yelled. I had to play it again—with the same result; in fact they refused to let me get on with the programme…Merely to restore order I had to play the march a third time."

Some time later Edward VII remarked that given the right words the tune would go round the world. The King was right. Using the second stanza of a poem by A. C. Benson, *Land of Hope and Glory* reached every corner of the "far-flung Empire" and several other places as well.

> Land of hope and glory, Mother of the free,
> How shall we extol Thee, who are born of Thee?
> Wider still and wider shall thy bounds be set;
> God who made Thee mighty, make Thee mightier yet.

At the Last Night of the Proms the audience listens appreciatively until the reprise of the great tune and then joins in lustily with Benson's words. Everyone knows that the Empire is long gone and the object of a great deal of debunking and facile humor, but many have tears in their eyes and some choke up completely. It's not just the Empire but a whole world that is drifting further and further into the past. Marred by self-interest, corruption and mistaken or misplaced ideals, it still trails clouds of glory or, at least, shreds of nobility. Perhaps we are feeling that mistaken ideals are better than no ideals at all and that the leftover trappings of imperial Britain are as genuine as a dude ranch and as inspiriting as dead men's clothing. Elgar was a very patriotic man but he sensed the shape of things to come and the chauvinistic tone of Benson's verses made him uneasy. His real feelings can be experienced in the great funeral march of his Symphony No. 2 and the valedictory Cello Concerto. The Funeral March was originally inspired by the death of a very dear friend, and later it became associated with the death of Edward VII, but to many of us it feels like a threnody for the passing of an Age and a way of life.

The title "Pomp and Circumstance" comes from Othello's despairing speech in Act III of Shakespeare's tragedy:

> "Farewell the neighing steed, and the shrill trump,
> The spirit-stirring drum, the ear-piercing fife,
> The royal banner and all quality,
> Pride, pomp and circumstance of glorious war…
> Farewell! Othello's occupation's gone."

Patriotic marches, and their associations with pride, pomp, circumstance, war and empire, don't seem to me to provide the right kind of background for a Waldorf graduation, even for those who experience the sense of leave-taking that permeates the splendor of Elgar's music. Love of one's country is a very good thing but there are higher virtues than patriotism—love of one's neighbor and the desire for truth and justice, for instance.

In the years when I was High School Administrator or Senior Adviser—sometimes I was both—we usually managed to avoid *Land of Hope and Glory*. One year we reached the opposite pole of absurdity and the graduates recessed to the strains of the Gallop from Rossini's *William Tell Overture*. "Strain" is the right word since it was played by the Junior Orchestra and they had to go so slowly that if the Lone Ranger had appeared he would have been riding a burro.

◆ ◆ ◆

Waldorf Schools seem to have a passion for perfervid nationalistic tunes. Cecil Harwood's *Wind in the Trees* has its good points but it's a very poor fit for the big melody from Sibelius's *Finlandia*. The poem was designed to fit a moderately paced three-in-a-measure tune, starting on the first beat of a measure:

> *Wind* in the *trees*,

Sibelius's melody is in a slow two and starts halfway through the first beat, so if we sing the tune as written we get:

Wind *in* the *trees*,

Similar problems occur throughout the song and the unfortunate result is that the rhythmic subtlety of the tune, which constitutes a great part of its appeal, has to be sacrificed to the needs of an unsuitable text and a mass of ignorant singers.

I don't know the history of *Wind in the Trees*, so I can only conclude that the poet didn't have this tune in mind, or that he was unaware of its actual rhythm, or that he didn't care.[33] After wrestling with the problem for a while I was driven to the conclusion that most teachers don't know and are either incapable of understanding the problem or consider that I'm making a fuss about nothing. This is a fair example of the general disdain for musical integrity that one finds both inside and outside anthroposophical circles. Few people would condone the application of this kind of treatment to Shakespeare, Goethe, Michelangelo or Renoir.

(ii)

Innocence

The loss of innocence is a great literary theme, but my own fall from naïveté, which is the same thing as innocence only in a manner of speaking, was really just a succession of minor bumps and enlightenments. In trying to characterize the painful discoveries that I made I have had to think about my childhood and upbringing. I experienced love, kindness, anger and sheer bloody-mindedness in the people around me but I was never conscious that I or anyone else was being manipulated. I can't say that I assumed that people said and did things because those were the things that they wanted to say and do, and not with some ulterior motive or, as we learnt to say thirty years ago, hidden agenda. The reason why I can't say that I *assumed* it is that I never thought about it. Such ideas were not part of my mental processes. I simply accepted the world as it appeared. This is not the same thing as saying that I believed everything that I was told. But I did think that the people who told me those things believed them to be true. It was a long time before I realized the extent to which people use speech to achieve a desired result without revealing what they are really thinking. It is possible that even in the days of my relative innocence I unconsciously used words in this way. One thing that brought the matter to my attention later in my life was that I was sometimes accused of doing it by people who claimed that they knew more about my mental processes than I did. Again, I can't assert that they were never right but I'll go far enough out on this precarious limb to say that it wasn't very often. Being the baby, by four years, in a family of people with strongly held views and a well-established pecking order, I had learnt the advisability of keeping my opinions to myself. But I thought a lot and, after some initial difficulties, read a lot, and when I did come out with something it was usually out of a sense of wonder or conviction—childish, no doubt, but deeply felt. As a child what I usually experienced in return was condescension or derision. Things were different in my student days at the Crypt and at Cambridge. There were still pecking orders, of course, but in both places I was lucky enough to find a circle of friends who took each other's beliefs seriously and discussed them as equals. Even when the discussions became fiery, which they often did, the heat arose from conviction and was focussed on the content, not on the individual. Occasionally someone would take up a position merely to provoke an argument, but it wasn't a matter of deception. Everyone knew what was going on. This is the essence of youth. There is time to discuss and debate, to crush your well-loved opponent with a beautifully turned phrase while refilling his coffee cup. Nothing need be decided yet. Tomorrow it will be back to the lecture room, the lab, the desk or the cricket field and, eventually, to the coffee table to set the world to rights again. Those sessions were as important to us as the time puppies spend rolling each other over in the grass, and more important than anything that happened in the classroom. Adults can get a lot of fun and some profit out of playing at being undergraduates, but such activities are no longer what life is about.

(iii)

Experience

In my first full year in New York I had a manageable schedule. I taught four physics main lesson blocks and their attendant lab courses, two math blocks and two math track courses. I was ninth grade adviser and this meant that I was on duty every lunch period, since the freshmen could not, I was told, be trusted to stay out of mischief for forty minutes in the middle of the day. This may well have been true, but it resulted in a situation that the ninth graders deeply resented. I didn't care much for it myself. Having been confined in classrooms for more than four hours already, they all had to troop over to the lunch room, even if they were not having hot lunch, and then troop straight back to the classroom to await the start of the next lesson. For one awful three-week period they had me for physics main lesson, math, lunch and lab. That works out at nearly five hours a day and it's a wonder that we survived each other. I had not finished making mistakes but the students were very tolerant and the inkblot seems willing to obliterate most of them—the mistakes, not the students. I was, after all, almost as fresh as they were. We got along very well indeed most of the time and a lot of good and funny things happened.

I am trying to explain certain things that I learnt about life in a Waldorf School and if you object that I am merely talking about life in one Waldorf School I shall have to admit that your point is well taken. There are, however, recurring patterns related to the peculiar nature of the Waldorf Movement. According to Rudolf Steiner a Waldorf School is supposed to be run by the faculty, and it is not necessarily a bad thing that no one seems to be able to give a definitive statement of what that means. "…Our schools will not be directed, but arranged in a collegial manner, administered as republics. In a true republic of teachers there will be no time for soft cushions and demands which come from the principal, but we shall have to have within us that which gives each of us the possibility to carry the full responsibility for what we have to do. Each one must be fully responsible."[34] Does "the faculty" mean "all the teachers", "some of the teachers", or "a few of the teachers"? Is it appropriate for the faculty, whoever they are, to appoint officials to do the administrative work for them? Should everything be brought to the faculty meeting or should there be faculty committees to discuss and decide things? If you agree to the formation of a committee and then disagree with its decision, is it OK to say so? (Not in the 1980's, when the movement was assailed by a highly infectious disease called the mandate system.[35] In this thinly disguised form of anarchy anyone could be on any committee and there were schools that ended up with more committees than they had faculty members.)

As that eminent barrister and memoirist, Horace Rumpole, has observed, "Our present masters seem to have an irresistible urge, whenever they find something that works moderately well, to tinker with it, tear it apart and construct something worse…"[36] In a faculty-run school we are all masters, so the opportunities for tinkering are endless. During the more than thirty years that I spent at the Rudolf Steiner School its organization cycled repeatedly between the centralization and the diffusion of responsibility. I have direct knowledge of the styles

·

and transitions of several other schools and reliable pipelines to a few more. In most of these places there have been broadly similar cycles of change, for which there are at least two reasons. One is that whichever system you adopt there are always insoluble problems.[37] Some teachers feel that the best thing is to accept the limitations of the prevailing mode of government, and do their best to make it work. Others, usually a vocal and obstinate minority, are always wanting to tinker with the system and taking up enormous expanses of time in the faculty meetings. Since one of the problems is that the meetings are too long for the endurance of the teachers and too short to get all the business done, while the vocal minority always seems to have enormous staying power, the tinkerers often get their way through sheer attrition.

Changes are sometimes catastrophic, in the geological sense, rather than gradualistic. Periodically in the life of almost every school there appears a new kid on the block who wants to turn everything upside down and remake the school according to his own vision. This happened more than once in New York so it is something of which I have vivid firsthand experience. The individual in question usually has an anthroposophical pedigree and what might be called selective charisma. The number of faculty members who succumb is usually quite small but the effect is amazing and in some respects resembles that of cocaine. The victims become energized and self-confident. Previously inoffensive people become point men in faculty discussions. People who were previously vocal tend to become strident. And X, who is the origin of this access of energy, is presented as the one great hope for the future of the school. Finding that the faculty as a whole will not accept X as their savior, X and his supporters broaden their offensive, working the parking lot, the Board of Trustees and even the students. When this happened in New York the school proved remarkably resistant and X, having become too much of a known quantity, decided to go elsewhere—not, however, before a great deal of damage had been done to the school as a whole and, in particular, to those who were closest to X, some of whom seemed to need quite long rehab periods.

◆   ◆   ◆

Until about 1990 the decision-making body at the Rudolf Steiner School was called the Faculty Council. Francis Edmunds, a pillar of Waldorf education from Michael Hall in England, had given some guidelines for membership of the Council, which he regarded as the equivalent of a College of Teachers, but they were not strictly applied. There was a general understanding that the qualifications included having been at the school for a year or two and having a commitment to Waldorf education. I was asked to join at the beginning of my first full year, however, and there were several teachers there whose commitment seemed to me to be to the school in particular rather than to the ideals of the Waldorf Movement. I don't think that this was a bad thing.

Werner Glas used to say that when he was asked to join the College of Teachers at the Edinburgh Rudolf Steiner School it was made quite clear to him that for the first year he should be seen and not heard. Those of you who knew Werner will realize that the first instruction must have been much easier to obey than the second. I was not given any particular advice but I found some of the members of the council quite intimidating and I often held my peace at times when I really ought to have spoken. In such circumstances silence is not golden and speech delayed until after the tide has gone out is often worse than useless. There were several members to whom I could talk easily without worrying about stepping on a mine. John Root, Amos Franceschelli and Joseph Dipper, who taught high school history, math and French respectively, and Swain Pratt, the High School Administrator, all had well developed opinions about the ins and outs of Waldorf education but anything was possible as far as discussion was concerned. Virginia Paulsen, who was teaching fifth grade at the time, was equally approachable as long as you remembered to avoid tangling with her on the subject of English grammar and usage. I loved Virginia dearly, even though she once threatened to punch me on the nose. Rudolf Copple had been the devoted class teacher of my freshman class, which, according to him, consisted entirely of fine boys and lovely girls. His enthusiasm knew no bounds until it was blunted by one of the X's, and he was not in the least scary. With William and Dorothy Harrer, two veteran class teachers, things were slightly different. My relations with them were never less than cordial but I was fairly confident that if I did not watch my step that situation might change. William had strong ideas about form, behavior and academic standards, and presented them in no uncertain terms at times when he thought things were getting loose.

"Looseness" was something that worried Henry, as well as the Harrers. It appeared, in particular, that the high school was loose. It lacked form, the students were becoming ill-mannered and unkempt, academic standards were not what they should be and excellence was in short supply. I thought that William, Dorothy and Henry could use a little loosening up themselves, but I didn't dare say so. William, with his choleric countenance, his stocky figure and his Schwabian[38] accent, was an impressive speaker even when his ideals sounded more like the results of a strong conventional upbringing than the insights of the education philosophy to which he had devoted most of his life. Dorothy was of a more equable temperament and her presentations of Waldorf pedagogy verged on the sentimental, but the steel was always there when she needed it. Henry was rather preoccupied with the idea of form. It was something that people and institutions always needed. Being the manager, he had to find some way of reconciling the uptight with the over-loose, and his natural inclination was towards the former. If the occasion warranted it and reasonable discussion didn't do the trick he would indulge in a certain amount of browbeating. I found William's oratory and Dorothy's steely determination rather daunting, but when Henry started banging on the table with his fist I usually began to see the funny side of things. In the long run none of it made much difference to anything. Most of the real managing went on behind the scenes.

(iv)

MIA

When I first appeared at the New York Rudolf Steiner School I was welcomed by Blanche Rossé, a very youthful septuagenarian who functioned as high school receptionist. Blanche was a devoted and knowledgeable student of Rudolf Steiner—not a rigid and conventionalized anthroposophist but someone with an independent spirit, a heart of gold and a somewhat rough exterior. Blanche was never afraid to lay down the law, which she often did in loud, unmodulated tones that echoed throughout the ground floor, and her judgements were generally based on the needs of the immediate situation rather than rules and regulations. On one occasion, while taking part in one of Steiner's mystery dramas, she suffered a memory lapse and, after waiting in vain for help from the prompter, demanded loudly, "Will someone give me that damn' line?"

Her voice was the cause of some concern, since it was the first sound that people who telephoned or visited the school heard. Her telephone manner was certainly brusque and it lacked the obsequious "How may I help you?" tone that often induces a slight feeling of nausea and makes one long for a little brusqueness. Most of the complaints that I heard came from the higher echelons but I'm sure that many people lower on the rungs of power had their ears put out of joint. Another problem was that the students and most of the teachers loved Blanche and there were always people sitting or standing around in the front hall talking to her. "The front hall is a business area", we were informed, "not a place for kibitzing. The receptionist has work to do." Naturally the students found their way past Blanche's rough exterior and into her tender heart. I can still see her dispensing coffee and zwieback from the tiny supply closet. Both were supposed to be for the teachers but the students often wheedled successfully. Clearly the situation in the front hall was a source of "looseness" and there were all kinds of rumors going about, one of which was to the effect that Henry was under pressure from certain senior colleagues of the "Either she goes or I go" variety. Eventually Henry mentioned the matter at a Council meeting and told us that he had had a "good talk" with Blanche. Not realizing that "good talk" was a euphemism I thought he meant that he had persuaded her to change her ways, so the next time I saw Blanche I was shocked to hear that she was leaving. When I asked her about it she told me that she had been fired—not in so many words but in effect. I asked her why she hadn't put up a fight, and suggested bringing the matter to the Council but she told me that she had been overwhelmed and did not have the strength to fight. She was broken-hearted and never forgave the school or Henry. The school received its comeuppance too. In the following twenty-five years the high school never found a receptionist of anything like Blanche's efficiency. During this time the telephone may have been answered in a more servile manner but the "looseness" in the front hall continued unabated and hundreds of messages failed to get through.

If this report gives the impression that the school treated Blanche badly it is probably because that was the way I felt at the time. Although I never entirely changed my mind on that score I did find that many years of experience in administrative positions made a considerable difference to the way in which I understood the incident. If you are a Faculty Chair or administrator you frequently find yourself trying to decide in your own mind what is the right course of action while being forcefully subjected to a wide variety of mutually incompatible views from faculty members. The position taken by a chairman often seems to depend on who was the last person to speak to him. Sometimes the Faculty Chair knows things that most of the teachers don't know and can't be told. Sometimes the Chair seems to be the only one who doesn't know something that is common knowledge to everyone else. There are situations in which if you wait for the College of Teachers to make a decision you may wait forever. When it is a case of deciding either to make some change or to leave things as they are, those who favor the latter course have a great advantage, since the inability to come to a decision actually amounts to a decision. Sometimes the person entrusted by the teachers to perform the only too vaguely describable duties of Faculty Chair has to take some action in order to avoid, or at least to postpone, the onset of chaos, and no matter what you do you often end up in the middle of some serious crossfire. If you become a Faculty Chairperson it is as well to remember that the last thing you can expect is gratitude for your efforts. This remark may be taken in its usual sense or interpreted as meaning that people will finally say "Thank you" on your departure from office and you will probably have the impression that that is what they are thanking you for.

In the meantime one or two other people had "good talks" with Henry, and the phrase entered the argot, at least for a few of us. In those days Henry had not yet discovered my waywardness and when my class graduated he pulled the right levers to have me installed as High School Administrator. It became necessary for me to meet with him frequently, and if I happened to encounter Johnny Root on returning from one of these sessions I would say, "Oh, I just had a good talk with Henry", to which Johnny would usually reply, "Oh, when are you leaving?" He occasionally varied the formula with, "Oh, when is *he* leaving?"

People are full of contradictions, and so are the institutions and communities that they build. Successful institutions need people with strong wills and strongly held convictions, but one person's convictions may be incompatible with another's even when they are working for the same ultimate cause. The first thing a principle is apt to do (apart from killing someone) is to contradict another principle, and it is often quite difficult to find the higher principle which encompasses both. The United States of America, the Waldorf Schools and many other institutions share the difficulty of reconciling principles of order with principles of freedom.[39] Rudolf Steiner gave some guidance on such matters in his *Threefold Commonwealth*, but he did not relieve the individual of the task of working through each situation on its own merits. There are no obvious and effective fixes. Like bombing Hanoi or shooting a few soldiers to encourage the others[40], expelling a few high school students so that the rest will know that we are serious about enforcing the rules is unprincipled and ineffective, and would still be so even if the school were the only show in town. That way safety lies, it might be said, but running a school under martial law is not conducive to the kind of atmosphere in which creative work can be done. We must not forget that education is an art. The opposite extreme, abolishing the rules, is equally bad for the ambiance. I have never questioned the need for order in the classroom and structure in the school as a whole. The problem is how to obtain these desirable commodities. Getting order in the classroom is something that each teacher has to figure out how to do or quit the profession. You can get advice, of course, but what works for one teacher is not necessarily going to work for another. Dorothy Harrer and Virginia Paulsen, for instance, had quite different ways of running their shows, and you might need something different again. The only functions of extraneous disciplinary recourse, such as detentions, suspensions and expulsions, are to get the beginner through the first year and to give the old pro something to fall back on when something extraordinary happens. Teaching is a tough and exhausting profession even for those who happen to have the inscrutable inborn gift of intimidating students. Being old and ugly helps but some people have it right from the start. Some students work better when intimidated. Some don't work at all unless constrained. Others find their creative impulses paralyzed by intimidation. Something similar can be said about teachers. We all work in different ways. Occasionally we encounter a colleague who prefers to avoid work. My mother used to use the phrase "piece of work" to mean a to-do of some sort, a serious quarrel or a heated discussion. "There'll be a piece of work about that", she would say, when someone illicitly borrowed someone else's what's-it and lost or broke it. What a piece of work is man!

Some of the teachers whose opinions and modes of operation were difficult for me to swallow were largely responsible for the fact that the school existed. Bringing a school into being and keeping it alive during its infancy and childhood is a heroic task requiring admirable qualities of vision, persistence and endurance. Many of us who were there in my early years have died and the rest of us will be gone quite soon. May I say that I bless you all and hope that you all bless me. Major differences of vision are not incompatible with respect, admiration and love. Being a little lower than the angels makes us a little higher than the animals, so we wander around between earth and sky, between matter and spirit, and do our best whenever we can manage it. Sometimes we have the feeling that we are responsible for the future evolution of the human race, an idea that can lead to humility, pomposity or despair. So let's remember that laughter and good company are just as important for the future as all the things that sound more urgent.

> If here today the cloud of thunder lours
> Tomorrow it will hie on far behests;
> The flesh will grieve on other bones than ours
> Soon, and the soul will mourn in other breasts.
>
> The troubles of our proud and angry dust
> Are from eternity and shall not fail.
> Bear them we can, and if we can we must.
> Shoulder the sky, my lad, and drink your ale.[41]

(v)

Keeping the Peace

Rudolf Steiner spoke disparagingly about people who enjoy feeling comfortable with their positions in life, their beliefs and their conditions of soul. While such complacency is not likely to lead to a life of spiritual seeking, it is often accompanied by the sense of a mission to put others on the right track. Many of us, however, have very little experience of the kind of comfort that Steiner was speaking about and would give our eye teeth for a few moments of it, no matter how anthroposophically incorrect it might be. In the absence of comfort one can legitimately strive for tranquillity, a goal endorsed by Steiner in *The Knowledge of Higher Worlds*. I don't think that a preference for peace and quiet requires any justification. It is true that quietness can be oppressive and that some people find it difficult to endure. I confess to a liking for loud, violent music, but not when I'm working. The trouble with peace and quiet is that they cannot be commanded. A *fiat* against outer disturbance ("Hold thy peace, varlet") results in a great deal of inner noise, and getting rid of inner noise is a meditative process. Since I have not reached the angelic condition it is hard for me to be at peace with you if you are not at peace with me.

One thing that I learnt at the Crypt is that teachers have opinions about everything. In the course of my early encounters with the people at Wynstones I realized that the same can be said about anthroposophists. So anthroposophical teachers have this characteristic raised to the second power. The combination of anthroposophy, the Waldorfian ethos and a certain kind of personality takes us into that higher order of magnitude already identified as X. The people at the Crypt were rather like the undergraduates of my youth at Cambridge, but with less intensity. No one would dream of inconveniencing anyone else by actually putting his opinions into action.

Anthroposophists direct most of their gripes at the unenlightened, non-anthroposophical world. When they do tangle with one another it is most often over the right way to run an anthroposophical endeavor, such as a Waldorf School, a Eurythmy School or an outpost of the Society on which the Sun Never Sets. I am not proposing that these quarrels should be suppressed. Such things were already happening in Rudolf Steiner's time. He expressed great sorrow, but he couldn't or wouldn't suppress them. I have not concealed the fact that the faculty meeting at the Rudolf Steiner School was often the scene of a great deal of bickering. I use that term rather than something more neutral, such as "differences of opinion", because that's what it often was, although I must say that as long as Henry was in charge the proceedings generally remained quite civilized. Henry was very patient. He would let the discussion continue until everyone else was exhausted, and then he would say his piece. People would then realize that what Henry said was the way things were going to be—mostly. As teachers and anthroposophists we had a double dose of opinions, but nobody really wanted to start a war. Anyone who broke the bounds of normal persistence was apt to end up having a good talk. It was only the third combination, referred to as X above, who caused hostilities to break out. This didn't happen until the very end of Henry's tenure. Henry did a lot of good things, one of which was to keep the school relatively peaceful, so that we could do our work in the classroom without continually wondering when the next explosion would happen. When I was a child and things were difficult in the home, my mother used to say, "When I'm gone you'll be sorry." Virginia Paulsen did an outstanding job as Henry's successor and several years went by before the real eruptions started. Later, when times were bad, I thought about my mother's words and felt quite nostalgic about the old days when Henry had ruled the roost.

My predilection for peace and quiet went with an innate dislike for making people feel bad.[42] I sometimes found it difficult to be as mean to the students as the situation demanded and I was kind to the more downtrodden members of the faculty and staff. As High School Administrator I kept my office door open. Students and teachers knew that they always had somewhere to go when they needed a good supply of Kleenex and someone to listen. Having been called "Diction'ry" in my childhood and "Parson" in my youth, I now became known for a while as "the Peacemaker". Some of the students called me "United", which I still don't get.

In functioning as a peacemaker I was following in the footsteps of Swain Pratt, who gave up the position of Administrator in 1969 and left the school in 1970. Swain had always been an immensely reassuring presence and although he undoubtedly had battles to fight with the opinionated and the influential, he seldom allowed any of the undercurrents to rise to the surface. I was never given a job description so I simply took over everything that I had observed Swain doing, with the exception of college guidance. I was responsible for the yearly schedule of the whole school, including changes that had to be made in the course of the year, and for day-to-day coordination in the High School. I met very frequently with parents who had problems or complaints and had not managed to get satisfaction from their children's teachers and class advisers. Students, singly or in groups, brought their troubles to me, and I soon learnt how difficult it is to discuss things with students when you know that their complaints about certain teachers are justified. Most of the teachers regarded me as the institutional source of disciplinary satisfaction when they were unable to deal with misbehaving students. Like Swain I was responsible for High School admissions, and I was the recipient of all mail and telephone calls that had anything to do with the High School. I made up for not doing the college admissions by teaching almost a full schedule and, in some years, by being a class adviser. The only part of the job that I really didn't enjoy was dealing with the paper work, which often kept me in my office for several hours after most of my colleagues had left the building.

One thing that Swain and I noticed was that although some teachers objected to the very idea of an administrator, once there was one in place almost all the teachers were happy to allow him to take care of things that they would have been perfectly capable of attending to themselves, including small disciplinary matters, minor disputes and communications with parents—"Well, I think it would be better if it came directly from the Administration." That may have been true sometimes, but more often the philosophy seemed to be, "Why keep a dog and do your own barking." I sometimes caught myself thinking that if I had encountered a similar attitude among the students I might have called it laziness.

◆　　◆　　◆

One of my tasks was to try to keep the peace between the high school and the elementary school. It occurs to me now that my position was rather like that of the English Deputy Headmaster described in a certain English novel.

"Deputy Headmasters, like most of God's creatures, come in all shapes, sizes and conditions, but they have in common certain tendencies brought about by their position in life; inoffensive entities, like so many gowned and peripatetic Belgiums, repeatedly caught between warring powers and bearing the scars of incessant conflicts which they have done nothing to provoke. Moreover, unlike that unfortunate nation, the DHM is expected to support all sides, solve the problems and pacify the combatants."[43]

The elementary school was ripely middle-aged while the high school was still in its childhood. Class teachers who had picked up their flocks from the kindergarten and shepherded them through the eight grades were not always happy with the sequel. This is not unusual. *Beverley Hills Cop I* and *II* were great movies but *BHC III* was a bummer. Parents who have quite enjoyed their children's infancy and childhood often find that adolescence is nowhere near such a good show. The elementary school class is a little kingdom. It maintains friendly relations with as much of the outside world—other students, teachers, parents and the school administration—as concerns it, but it has a high degree of autonomy. The older the children get the more they want to burst the bounds of their microstate. The skill with which the class teacher handles this stage of the lifelong process of transition has a great influence on the decisions of parents and students to enter or not to enter the high school and on how they fare when they get there or somewhere else. There is no better example of the perils of extrapolation than the way in which students and parents are apt to view the high school through the telescope of the elementary school. High school teachers become desperate when they find that the parents of children whom they would like to welcome into the ninth grade are under the impression that the class teacher system continues through twelfth grade, and that many of them are unwilling to attend open houses and conferences in order to find out what really happens. It is even more shocking to learn that some of one's colleagues in the preschool and elementary school are no better informed than the parents. When elementary school teachers have a somewhat high-nosed attitude towards the high school it is not surprising that parents often choose to send their children elsewhere.

Children—and there are many of them—who have felt "cabin'd, cribb'd, confin'd", are apt to break out when the different structure of existence in the ninth grade makes this easier. This is the natural order of events and will cause problems no matter how skilled and insightful the teachers are. When we add human frailty we get a very volatile mixture and we start blaming each other when things go wrong. "It took me eight years to bring the class to this point and you've ruined it in six months." "If you had been a bit more flexible over the last two or three years they wouldn't be so rebellious now. And maybe Bill, Jill, Maria and Cliff[44] would still be here instead of at Dalton and PS9." "When I had these children they always dressed nicely and did beautiful work. Now they look and behave like slobs. And I certainly wouldn't want to put their main lesson books where anyone could see them." There was no short answer to these last remarks. A whole treatise on adolescence would have been required, not to mention a few home truths about the quality of the notebooks issuing from the elementary school. The discussion, in any case, was lopsided. Clearly the high school was young, inexperienced and in need of correction. The elementary school teachers felt that their complaints were just and enquired why the high school teachers were so defensive. The high school teachers felt that their responses were just too, and that it is natural to defend oneself when one is being attacked, but they were restrained by the fact that they were speaking to the elder statespeople of the school. Open criticism of the likes of Mr. and Mrs. Harrer was hardly to be contemplated. So we often just sat and stewed and thought, "Unfair, unfair!"

◆ ◆ ◆

Henry had quite a number of suggestions about improving the high school. Sometimes they were his own ideas and sometimes they were bullets that he had consented to fire for other people. He expected me to present these suggestions at the high school faculty meeting and I was perfectly willing to do so when I thought that the ideas were good and practicable. There were, however, proposals that sounded reasonable in the abstract but would obviously not do in practice because they were not based on any insight into the workings of young people's minds. It is no use trying to regulate a high school as if it were an army—as far as high school students are concerned, theirs *is* to reason why.

After some experiences of getting into difficulties with teachers and students through acting as a pipeline for ideas originating in the elementary school I changed the system a little. When I was being asked to make a proposal of which I thoroughly disapproved, and I could see that it would be impossible to explain to Henry why the high school teachers or students, or all of the above, were going have strong objections, I usually managed to persuade him that it would be better if he made the presentation himself and experienced responses directed at him and not at me.

I believe that most people figured out that when I said, "Henry has a proposal…" it was something that I wasn't very happy about. I suspect that this counts as manipulation. If so I am guilty many times over. I can't help feeling, however, that Henry, bless his heart, deserved it. I'm sure he caught on to what was happening but there really wasn't anything he could do about it short of relieving me of my duties as High School Administrator or having a "good talk" with me. Pressure did in fact mount for me to give up the administration, but I went when I was good and ready. I don't believe that Henry wanted me to leave the school. I'm sure that I was just as much of a disappointment to him as he was to me, but in our funny ways we rather liked each other.

7

The First Time I Left the Rudolf Steiner School

The Waldorf movement is threatened in many ways. Governments want to force unacceptable curricula and testing programs on the schools and many individuals object to the whole idea of independent education. Misinformation about anthroposophy and Waldorf education is widely circulated and it is very difficult to attract capable people into the movement. And yet, against all the odds, schools grow up and flourish. When teachers work together the external opposing forces can be resisted effectively, if not defeated. Bitter experience has taught me, however, that these periods of well-being do not last, and that when things go bad they do so from the inside. People are reluctant to take notice of warnings, and often it seems safer, if not better, to keep quiet; but I tell these stories just in case there is someone who wants to listen.

That was the introduction to the next section, which in its original form was the most instructive part of the book, possibly because it had the most to do with human frailty. Unfortunately it is this aspect of the story that makes publication impossible, or, at least, imprudent. Reports of actual events involving particular individuals are much more likely to make people think and do a little self-examination than generalized statements of principles and goals, but they are also very likely to stir up dust, resentment and accusations of partiality. Rudolf Steiner spoke a great deal about the Karma of Untruthfulness. If you have lived through a series of events and find that people generally give false pictures of what actually happened you may be tempted to stand up and say, "Excuse me, but it wasn't like that at all. This is what really happened..." But there is a Karma of Truthfulness too. Steiner spoke of it implicitly all the time, but I sometimes wish he had given us some explicit advice. Knowledge of the truth about the past may be essential to the task of doing better in the future, but what if the telling of it is inevitably accompanied by pain, controversy and disbelief? All I feel able to do is to give a very rough and not very concrete indication of difficulties that appeared in particularly virulent forms at certain times and were rarely entirely absent.

Telling the story this way involves a certain amount of overlap with an earlier section, but the perspective is slightly different. It also makes it harder to explain how my involvement in music got tangled up with questions of leadership. That story has had to be drastically pruned and placed in a separate section.

(i)

Respublica, Demokratia or what?

People who start a speech or an article by dwelling on the derivation of a key word often end up chasing a wild goose into a mare's nest. My Latin master, "Fishy" Walton, used to hoot with laughter every time a visiting speechifier, having derived "education" from "*e-duco*", concluded that education must therefore be a process of "drawing out" what was already in the pupil rather than stuffing things into a vacant space. If the word were really derived in that way it would be "eduction". (*Duco, ducere, duxi, ductum,* as I'm sure you all remember) The Latin verb "to educate" is *educare*, not *educere*. Partridge says *ducare* is a durative form found only in compounds, which makes it sound like a chemical. "Durative" is found only in larger dictionaries, but if you haven't met it before you can easily guess what it means. So maybe if you go back far enough you can make a case for *educere*, but then you have to reckon with Rudolf Steiner who, in speaking of the Socratic method, remarked that you can't draw out something that isn't there. I have found that many students are highly absorbent and that others are more malleable[45] than ductile. What all this is leading to is the proposition that, with all due respect to certain Authorities, if we are trying to understand the politics of a Waldorf School not much help is to be expected from an etymological study of "republic" and "democracy"

◆   ◆   ◆

One thing that I was told in the earliest days of my training was that a Waldorf School is run by the faculty. A little later I learnt that a Waldorf School is not governed democratically. My experiences at Garden City and Kimberton confirmed the second proposition and cast a great deal of doubt on the first. As I have already indicated, the situation in Manhattan was not quite so clear-cut. The Faculty Chairpeople at Garden City and Kimberton were really Principals whose positions were maintained by some power other than the will of the Faculty. In Manhattan the Chairman was chosen by the Faculty Council but the election process bore some resemblance to those of certain nations in which everyone votes and there is only one candidate. Waldorf literature used to make a big point of the "faculty-run" school, but for a long time I remained unsure as to whether I had ever seen one in action and whether I should actually recognize one if I did.

According to Rudolf Steiner "...Our schools will not be directed, but arranged in a collegial manner, administered as republics. In a true republic of teachers there will be no time for soft cushions and demands which come from the principal, but we shall have to have within us that which gives each of us the possibility to carry the full responsibility for what we have to do. Each one must be fully responsible."

As an individual teacher the way in which you do your work is governed by your understanding of what is best for the children and of how to work with their parents and your colleagues. It has to be realized, however, that no matter how much you have studied the pedagogy, and no matter how much you have discussed the problems of individual children, classes, teachers and parents, you and your colleagues will encounter situations to which you respond in very different and sometimes incompatible ways. Should the student who makes it so hard for any learning to take place be asked to leave? (Waldorf teachers are reluctant to say "expel".) Should the teacher who is having a really difficult time with his class be replaced? Should a certain person be allowed to come and speak to the students? Is it proper for a teacher to give a main lesson block on South American geography instead of the usual European geography? You may take the individual responsibility for the way in which you conduct your classes and work with the parents, but you can't be individually responsible for expelling a child, dismissing a colleague, inviting a speaker or making a radical change in the curriculum. And if you are not, who is and how are the decisions made? Steiner says (or the translation makes him say) that the schools "will be arranged in a collegial manner, administered as republics" and this way of saying it makes an excellent illustration of the use of the passive voice. You can say *something must be done* without having to say who is to do it. It would not sound half so grand to say, "*Somebody* will arrange the school in a collegial manner and administer it as a republic." Unless *somebody* turns out to be *everybody* we have to decide who *somebody* is.

◆　◆　◆

In trying to discuss how things work out in practice I continually run into the difficulty that the picture of Waldorf administration which somehow formed in my mind and which seems to be a good picture as long as I don't probe it too deeply, doesn't correspond to anything that I have ever encountered in an actual school. We have to start somewhere, however, so I'll describe the bare essentials of the picture and then I'll mention some of the questions that arise.

Let's say that we have a school in which there are perhaps three hundred students, forty teachers (some part-time) and a staff of a dozen people doing financial, secretarial and maintenance work. There is a College of Teachers consisting of about twenty people—about half the faculty—who fulfill certain requirements; each has been in the school for at least a year and has made a commitment to Waldorf education in general and to the school in particular. This involves at least a working relationship with anthroposophy. The College is responsible for all decisions on all aspects of the running of the school, and becoming a member of the College is not a matter to be taken lightly. (The process of becoming a member has been the subject of lengthy and inconclusive discussions.) Since it would be impossible for a body of twenty people who have full time teaching schedules to supervise the day to day running of the school, the College deputizes certain teachers and gives them specific areas of responsibility. One of these areas includes chairing the meetings, serving as the person of last resort for troubled teachers and parents and representing the school to the public. The teacher chosen by the College to perform these duties is called the Faculty Chairperson.

This picture would not satisfy an elementary school painting teacher, since it leaves most of the paper blank. It also raises several questions that I can't answer in this article:

Should membership in the College be restricted to teachers?

Can teachers apply for membership or should they wait to be asked to join?

Should the College be responsible for *everything*, or should it leave financial matters to the Board or to some other body?

Should the College concern itself only with spiritual and pedagogical matters or is the distinction between the "spiritual" and the "mundane" artificial and meaningless?

Should there be a College Chair whose duties are purely internal to the College or is the Faculty Chair the same thing as the College Chair?

Is it part of the job of the Faculty or College Chair to form policies and to decide on the relative urgency of agenda items, or is it just a matter of "facilitating" discussions?

What I am concerned with first is the question of how people get into these or other leadership positions. (What they do when they get there is a matter for later consideration.) References by Steiner and other writers make it necessary, although not very helpful, to refer again to the question of what we mean by "republic" and "democracy", not from the point of view of derivation but from that of usage.

◆ ◆ ◆

Most standard reference works agree that the main point about a republic is that it is not a monarchy, to which they add that a republic is usually governed by the representatives of a broadly based electorate. Webster (1969), however, says nothing about monarchs and insists on the people's right to vote for their representatives. Descriptions of democracy are characterized by a greater emphasis on the role of the people and on their inalienable natural rights, the absence of a monarch being taken for granted. Oddly enough, among all the references I have looked at I have found only one in which the words "republic" and "democracy" occur in the same paragraph. If it weren't for Webster we might get the idea that a democracy is bound to be a republic but that a republic is not necessarily a democracy. We can, in any case see why the workings of a Waldorf faculty cannot be regarded as democratic; it does not elect its leaders by popular vote. We can also see that talking about republics and democracies is not going to help. I only mentioned them because people often do when discussing how Waldorf Schools should be run and I wanted to get them out of the way.

(ii)

Consensus and Decision

Members of anthroposophical institutions don't like to vote and rarely do so unless compelled by legal requirements or by unwillingness to continue banging their heads against a brick wall. The brick wall is the occasional impossibility of arriving at consensus. Government by consensus is a wonderful thing if you can get it, but it has its problems; consensus is supposed to mean "general agreement" but it often amounts to "absence of audible disagreement" and sometimes the system, having rejected majority rule, allows decisions to be dictated by a determined and vocal minority. This is called government by nonsensus.

◆ ◆ ◆

A College of Teachers is sitting in a circle and trying to decide who shall be the class adviser of next year's ninth grade. There are two people in the room (A and B) who would very much like to do the job and another one (C) who could do it very well but would be quite happy if someone else took it on. It is at times like this that we have to face an unpalatable fact, one which is often not considered when consultants come to help the school through its spiritual and organizational difficulties. When it comes to the ordinary human weaknesses, we cannot assume that anthroposophists and Waldorf teachers will be any better than average for the human race as a whole. Since there is a tendency for anthroposophy to bring out the very best or the very worst in people, the deviations from the norm are greater than usual, and this only compounds the problems of making good decisions and keeping the school on course. The College meeting I am talking about is not altogether imaginary, so when I say that ambition and partisanship play a considerable part in the discussion I am not speaking theoretically. A and B are both quite determined and each has his supporters. C would rather stay out of it, but P, Q and R see that the only way out is to choose neither A nor B, and eventually C reluctantly agrees to be appointed.

One of the most remarkable aspects of the discussion is that the individual and personal qualities of A, B and C are hardly mentioned at all. A's supporters think that B is too much of a *laisser faire* type and is far more interested in keeping the students happy and friendly than in insisting that they live up to their responsibilities. Privately some of them think that he talks a lot of idealism but actually has his own agenda. They think that A has the strength of will and purpose to keep the students in line, even at some cost in personal popularity. In later years, they say, the students will look back and be grateful. B's backers see A as too much like an old-fashioned dominie, insistent on rules and regulations and devoid of spiritual insight. The students, they believe, will find it impossible to talk freely with him and will go elsewhere for advice. They think that B has the knack of getting close to the students, understanding their problems and talking them through the difficult passages of their lives. There is some truth in these opinions but the more extreme ones are quite unjust. That is the way of partisanship. Now, as I have said, the odd thing is that all these thoughts are hovering about the room, but the discussion is almost entirely devoted to the technicalities of the situation—workloads and scheduling matters. Is it necessary for the ninth grade adviser to teach the class on a regular basis? Would A, B or C have to drop a course in order to take on the advisership? Someone mentions that A taught the class a main lesson in the eighth grade and that it went very well. Someone else mentions that B has often supervised the class at lunchtime and has a wonderful relationship with them. But that's as far as it goes. No one is anxious to get into a discussion of personal strengths and weaknesses, so the real issues stay in some astral limbo where they remain unresolved and do immeasurable harm. Either A or B might well have been a very good adviser but the only way of pacifying their supporters is to choose an unaligned third party who will be good and efficient and relatively unengaged. Relative unengagement is, by the way, not necessarily a bad thing.

If you are now expecting me to say that it would be much better to let all the personal stuff hang out I'm afraid you are going to be disappointed. Although this didn't happen very often in my experience, it was often enough to make it clear that most people are not equipped to handle the consequences. I have heard of rather more frequent cat-and-dog fights taking place in other schools with unpleasant and unproductive results. Not many people can cope with having their motivations, attitudes and actions probed and dissected in a meeting.

I know of only one thing that will help with situations like this—the constant effort of all involved to strengthen and purify their inner lives. This is a long, slow process of prayer and meditation, but I think that even the first step—recognizing where the problem really lies and making an inner commitment—will have an effect. A consensus in which two factions have joined simply because "well, at least *they* didn't win" leaves a residue of bad feeling that is only going to crop up again and again in different contexts.

What I am suggesting is not easy, partly because before deciding to turn over a new leaf you have to admit that there is something wrong with your old one. But it is something that has to be attempted. Old-fashioned Christians talk about a conviction of sin. All our leaves are torn, stained and dog-eared, but we know that we are not alone in our effort. As anthroposophists and Christians we acknowledge the presence of Christ. Although it was not my conscious intention the fight over choice of advisers sounds something like a tug-of-war between the Luciferic and Ahrimanic tendencies within the College as a whole, although not necessarily within the individuals who are being discussed. This is a small domestic problem compared with the cosmic issues that human beings are involved in, but a picture nonetheless. If we can tidy up our inner selves sufficiently to go beyond acknowledgement and actually *feel* the presence of Christ, perhaps we can take a little step in becoming able to cope with the enormous problems of the temporal world and the task, as Rudolf Steiner described it, of safe passage into the spiritual world, where without Christ to guide us we shall have no chance of steering a right course between Lucifer and Ahriman.

(iii)

Leadership

The process of deciding about the leadership of the school, which may involve choosing the members of an administrative committee and asking someone to become Faculty or College Chair, is usually beset by the same problems as the ones that came out in the episode that I have described, only in many people's minds the stakes are higher. One approach is to make a list of desirable characteristics for a leader. It might be thought that these would include such things as freedom from personal ambition, the capacity to maintain good relationships with one's colleagues and the ability to treat all members of the community with equal respect for their humanity, as well as commitment to anthroposophical studies, knowledge and experience of Waldorf education and some skill in dealing with outside authorities. Although some people feel that the former group of characteristics is, if anything, slightly more important than the latter, and some see that where both are necessary it is meaningless to assert that one is more important than the other, the tendency is to dwell on the second group and to ignore the first. Others are willing to take advantage of the fact that such a list can be tailored to fit the particular candidate of their choice. In any case, although the qualities that enable the individual to foster a sense of comradeship and joint purpose in the community may be discussed, their conspicuous absence in one of the candidates seems to be impossible to mention.

I remember a meeting at which the College was told by a departing Chairperson that the Faculty Chair must be someone who "has a profound knowledge of anthroposophy and the pedagogy, is fluent in German and is well known in European Waldorf circles." It may well be that when a list of requirements like this is announced everyone realizes that there is only one person in the room who fits them. Some people suspect that the list has been compiled with this in mind and consider that if personal characteristics had been included it would have been necessary to acknowledge that although the individual in question has many great qualities he is also ambitious, egoistic, divisive and full of hot air. It seems impossible to say these things, so the discussion stays largely in the abstract and when the time is ripe for consensus those in opposition find themselves speechless. All the things that *can* be mentioned are favorable to the proposal and all the things that *can't* are unfavorable. Since silence is traditionally supposed to indicate consent the new Faculty Chair is duly installed, and if things turn out badly the silent and the vociferous are equally responsible.

At this particular meeting one brave soul found the courage to speak out and prick the bubble ("Don't you think we should have someone…more mature?") and those who had made the proposal were reduced to silence. That same brave soul was then asked, much to her surprise, to take on the chairmanship, and for three years she did a wonderful job. Unfortunately, in that case the three years of productivity and relative peace were followed by a period of discord which led to another outbreak of the old scenario. Resistance was just as strong as before and this time it was more vocal. Soon after that the teacher in question took a job at another Waldorf school, leaving the faculty bitterly divided and the school seriously damaged. One might have thought that everyone would have learnt something useful from these episodes but subsequent events suggest that the lesson is simply too difficult.

I remember very well the fervor with which we were told that people must recognize their leaders and appoint them by consensus rather than by democratic election. Failure to make this recognition, it was said, was a serious fault and if we didn't get it right the younger generations of teachers would rise up against the grey-heads who made the wrong decision. These remarks were made in a moment of extreme disappointment and frustration and can easily be excused. It is at moments like this, however, that people are likely to say what they deeply feel, if not what they honestly think, since thinking often does not have much to do with what emerges. Sometimes the feeling is so deep that it emanates neither from the head nor the heart but from the stomach, becoming not so much a matter of "I feel" as of "I want".

One of the problems of communities is that different people or groups of people often have very different and opposing perceptions of the qualities of the individuals who may become leaders. *We* recognize the new leader and so do *they*. Unfortunately *we* and *they* are recognizing two different people. The most difficult and dangerous character is the one who recognizes *himself*, not perhaps in so many words, but in his actions and in the way he relates to parents, board members, colleagues and sometimes, I'm sorry to say, students.

◆   ◆   ◆

In discussing our problem we find that we avoid the human issues because they are simply too difficult to mention, and concentrate on more formal, abstract or pragmatic matters. The difficult things are certainly discussed, perhaps too much, but the discussions take place outside the meeting. Eventually, as in the case of the class advisers, it may be that another individual, steady and reliable and with no particular ambition or vision for the future (or, to put it more crudely, having no axe to grind) has to take on the job. Such an outcome has several things to recommend it. One is that the visions of the flaming enthusiasts are often lop-sided and impractical; another is that the steady and reliable individual may have a talent for fostering initiatives from the community as a whole, or if not a talent, at least a wish to leave the appropriate space in which such initiatives can appear.

This sounds like a workable solution, but it may fall short in a number of ways. One is that the pot may need to have a fire placed under it, or at least to be given a periodic stir. Our chairperson may be regarded as a facilitator, but facilitation includes the art of keeping a sense of direction and administering a good shake from time to time. People who teach full time and have to attend several weekly meetings sometimes appear to be inert or even complacent, but the real problem is usually that in addition to being exhausted they have too many other essential things on their minds; so the shake has to be good-humored and not accusatory. Another problem is that the flamingly idealistic enthusiasts who did not get the job are still present and may have some difficulty in channeling their will forces cooperatively. Waldorf communities make very convenient homes for loose cannons and I know of no recipe for dealing with the situations that they create. It all depends on the strength of the faculty as a whole and there is little that the leadership can do except to try to make sure that essential business is not neglected and that victims are protected and succored. I remember several occasions when the work of the College ground to a halt for weeks or even months because of implacable bees in the bonnets of one or two members. I remember other occasions when good people left the school because they couldn't stand it any more.

◆   ◆   ◆

I have often heard that a leadership structure can conveniently be represented by a triangle with a horizontal base and a vertex at the top. The leader, or CEO sits at the top (an uncomfortable, prickly kind of place, we might think) and his directives stream downwards to larger and larger groups of managers—upper, middle and lower—before finally reaching the people who do the actual work. (I apologize to those who have seen and heard this picture over and over again.) Some people think that this set-up is analogous to the human nervous system. So the CEO (the brain) sends out a signal which eventually finds its way down to one of the workers (the big toe, perhaps) and the big toe (or worker) wiggles. One of the CEO's greatest problems is knowing what is actually going on down below, so the analogy adds sensory nerves to motor nerves and information about what the big toe is doing eventually finds its way back to the top. I don't wish to comment on this picture of the way in which the corporate world works or to mention Rudolf Steiner's different view of the workings of the human nervous system, but I do have something to say about the opposite picture, the upside-down triangle which may be thought to represent what happens in a Waldorf school, where all members of the republic are equally responsible.

The teachers are, of course the front line. The most important thing in a school is what happens in the classroom—an idea which occasionally seems to escape people's attention. (I have often been amazed at the way in which good work continues to be done in classrooms while the rest of the school is in one of its periodic crises.) The teachers handle everything that they can, but when things get tricky they sometimes have to turn to the class adviser or class teacher for help. If the situation is so difficult that these worthies can't cope with it they will probably bring it to the College of Teachers. Eventually the College may come to a decision, and this decision has to be explained to the parent, the child, the classroom teacher and anyone else involved. It may be a difficult or unpleasant decision that will not be easy to communicate or to receive. There may be a big fuss. The individual who has to present the verdict—often the Faculty Chair or someone involved in administration—has to do something that CEO's hardly ever have to do; that is, to communicate a decision directly to those who are personally affected by it and may bitterly resent it. The reason why the triangle is upside down is that we start in the most important place and see that whatever can't be digested there passes down to the next level, and whatever defeats digestion there passes down again, and so on…The analogy is obvious and there is no seemly way of expressing what it is that eventually falls on the Faculty Chair or whoever[46] it is who eventually has to make the final sacrifice.[47]

Analogies are fine as long as they are kept in their place. They often help students to grasp the overall form of a train of thought—in other words to take in what the teacher is actually saying. They have to do with structural relationships rather than content. Sometimes the use of analogy gives us and our listeners the feeling that we really understand something when we actually don't. Sometimes what is presented as an analogy is a distortion or an oversimplification. I think the main point of the upside-down triangle is that it gives people some idea of what it's really like to be Faculty Chair. (When you come to think about it you realize that the position is well named.) But the way in which the organism functions is much too complex and fluid for plane geometry.

(iv)

Footnotes

I'd like to comment on the reference to the "grey-heads" who were alleged to have prevented the young teachers from getting the leadership they wanted. My experience in the Waldorf movement is that there is very little correlation between the young-old, the radical-reactionary and the liberal-conservative axes. In society as a whole radicals are at least as likely to be conservative as to be liberal, and a liberal may be regarded as reactionary if he wishes to maintain the visions that so many of us embraced fifty years ago. So we have old reactionary liberals and young radical conservatives rubbing shoulders in Washington with the more traditional old reactionary conservatives. The young radical liberals don't call themselves by that name and tend to be absent from Capitol Hill. In the Waldorf schools, as I have experienced them, if there is any tendency at all it is for those who want to try doing things differently in matters of pedagogy, organization, public relations and so on to be the youngest and the oldest, and for those who prefer to keep things as they are, and perhaps always have been, to be going through that ill-defined region of life known as early middle age. But this is only a weak correlation and is overridden by the tendency of young people to develop characteristics such as a liking for change and experimentation or a strongly conservative outlook, and maintain them for the rest of their lives. When it comes to leadership questions you might have expected that it would be the older teachers who had developed some resistance to those charismatic and fallible would-be leaders who appear from time to time, but experience teaches over an over again that there is no correlation. Young, middle-aged and old are equally likely to succumb. Rugged individuals who maintain independent judgement seem to be born, not made, but it is something you can work on.

◆　◆　◆

It is generally fruitless to try to solve leadership problems and other difficulties arising from the interactions of human beings by tinkering with forms and structures. This is not because all forms are inherently equal but because, whatever the form, most people will find good ways of working with it, but someone with a powerfully projected personal agenda will have no difficulty in defeating its intentions. What really saves a school is the strength and selflessness of its individual teachers and staff members.

◆　◆　◆

In the early Christian Church one of the conditions for becoming a bishop was *Nolo episcopari;* "I don't want to become a bishop." Well, it's easy enough to *say* that you don't want to become a bishop, but even taking this into account I thought at one time that a similar commitment might be asked of potential leaders of anthroposophical institutions. I realized, however, that the wish to undertake the task may well be regarded as an essential qualification, provided that it is the right kind of wish, being based on "love of the deed" rather than any feeling of superiority, desire for control or enjoyment of shining in public. Since we are all fallen human beings we cannot rid ourselves entirely of such baser motivations but we can recognize them for what they are and concentrate or meditate on the real purpose.

◆　◆　◆

You may be wondering why this section has the title *The First Time I Left the Rudolf Steiner School…*

8

"From Harmony, From Heavenly Harmony…"

There is something peculiarly appropriate about starting this chapter with a quotation from a poet whose work fills me with inertia. When I think of Dryden I have a vision of dried-up ink-blots.

(i)

Allegro Energico

After my first year at the Rudolf Steiner School, Barbara and I went to England for part of the summer. It's good that we did it then since we've never been able to afford another such trip. Some time in August I received a letter telling me that the music teacher had left and requesting me to take over the high school chorus, the junior chorus and some of the music lessons. Since I had already added two earth science main lessons and eleventh grade English to my previous workload I realized that I was going to have enough to do, but I have always found it hard to turn down a challenge and I really wanted to do the music. As it turned out, my colleagues were pleased with my efforts, and the high school chorus and I stayed together the following year while the new music teacher concentrated on the elementary school programme. It is worth noting that I and the other people who filled in for the missing teacher saved the school a whole salary for one year, an achievement which, as was only to be expected, went entirely unrecognized.

We covered a wide range of repertoire from mediaeval chant, renaissance polyphony and Bach cantatas to Bartok, Britten and Broadway, and although we were by no means perfect, people noted that my chorus sang in tune and that every word could be heard clearly. Rehearsal time was very limited and hardly any of the students had any notion of sight-reading, so there was not much time to work on voice production or niceties of interpretation. I found, slightly to my surprise, that I could depend a great deal on natural musicianship and the power of imitation. One of the most important qualifications for a high school choral director is to be able to sing. It takes much less time to sing a passage for a group than it does to explain in words about the phrasing, articulation and dynamics that you want, and in my experience it's far more effective. The students pick up something in the music that goes beyond words.

After I had been doing this work for a few years something changed. The chorus had, in fact, improved, but I began to get the silent treatment from the management. Other people weren't silent. We had the custom of reviewing all special events at the faculty meeting. On one occasion there had been a good concert by the high school chorus and several people spoke positively about it. One person—it happened to be one who had "a profound knowledge of anthroposophy and the pedagogy, was fluent in German and was well known in European Waldorf circles"—agreed rather reluctantly that the performance had had its good points but he went on to say the there had been something missing. He didn't say what it was, but I got the message. After a while I began to hear comments to the effect that the school really needed a professional to direct the chorus. When I asked in what respect the work was less than professional all I could find out was that it lacked an indefinable something. Whether it was the same *Je ne sais quoi* as the one already mentioned I never discovered. I was quite curious about this as when I first came to the school the chorus had been directed by a professional and he was fired for some reason that remained obscure. There was, it seemed, no clear definition of professional status. History shows that during my tenure in Manhattan three different "professionals" directed the chorus and lasted a total of four years between them. Perhaps the problem was that although they were professional musicians they were not professional teachers. Two of them also had the disadvantage of being unable to sing very well. I took the remarks about the need for a "professional" to heart, however, and worked very hard with my willing and enthusiastic group to improve certain aspects of our singing which I deduced might be audible to the complainers. I continued to emphasize tuning, diction, tone and phrasing, and did some extra work on unanimity of attack, precision of rhythm and such relatively mundane items as how to enter and leave a room, and how to stand up and sit down. After the next concert I was told that the chorus seemed too much like a professional group.

From all this I drew one conclusion, which was that as far as the management was concerned I was no longer *persona grata*. This phenomenon—losing the favor of the powers that be—is no easier to explain than the opposite process. There is nothing peculiarly Waldorfian about it. Heads of State have always had a strong tendency to take favorites and periodically to exchange the old for the new. The main difference is that in modern times one is sent to the doghouse instead of the Tower. The few of us who used to talk about such matters observed parallels with the process of falling in and out of love. Certain "heads of state" were partial to certain personal characteristics, but alliances were often inexplicable, contrary to common sense and counterproductive as far as the school was concerned. A degree of personal attractiveness and a clear identification with the goals of those in charge or a vision that you are able to sell are certainly useful assets to anyone wishing to gain favor, but I can't account for the blindness of love or favoritism except in terms of some kind of astral exudation, resembling pheramones perhaps, that disables people's critical faculties. If you have an eye to the mainchance you can cultivate some of these qualities consciously, and when things go wrong you may be able to identify your mistakes and kick yourself for them. If, however, you got into your favored position by accident and unconsciously, as I did, you will probably have no more idea why it ended than you did why it started—that is, until you begin to think it over. I don't think, in fact, that I was aware that it *had* started until after it had ended, and in any case, I am sure that it was all the result of my having been mistaken for something that I never was and never could have been.

◆   ◆   ◆

When I had been around longer I realized that official responses to artistic events usually have more to do with politics and ideology than with the quality of the presentation. If you are in the doghouse even a supremely good performance will not get you a good notice. If, however, you happen to be "in" with the powers that be even the most egregiously awful performances will be found to have merit. Throughout my thirty-two years at the school people wrung their hands over the lack of an effective program of instrumental music. At the time of which I am speaking several teachers had, through a misunderstanding and misapplication of Steiner's words, become excessively, in fact obsessively, preoccupied with the development of the instrumental program. The program certainly needed developing, but the zeal and fervor with which the ideas were put forward would have been somewhat more appropriate for a religious revival. There was a great deal of talk about the need for children to "experience the string tone", and among the new instrumental teachers was a very fine violinist. In the course of a few years this teacher built up a small string orchestra in the elementary school and they performed a group of Schubert waltzes. These waltzes, originally written for the piano, are simple, poignant, tender pieces, which the orchestra murdered in cold blood. The general effect was that of an ill-tuned bulldozer ploughing through a rose garden. The performance was so bad that I could hardly believe my ears, but I was not surprised to hear the management singing its praises at the next faculty meeting. "The children", we were told, "genuinely experienced the string tone." Clearly those who are "in", and who tread the official line, can get away with anything. That, however, was only one of the painful lessons that I learnt. These lessons applied to all artistic events in the school—music, eurythmy, plays, festivals and assemblies.

Lesson One: in most cases the artistic quality of the event is of minor importance. The audience consists largely of those who can't tell the difference and those who won't.

Lesson Two: everything will be fine as long as the children look cute. Nobody ever commented on the fact that the Junior Chorus always sang out of tune.

Lesson Three: it is not a good idea to do anything new, challenging or even faintly controversial. The students may be excited and enthusiastic about it but we can't risk offending the traditionalists. This is a problem that afflicted two of our most talented eurythmists much more than it did me. One of them had to be given a good talk. So did the director of the high school orchestra, who had the nerve to include Holst's *Fugal Concerto* in his program.

Lesson Four: if you are not "in", an excellent performance is an even riskier proposition than a poor one. Excellence promotes professional jealousy and merely serves to inflame the opposition.

Lesson Five: there is nothing that can be done about any of these facts of life. One might simply withdraw. I like praise as much as anyone else but I decided that I could do without it and I went on doing the best I could for as long as I could. Whatever we achieved was a matter for me, the students and the spiritual beings who hover over the school. Others were welcome to listen if they wished.

At this remove of time it is possible to report these things neither in sorrow nor in anger, but in a questioning frame of mind. Are such goings on the inevitable result when anthroposophy interacts with human nature? Perhaps it isn't just anthroposophy but anything that makes people think that they know better than everyone else.

(ii)

Cantate Angelis Puerisque

One of the best things—and there were many good things—about my time at the Waldorf Institute at Garden City was that I was allowed to sing with George Rose's excellent high school chorus. George knew how to get the best out of his talented group of about thirty students and they had two inestimable advantages. One was that they rehearsed three times a week—two full periods during school hours and another period after school—and the other was that they had the full support of the community, which they absolutely deserved. What the rest of the high school students were doing while the chorus rehearsed I never found out, but clearly the chorus had priority over whatever else was going on. Things were different in Manhattan. The chorus met for thirty-five minutes once a week in school time and for one hour after school on Monday afternoons. Besides being too short, the thirty-five minute rehearsal took place at the same time as the Student Council meeting so several chorus members were always missing. The good thing about the Monday afternoon rehearsal was that students stayed for it only out of the desire to sing. I was quite surprised at the size of the group, at their enthusiasm and at their willingness to sing anything I put in front of them.

During the first six or seven years of my tenure as choral director a lot of funny things happened, but as far as I know no one ever questioned the chorus's *raison d'être*. After a few years, however, the Monday rehearsal had ceased to be a practical proposition. The two main reasons for this were that more and more students were taking afternoon jobs and that the sports programme expanded to the point where any day of the week was likely to be a game day. Swain Pratt, who was High School Administrator and schedule maker for my first five years at the school, was extremely helpful and for a while we rehearsed twice a week in school time while the students who were not in the chorus had study periods. For several years more than half the students joined the chorus and we topped fifty on a couple of occasions. Unfortunately this move was not as popular with the faculty as it was with the students. Teachers did not like being in charge of study periods and some people grudged us the time we were getting. When I became the schedule maker the complaints got louder. It was much more acceptable for Swain to give the chorus the time that it needed than it was for me to schedule it myself. It was at this point that the real questioning began. If the *whole* high school sang together there wouldn't be any need for study periods and the rehearsal times could be cut because no one would expect the whole school to give the kind of thoroughly rehearsed, extended performances that the chorus gave. Fortunately there were a lot of teachers, as well as students, who loved what the chorus did. People used to tell me how they counted on the Christmas Concert, which always attracted an overflow audience, to put them properly into the festival mood. I could see the difficulties, however. Some of the questions were genuine and needed serious consideration. My sticking point was the observation, which nobody ever quarreled with, that the high school chorus was the only group within the school where students could have the experience of tackling complex masterpieces like Bach cantatas or Kodaly's *Jesus and the Traders* and performing them with conviction and commendable accuracy. But the pressure mounted and before long we were down to one rehearsal a week. Meantime I heard from George that his group had been reduced to twice a week and he was very upset about it.

(iii)

Musica Ficta

My fall from grace was accompanied by a great deal of talk about improving the instrumental program and unifying the teaching of music in the school. I agreed with much of what was being said. Playing an instrument does something vital for the child's development that is different from the effect of singing. Instrumental music, as Steiner said, becomes more important as the child grows older. It does not at any time, however, become more important than singing.

Visits by orchestras from the Garden City Waldorf School and the Green Meadow School added fuel to the fire. These were very good groups whose directors had the sense to choose repertoire that was well within the capabilities of the students. Most of it came from the Renaissance and the Baroque and any arranging that had been done to suit the available instrumentation had been achieved with minimal damage to the integrity of the music. Many of our teachers looked enviously at the visiting orchestras and wondered why what was evidently possible for other schools seemed impossible for us. I looked at them apprehensively. I knew that under certain conditions it might be possible for us, that these conditions were unlikely to be fulfilled, and that no amount of explanation would have any effect.

The general idea was that there should be an instrumental program in which every student took part. Children would, of course, play recorders in first and second grade, but the real work would start with group lessons in third and fourth grade and after that all the children would have to take individual lessons. This would become a difficult matter for many of the parents, since instruments were needed, lessons had to be paid for and not everyone could be convinced of the value of the program. This regime was to advance through the school from year to year until all the high school students were involved. There would be various orchestras at different levels and every child would eventually be in an orchestra of some sort. It was predictable that scheduling all this would be a nightmare. At the time when all this ferment was going on I had been making the schedule for the whole school for seven years, so I had some idea of what I was talking about. A schedule that includes main lesson blocks, track courses and afternoon blocks, some of which are tied to science main lessons, is a very tall order anyway. Teachers' demands tend to be excessive and conflicting so, as with most things at Waldorf Schools, you do your best and try to dodge the bullets. Now it became necessary to clear the decks[48] completely for several periods a week in order to accommodate the music programme. Apart from considerations of available time this was excruciatingly difficult because the only spaces in which an orchestra could rehearse were the high school eurythmy room and the elementary school library, which also served as the elementary school eurythmy room. These rooms were already in constant use. In the past it had been difficult enough just to schedule rehearsals for the high school chorus, but now I suspected that this would no longer be a problem. It looked as if the high school chorus was to be abolished. All that was needed was someone to take charge of the whole programme.

That was the situation when the school received a visit from a quartet of musicians with strong anthroposophical connections.

(iv)

Allegro Allergico

The quartet played beautifully and I was particularly impressed by some arrangements of American folk songs, which struck me as being exactly right. Having done some folk song arranging I knew that suiting the harmonies and textures to the mood and style of the song is not the easiest thing in the world. It turned out that the arrangements had been made by one of the members of the group, so I realized that this person's musical accomplishments were not limited to being an excellent instrumentalist.

Some time after this performance, and in the midst of all the talk about reorganizing the music programme, two new elements entered the discussion. One was the idea that what the school really needed was one teacher who would take responsibility for the whole music programme from bottom to top, and the other was that the instrumentalist who had arranged the folksongs—hereinafter referred to as "Deuce"—was interested in teaching at the school. Putting one and one together I could see that the answer was probably going to be one, and that I and the high school chorus would no longer be needed. Nevertheless I sat with all the interested parties and discussed the shape of things to come. The general principles were as I have already described them. The school would turn itself into a pretzel to accommodate all the instrumental lessons and group rehearsals that were required. The junior chorus would continue, since it had always rehearsed outside regular school hours and made no demands on the schedule, but for the high school there would be what Deuce referred to as "the choral experience" in the tone of voice that one uses in speaking about matters of minor importance.

There is no need to go into the details of our discussions. Deuce's vision of the music programme and his own part in it led him to make extraordinary demands on the school community, but he had a great deal of support from people who were unable or unwilling to figure out the consequences. "This is what you want", I thought, "and this is what you're going to get. And when you find out what it's really like you'll regret it." So I did my best to clarify the scheduling problems and explain why I thought the proposals wouldn't work out very well, but I knew it was no use making a big song and dance about it. The one thing that I found impossible to explain was my perception that in spite of Deuce's outstanding qualities as a musician he would be a difficult colleague, wanting things that the school could not and should not give, and that there would be serious trouble. I have made my share of mistakes, but when it comes to forecasting the future I am rather like Cassandra. Nobody ever believes my prophecies but they usually turn out to be correct.

Between them the school's managers and their protégés had turned the Rudolf Steiner School into a place where I didn't want to be. Unlike Cassandra I decided to leave Troy before the Danaans[49] emerged from the wooden horse. The *lares* and *penates* didn't seem worth salvaging, so all I took with me was another Clerihew.[50]

> Mr. Francis, Keith,
> Being fed to the teeth,
> Could see little use
> In working for Deuce.

(v)

Adagio Lamentoso

I wasn't left in peace for very long. My family couldn't afford it, and the school seemed to keep on needing me for one thing or another. One was bailing out a fifth-grade teacher who was in deep trouble with her math classes and another was helping the new physics teacher, who was having trouble with physics. After a year of what people used to call living in straitened or reduced circumstances[51], I got myself a job at the Lenox School as a part-time math teacher and another job at the SUNY College of Optometry as a part-time demonstrator. My work at Lenox was rather trying, since the students were much nastier than the ones at the Rudolf Steiner School and this was only partly compensated for by the fact that the teachers were considerably easier to get on with. The work at the College of Optometry was very rewarding and I learnt things about the eye that I should never have found out from any other source, either orthodox or anthroposophical.

Since my wife was continuing as a class teacher and my sons, both in the elementary school, were talented instrumentalists, I was kept very closely informed about the music program. There is no need to make a long tale of what ensued. The school did a great deal more than it should have to accommodate Deuce's demands; so much, in fact, that parents and students began to ask if they were enrolled in a music school. It was never enough, however, and after two exhausting years a thoroughly disgruntled Deuce left for foreign parts.

The odd thing is that I agreed with a very large part of the rationale that produced these years of turmoil and yet I knew that the results would be lamentable. Why was it possible for our neighbors at Garden City and Green Meadow to have worthwhile orchestral programmes and not for us? It was partly a matter of personalities and goals. If we had been content to stick to the kind of repertoire played by our visitors we should have had a much greater chance of success. Deuce hired a platoon of instrumental teachers and tried to put together a whole symphony orchestra, and although he came remarkably close to success it was only by bending the life of the school out of shape to an extent that could not possibly be sustained. The directors from Garden City and Green Meadow were happy—and rightly so—that their groups could give spirited and enjoyable performances of renaissance dances and the minuet from *Berenice*; Deuce wanted to play the *New World Symphony*. He had one great success. After months of intensive rehearsal his orchestra gave several rousing performances of an only slightly truncated version of Glière's *Russian Sailor's Dance*; but the finale of the *New World* suffered a fate worse than death. It is possible to tolerate a certain amount of re-orchestration, but the piece was cut and mutilated to the extent that the students can have had very little idea what Dvořak was driving at. Most of the audience, being unfamiliar with the symphony and, as Sir Thomas Beecham put it, not caring much for music but liking the noise that it makes, loved it. The effect it had on my cello-playing son was that several years elapsed before he could bear to hear another note of Dvořak.

The other major difference has to do with the contrast between a school occupying overcrowded buildings in a pulsating metropolitan environment, and a spacious suburban school in a calm and peaceful setting. It makes a big difference if you have dedicated rehearsal spaces for music and eurythmy, a library which is always a library, your own playing fields and your own gymnasium. In Manhattan the elementary school library was also the eurythmy room, the music room and the assembly room. It was often hard to keep any communication going between the left hand and the right hand. The music department sometimes scheduled things without regard for other school activities. I shall never forget the day when the high school eurythmist arrived with her class at the high school eurythmy room only to find it occupied by the elementary school wind ensemble. The political situation was such that the eurythmist had to give way and find a space for her class by pushing the desks up against the walls in a regular classroom. Anyone familiar with the position of eurythmy in the Waldorf schools will realize that this was an epoch-making event. For high school students who are not dependent on the school bus it is (or was, at any rate) much easier to schedule activities outside regular school hours in rural and suburban areas than in the middle of the city.[52] I strongly believe, however, that if the discussions had taken place on the basis of pedagogical needs and practical common sense, instead of ideology and ambition, the school could have built up an adequate orchestral programme.

When the school once again found itself needing someone to teach physics and math I agreed to return. I'm not sure how much my decision had to do with Deuce's departure.

(vi)

Come Prima or As I was saying...

I wasn't gone long. Some people never realized that I had been away at all. During the two years when I was largely absent my picture continued to appear on several different pages in the school yearbook. Some of the students and teachers thought I had been on sabbatical.

Somewhat to my surprise the high school chorus had maintained a foothold in the school. I was even more surprised to find myself asked to take the place of the excellent professional musician who had been leading the group and who, unlike previous professional imports, had lasted two whole years. By the time I discovered that the chorus was utterly absent from the schedule for the new school year I had already agreed and started planning repertoire.

After-school rehearsals had become impossible, so we met as often as we could in the lunch period. This meant that we could never rehearse for more than half an hour at a time, we rarely had the services of an accompanist or even a piano, and the students often had to sing with their mouths full. Buoyed by the presence of an extremely talented freshman class we did a marvelous Christmas Concert and in the spring we tackled Vivaldi's Gloria. The total number of performers was twenty-seven; sixteen students and three teachers in the chorus, an instrumental group of seven (four students and three teachers), and one conductor. Using flutes instead of trumpet and oboe, we made a virtue of necessity by taking the quick movements at an exhilarating pace, and still achieved a measure of grandeur where it was needed. The student soloists were magnificent and the performances were greeted rapturously by all who heard them. These were possibly the only performances of the piece ever to have been conducted with a steel knitting needle.

I mention these things partly because I want to blow my own trumpet (or flute) a little, partly because someone out there may find them instructive, and not at all because I want to needle anyone.

9

Finance

Rorschach's blots are a uniform black and have an axis of symmetry. You will already have noticed the tendency of my blot to develop purple passages and strong directional preferences, but don't worry. It won't go on for ever.

(i)

Less is Less
or
Who Steals My Purse Steals Trash

"Annual income twenty pounds, annual expenditure nineteen nineteen six, result happiness. Annual income twenty pounds, annual expenditure twenty pounds aught and six, result misery."

—(Mr. Wilkins Micawber, *via* Charles Dickens, *David Copperfield*)

When I joined the faculty of the Rudolf Steiner School the starting salary was $4,800 per annum. Six annual raises of $150 brought the total to $5,700, which is where it remained for the rest of one's natural life or tenure, or until the scale was amended.[53] Barbara was starting her second year, so she had reached the dizzy height of $4,950, and that is what I was offered, ostensibly on account of my age—31—and previous teaching experience—seven years. These assets were evidently valued at approximately $3 a week. I am quite certain that in reality I was given this modest step so that the husband would not be receiving a smaller salary than the wife. Our joint monthly net income was about $800 and the rent for our two-room fifth floor walk-up was $135, so we managed quite comfortably as long as we were both working. Barbara saw her class through fifth grade, but at that point, as people used to say, there was a change in our domestic circumstances. I became the sole breadwinner and the number of people requiring bread was about to increase by 50%. By this time my monthly salary was $800 but even that sounds better than it really was, since we were paid for only the ten months of the year in which we taught.[54] Some teachers actually managed to obtain unemployment benefits for the summer months. I have a vivid memory of walking home—we couldn't afford to travel by bus—and, as I turned into our block, getting out my check and looking at it. The number, $622.84, is permanently engraved in my memory. We had moved into a slightly bigger apartment in what was then a very sleazy neighborhood. The rent was $225, so we were left with less than $400 not only to see us through the month but also to provide something for the summer. Just thinking about it, thirty-five years later, brings back the feelings of depression and despair that, in spite of the wonder of having a child, were never far away. We furnished our apartment largely off the street. Barbara had a genius for making a room attractive even when old wooden boxes served as bookcases and the living room table, courtesy of some unknown neighbor who had evidently been able to afford a new one, had to be unobtrusively propped up because the legs were falling off. I had never tried to be one of America's best-dressed teachers but now I almost stopped buying clothes altogether and my sartorial reputation plummeted to a depth from which it has never arisen. Barbara made most of the children's clothes and haunted the thrift shops. In spite of all our economies we couldn't avoid going seriously into debt even though I worked every summer for the next ten years. Looking back on this period I am at a loss to know how we survived it. We may have thought that this was the way Waldorf teachers had to live, but we couldn't help noticing that a lot of our colleagues didn't seem to have any financial worries. They had real furniture and smart clothes and they took vacations in Europe. Some of them had wealthy parents but it turned out that that wasn't quite the whole story.

(ii)

The System

Some of the basic laws of physics are quite well known. Water doesn't flow uphill and heat doesn't flow from a cooler body to a hotter one. Money is different. Most of the money spent by the poor ends up in the pockets of the rich or, at least, the relatively wealthy, but, *pace* Ronald Reagan, money spent by the very wealthy rarely trickles down to the poor; it merely recirculates among the fairly wealthy. This law of economics is seldom mentioned, perhaps because it is too obvious for the experts to bother with, but it may explain the peculiar system by which the salary scale at the Rudolf Steiner School was, and for all I know, still is calculated. How the system was arrived at in the first place I don't know, but I do know how it was recalculated from one year to the next. The point of reference was the school's estimated income for the following year, based on projected enrollment, a tuition scale which was subject to very modest increases, annual giving and financial aid. From this all the necessary expenses—administration, supplies, building maintenance, insurance and so on, were subtracted. Whatever was left was the amount available for teachers' salaries. This is obviously the real meaning of trickle-down economics.

At that time placing the school's greatest asset last on the list was to some extent justified by the fact that all other expenses were kept to a bare minimum. Administrative expenses were far lower than they have become in recent years. We managed without the army of administrators, development and public relations officers, registrars, associates, secretaries and assistants that seems to be necessary now, and there were no class distinctions. The business manager, for instance, was on the same salary scale as the teachers, and somehow Henry Barnes and the business and secretarial staff survived without air conditioning. In the 1960's faculty salaries accounted for about 70% of the whole budget. By 1995 this figure had dropped to about 50%.[55]

As long as the new budget was worked out by making adjustments to the current budget there was no possibility of making any significant changes. It wasn't until about 1994, at a time when a financially dictated reduction in the number of teachers had been counterbalanced by an increase in the administrative establishment, that I managed to persuade the finance committee to try doing things the other way around. We did our best to devise a salary scale that would enable teachers with no other source of income to live slightly above the subsistence level, and incorporated it into the budget with all the other expenses. When it was all worked out we found that some economies in other directions were needed, one of which was that the administration's request for another assistant would have to be denied. This caused something close to a revolution. I can't remember how that element of the puzzle turned out, but what I am sure of is that in the long run we had very little to show for our efforts.

According to Mr. Wilkins Micawber the difference between happiness and misery in nineteenth century London was about a shilling a year. I estimate that for someone trying to live on a Manhattan Rudolf Steiner School salary around

1970 it was about $2,000 a year, but I can't be sure because we never had the chance to try it out. In 1968, allowing for part-time teachers, the faculty establishment was equivalent to about thirty-five full-time teachers. There were 307 students (46 in the kindergartens, 186 in the elementary school, and 75 in the high school). A uniform increase of $2,000 for the teachers, the building manager and the five people[56] involved in administrative work would have cost the school about $85,000 and would have required an average increase in tuition of $280. It was often loudly proclaimed within the school community that raising teachers' salaries was the first financial priority. Could the parents at that time have managed another $5.40 a week, or would such an increase have sent them scurrying off to other independent schools, most of which had considerably higher tuition? That's another thing that we'll never know. Financial decisions were at that time largely in the hands of people who had money in the bank and sources of income outside the school, people who would visit our apartment and say things like, "You know you really ought to get your kitchen done over. For a couple of thousand dollars it could be really nice." As far as we were concerned it might just as well have been a couple of million dollars. We were using a disgusting old refrigerator discarded by another tenant because we couldn't find a couple of hundred dollars to buy a new one. I had an idea which was never adopted, possibly because I was very diffident in putting it forward: let the salaries be calculated by those who actually had to live on them.

(iii)

Sunshine

At a certain point it was deemed necessary to go through the files in the administrative office and see if the enormous accumulation of paper could be reduced somewhat. This was a long job since each piece of paper had to be given at least a cursory glance before being discarded. A number of odd things emerged but there was one that really startled me. I had always taken it for granted that the salary scale had been applied uniformly, but this was not the case. It turned out that there had been some exceptions—not many, but enough to indicate a certain tendency. One might have thought that if there were exceptions they would have been in favor of people in desperate financial need, but the trend seemed to be more in the other direction. The strongest correlation seemed to be with personality. People who managed to get special deals were of the persistent, nagging, me-first, fur coats and holidays abroad persuasion. When I think about this I have to remind myself very forcefully that nothing really matters and I mustn't take it too seriously. I know from personal experience that the people who make financial decisions often find themselves not only in dilemmas, but also in trilemmas, tetralemmas and pentalemmas. What do you do when an urgently needed teacher says, "This is what I need. Without this special consideration I'll have to go elsewhere."? I sometimes wish I had tried it, but there are two reasons why I didn't. One is that I'm not built that way and the other is that at the time I didn't want to go anywhere else.

◆　　◆　　◆

According to Mr. Micawber we ought to have been miserable. The odd thing is that, although we had our moments of depression, a lot of the time we seemed to be a great deal happier than most of our more affluent colleagues.

10

Being a Teacher, Part 1

Some of the blots on the Waldorf landscape have been painted over or digested by time. Some of the others could be made to disappear by more respectable methods.

(i)

Tests and Such

In the course of my tenure at the Rudolf Steiner School one of the most frequently debated issues was the appropriateness of testing and grading in a Waldorf School. I say "debated" rather than discussed because the major participants often appeared to be proceeding from heavily fortified positions and arguing for victory rather than working together for understanding. It is a problem that I am not prepared to discuss here.[57] I have already touched on several thorny issues and you may have noticed that I am better at asking questions than I am at giving answers. One of the advantages of having a mathematical training is that you realize that many problems do not have answers in the real world. Mathematicians showed that it is easy enough to invent a world of imaginary numbers in which answers can be found. I was about to write that no one would want to invent an imaginary world of students, parents and teachers when it dawned on me that that is exactly what people with an axe to grind often do. What I wish to convey, however, is that debates and discussions often appear to proceed on the unwarrantable assumption that somewhere or other there is the one correct solution, if only we could find it.

If, at random, you write down an equation containing x^2 or some higher power of x, by far the greatest probability is that it will have no solutions at all in the world of real numbers. The next highest probability is that it will have at least two different irrational solutions. The probability that it will have just one real, rational, correct solution is almost indistinguishable from zero. Since life is very much more complex than mathematics it is hardly surprising that we spend much of our time groping around in semi-darkness and designing systems that work reasonably well most of the time as long as we don't expect too much. What *is* surprising is that there are still people who think that if we sit around and talk long enough we shall hit on perfect solutions for our problems. I was never in favor of abandoning tests and grades. I don't like them very much but I have never heard anyone propose alternatives that I thought were workable.

◆   ◆   ◆

When I taught my first main lessons at Kimberton I found that my ideas about what constituted appropriate tests and grades caused quite a problem. This was largely due to my not having caught on to the enormous difference between what I had been used to in an English grammar school and what I was encountering in America.

In the English system the only thing that mattered in the long run was how well you did in certain examinations. I am not talking about tests given by teachers at various points in their courses, or even about final exams. If you made it to grammar school as a result of the eleven-plus, the next momentous event did not occur for another four or five years. This time was spent preparing for the School Certificate (later the General Certificate of Education) examinations which you took at the age of fifteen or sixteen. Hard work and talent would help you to do well, but if for some reason you happened to crash you would have nothing whatever to show for all your efforts.

The tests were designed in such a way as to limit severely the degree to which a student could depend on memorization. The Latin exam, for instance, required prose composition and the translation of passages from obscure authors whom the students were exceedingly unlikely to have encountered before. There was also a set book, which in 1949 was the *Aeneid*, Book VIII, from which the examiners chose quite a long passage for us to translate. We did not, of course, know which passage it would be, and our Latin master, Mr. Walton (known to us, obviously, as "Fishy") gave us a severe warning. If you made yourself thoroughly familiar with the vocabulary and the style, you would be able to translate any passage that the examiners put in front of you. Otherwise you might suffer the fate of a young lady at Ribstone Hall who, having decided that the only thing to do was to memorize all eight hundred lines, unfortunately failed to identify the given passage correctly and started in the wrong place. In physics and chemistry some of the questions required descriptive work, but many included calculations that demanded the understanding and application of principles. The tests were made difficult enough that even the very best students were unlikely to score above 80% and the average would be about 50%. This is the way to achieve the maximum differentiation over the whole range of accomplishment.

At Kimberton I was much too slow in realizing that although my style of teaching appealed strongly to the able students who did not require extraneous means of motivation, some of the others were left at the post. At that time Kimberton had a rigid system of three-week main lesson blocks. As a result of holidays and snow days none of the courses had more than fourteen sessions and one of them had only twelve. In order to keep a whole class up to scratch you have to be very quick off the mark, and I wasn't. I also hadn't grasped the idea that parents have to be kept informed about what's going on and are apt to be very annoyed when an unexpected D or F crops up. At the Crypt we didn't bother much with parents and in most cases that was what they preferred. At the end of my first main lesson block I was quite surprised to find that several students not only scored below 30% on the final but also produced main lesson books of negligible accomplishment. It dawned on me that a crop of F's would not be appreciated so I carefully renormalized the test so that the average was 80% instead of whatever it was really—somewhere around 55%, I believe—and reduced the standard deviation to the point where poor old Patti's raw score of a generous 10% was transformed into 49%. This allowed me to square my conscience sufficiently to give her and three of her classmates D's instead of F's. It also meant that I had to find an excuse for not handing back the test papers. There were several students who deserved A's by any standard, and the final roster consisted of four A's, two B's, four C's and four D's. I thought that I had made the best of a bad job but the school administration was not pleased. "We don't like D's", said Mrs. Lord.

I never caught the habit of grade inflation, but I did acquire some expertise in the matter of improving students' work habits and I figured out how to set tests that adequately reflected the efforts of those of whom one would have to say that the spirit was willing but the intellect was weak. As you will learn from what follows, it also became clear to me that the correlation between IQ and achievement was nowhere near as strong as I had thought.

(ii)

IQ—I Question

Suppose for the moment that we take the concept of intelligence quotient seriously. Defined positivistically the IQ is a number calculated from the results of a certain test. People who took it seriously thought that it was the measure of the general intellectual capacity (GIC) of a human being. GIC is a term that we were taught to use in the 1950's as a substitute for "intelligence". It is an example of the kind of terminology that helps to give the impression that you have some idea what you're talking about. Examination of the test questions indicates that general intellectual capacity has to do with the ability to acquire and exercise verbal and computational skills and to analyze geometrical forms. Given a large enough population, a graph with IQ's on the horizontal axis and the numbers of participants at each IQ level on the vertical axis, shows the notorious bell curve. If the test has been normalized properly its peak is at an IQ of around 100 and it is largely confined between limits of 60 and 140. In practice it is difficult to produce such a curve since there is no single test that can be applied to the whole population. A test designed to differentiate adequately between IQ's near the middle of the range will not work for IQ's nearer the extremes. I continually refer to IQ's rather than people because although the test undoubtedly measures something called IQ and I am supposing for the moment that IQ has some meaning in relation to the individual, I still find it hard to use such phrases as "people with low IQ's" or "people with high IQ's." An IQ is a number calculated from a test, not something that a person actually has. With this reservation, however, I'll have to submit to the need for intelligibility.

At the Crypt School the students had all scored in the top 30% of the eleven plus intelligence test pool. You have read about my perceptions of the C-streamers, so it may come as something of a shock to realize that all these hapless students had IQ's that were considerably above average. (It is said, perhaps apocryphally, that in the early 1950's a Labor Member of Parliament complained that in spite of the enormous amount of money being spent on education, half the nation's children still had below average intelligence.) In the early days of my tenure in New York some of the classes took standardized tests the results of which included an IQ for each student. Having doubts about the validity of such numbers and not wishing to have the students labeled, the teachers kept this information strictly to themselves. What I found intriguing was that on the basis of the numbers several members of each class at the Rudolf Steiner School would not have made it even into the C-stream at the Crypt. Furthermore, some of these students were doing quite well—in some cases very well indeed—and very few of them showed any of the more distressing symptoms that I had observed among the C-streamers at the Crypt. At the same time it was clear that, ignoring the IQ's and judging by classroom performance and written work, the range of abilities and accomplishments was much greater than anything that I had previously encountered within a single class. This suggests, admittedly on the basis of a very small sample, that students who would have been lumped together in a C stream do much better when the pool is not segregated in this way.

Unfortunately, lack of such segregation can cause another kind of problem. In the first class that I had the honor to advise there were three particularly troublesome students, all boys and all with IQ's that would have placed them in the A stream at the Crypt. Two of them left the school at the end of the freshman year and the other one after the sophomore year. The limited knowledge that I have of their subsequent histories does not say much for the predictive powers of the IQ test, and it is not the kind of thing I want to talk about. There is, however, an important question that is rarely raised among Waldorf teachers. These students were undoubtedly quick and often had to wait for long periods with their brains in neutral while their teachers struggled to engage the indolent and to aid the "intellectually challenged." How would they have fared in a class of intellectually gifted, highly motivated students, in which the discourse would not have kept losing its momentum and they might have had to work hard just to keep up? *Steiner's notion that it is good for the quicker students to learn to understand and help the slower ones is valid only as long as we realize that there is a limit to the amount of that kind of good that a student can take.*

The most gifted students in the class, whatever their measured IQ's might have been, often had to exercise great patience while the teachers attended to the needs of the less gifted and the obstreperous. My impression at the time, which has only been strengthened by subsequent experiences, was that one of the greatest problems of a Waldorf School is that of satisfying the needs of its most able students. I am not talking just about the three intellectually gifted young gentlemen mentioned above, but about all those who, without fuss, are able to receive new ideas, understand and apply new methods, whether mathematical, scientific or artistic, participate constructively in classroom activities and get their written work done on time. Let me emphasize that in a system regulated by IQ measurements many of these students would have been placed in lower streams where their talents would probably not have been recognized and developed. The difficulty to which I refer is caused by the disproportionate amount of time devoted to non-achievers, underachievers and students with severe behavioral problems. There is no secret about this. In faculty meetings and teachers' conferences enormous expanses of time are devoted to the discussion of children with all kinds of difficulties, while children who simply get on with their work without drawing attention to themselves are neglected, apparently on the assumption that everything is so easy for them that they neither need nor deserve any help. Yet in their inner lives and outer experiences they may be going through just as much turmoil as the child who continually disrupts the class, makes learning difficult for everyone else and absorbs most of the teacher's consciousness. Occasionally—every few years, perhaps—someone points out that this is not a healthy situation and that the able and cooperative students need as much attention as the difficult ones. I have never heard anyone disagree with this proposition, but it provokes about as much reaction as the observation that the weather has been bad recently. Everyone deplores it but no one does anything about it.[58] In this connection there are several questions that need to be put clearly by the faculties of individual schools.

Who attends this Waldorf School? Should we accept everyone who applies? At what point, if any, do we say, "We can no longer help this child" or, "This child has to go. He or she is so disruptive that it is becoming impossible for the other children to learn and several of them are planning to leave the school"? What are we to do for the student who masters the material before some of the others have finished copying it? Are we running a college preparatory high school, a school for all ambulatory applicants, or something in between?

There are teachers who believe that people are led to the Waldorf Schools by karmic connections and that it is therefore wrong to deny admission to anyone. One consequence of operating the school in accordance with this principle is that there will be many students who can meet neither the expectations of mainstream education nor those of Rudolf Steiner. Another is that many of the most able students, no less karmically connected, will leave the school. This does not mean that the principle is wrong, only that it has bumped into other equally valid principles. If all these principles are applied the school will have to have the resources to meet the wide-ranging needs of an enormously diverse student body. One or two "help classes" and a few tutors are not going to do the trick. There is no hope of getting an answer to these questions unless the faculty can decide what kind of a school they are running. This has to be done in terms of available buildings, faculty, finance and the desires of the community in which the school operates. I say "desires" rather than "needs" because parents often don't know what their children need whereas they are usually pretty clear about what they (the parents) want. This is not a criticism—it's just the way things usually are, and it's not meant to imply that the teachers always know better. A characteristic and embarrassing thing about Waldorf education is the spectacle of a young class teacher, fortified by partially digested anthroposophical training rather than life experience, laying down the law to a parent about what the child ought, or more often ought not, to wear, eat, read, see, and play with.

There are well over a hundred Waldorf Schools in North America and I have first hand knowledge of about a dozen of them. This dozen includes many of those that have high school grades. None of them could possibly cope with a situation in which the admission process was not to some extent selective. One element of selectivity is present whether the schools like it or not—most of the parents have to be able to pay. The effect that this condition of entrance has on the nature of the student body varies from place to place, and it has already cropped up in reverse in relation to the Crypt School. There the effect of intelligence testing was to produce a body of A-streamers drawn from fairly well defined sections of the community. Independent schools with largely fee-paying parent bodies draw on fairly well defined sections of the community and automatically eliminate some of the crippling environmental factors that tend to be associated with poverty. The children who attend such schools are not innately superior to other groups of children but they have generally had enough to eat—which is not exactly the same thing as being well nourished—and been kept warm in the winter, and grown up with some sense of security. Such things undoubtedly affect the way children perform at school, even though they may be thoroughly messed up in other ways. As a teacher you have to work with whoever[59] appears in the classroom. The divergences of ability and attitude may have been mitigated somewhat by the admissions process, but it is still wide enough to make teaching the class as a whole a difficult matter which only becomes more difficult as the children get older.

Very young children have a power of imitation which enables them to do amazing things, and which they gradually lose as they grow older. They never entirely lose it, of course, but the older you are the more choice you have about whether or not to imitate. For the young child it generally isn't a matter of choosing—just of doing. Some children stay in this stage longer than others, and some have difficulty in getting out of it, so that imitation becomes a substitute for the development of independent thinking. This can be very deceiving. Teachers often mistake the imitation for the real thing, partly because, earlier in the child's life, it *was* the real thing, and partly because imitation in some form or other remains such a big part of life in the Waldorf classroom. This last remark requires some explanation.

(iii)

The Curse of the Waldorf Schools

"What textbook do you use for geography [or history, physics, geometry or any other main lesson subject]?" asks the visitor.

"Well, actually we don't use textbooks", replies the class teacher, a shade nervously. He takes a certain pride in not using textbooks, but he knows that parents are apt to be a little skittish on the subject.

"So where does the material come from and how do the students keep track of it?"

"I provide the material and…"

"Where do you get it from?" This is a rather impatient parent.

"From my own reading and experience, and from older teachers. I present it to the class and we discuss it and later they write it down and turn it into a beautiful notebook. So, in effect, they make their own textbooks."

"So you spend a lot of time doing research, you tell it all to the kids and then they write it down. Do they put it straight into their notebooks or do you correct it first?"

"If they are copying from the blackboard it goes straight into their goodbooks. If it's a dictation I correct it and then they copy it."

In many Waldorf communities "goodbook" has become a word.

"And then you correct it again?"

"Well—er—yes."

"That's a formidable amount of work. Wouldn't it be much easier and more economical to use a regular textbook?"

You have certain objections to regular textbooks, one of which you share with teachers at other schools—textbooks are often badly written and full of errors. As a Waldorf teacher you have ways of getting into your subject that are at odds with the conventional approach. There are certain points of view to which you don't wish to expose your students until later. Furthermore, the creation of the main lesson notebook through the cycle of presentation, review and writing is central, archetypal almost, to the way you teach. It would be impossible to explain all this to a parent, especially one who keeps interrupting, in a single conversation, even if you thought it desirable. It's hard enough to explain the main lesson system in itself, without going into all these related matters.

"Don't they forget everything as soon as the block, or whatever you call it, is over?"

"Well, you see, forgetting is just as important as remembering."

"Really? They didn't teach me that when I was at school."

Suppressing the impulse to say, "Perhaps they did but you forgot", you suggest looking at some old main lesson books.

"Hmmm, very pretty. Oh, it's a physics book. What's that unicorn doing there?"

"Well, we encourage the students to make their books beautiful as well as accurate."

"But what does a unicorn have to do with physics?"

"I guess they get a little fanciful sometimes. We had been to visit the Cloisters."

"And then there are all these trees, flowers and crystals. Doesn't that take a lot of time?"

"Yes, but it's something they love to do."

"Maybe this one should have spent more time on physics. Look at these spelling mistakes. Didn't you say this was an old book?"

"Yes."

"It doesn't look as if anyone ever bothered to correct it. Aha! 'Beautiful work, Nicki, A+.' I guess you don't care as long as it looks nice."

I have attended countless open houses, exhibitions of student work, illustrated lectures and discussions. I have seen scores of notebooks, copied and illustrated with enormous care and devotion and riddled with all kinds of errors, placed where parents and visitors are most likely to see them. I can assure you that I am not exaggerating. The main lesson book can be a wonderful thing, but it causes problems which are rarely, if ever, addressed.

Class teachers have to cover an immense range of topics. A seventh grade teacher, for example, has to teach courses in mathematics, physics, chemistry, physiology, English language and literature, geography and history. Since most people have a specialized knowledge of at most one or two of these subjects this means an immense amount of research in areas where the teacher is at the mercy of his or her sources. I am not implying that you can't teach a subject without having taken courses in it. I am saying that if you have only a few weeks in which to prepare to teach a block in physiology or mediaeval history you may well find yourself simply copying what someone has told you or what you read in a few—maybe a very few—books. Very often the time available is considerably less than a few weeks. Having completed sixth grade you are in a state of exhaustion as you tackle your reports and approach the end-of-the-year faculty meetings. Perhaps you go to the Waldorf Schools Conference. It can be very uplifting, but now it is the beginning of July and you have eight weeks, if you are lucky, before the opening faculty meetings for next year. That means about one week of preparation for each main lesson block, provided that you don't take a vacation. Even with talent, hard work and the best will in the world this is not a good situation. Since you are talented and committed, some of the main lessons will turn out very well. In others you will simply be going through the motions. You will be copying a mentor or a textbook or, worse still, someone else's old main lesson book. The children will copy you, you will correct their work and then they may have to copy it again, making a new batch of mistakes. You may or may not correct it again. I won't blame you if you don't. Writing all that stuff on the board and having to correct it over and over again must be a weariness of the spirit. But check the books that you put in the exhibit!

I have touched on a number of problems connected with preparing and teaching main lessons. Some of them are in the nature of the Waldorf School as it was created by Rudolf Steiner. The effort to do all that is necessary for the healthy development of the child results in contradictions. If you don't believe me, pay attention next time you are at a faculty meeting. All you can do is to live with the contradictions, try your hardest, and avoid the contentious spirit that often invades the room when teachers are vying for the children's time and attention, for the use of the one available room and for the more advantageous spots in the schedule. Contradictions are the stuff of life. If they don't kill us perhaps they will make us strong. Eventually we may understand the over-riding principles that make sense of the contradictions. Later on I may focus on other problems but for the moment I want to talk some more about copying.

Copying is the curse of the Waldorf Schools. There is altogether too much of it, and it is not confined to the elementary school. In the high school, where there is much less excuse for it, it still goes on. The way in which many teachers organize their work implies that they consider that the whole object of the course is the creation of a gorgeous notebook. And the way in which some teachers judge the work of other teachers implies the same thing. It's a terrible mistake but it has a number of dubious advantages, one of which is the reason for bringing up the question at this point. The main lesson book system makes it possible for any child who is willing to do the copying to give the appearance of doing well in the course. "Amy just isn't good at taking tests—for some reason she blanks out—but she does beautiful work and I'm sure she really understand everything." The teacher may or may not know better, but it's hard to tell Amy's—or Jack's—parents that their child has a learning difficulty, especially if you haven't realized it yourself.

This is a situation that many class teachers will tolerate. Amy and Jack sitting there, carefully, painstakingly and slowly copying things down while everyone else is having a good time, make a heartwarming sight. Meanwhile Maria and Cliff, who understand most things before their teacher has finished explaining them, who lose interest while the long and painstaking explanations continue, and whose notebooks look like the efforts of cross-eyed English schoolchildren with bent J-nibs, command much less sympathy. Amy and Jack must be very artistic children who are incarnating just a little slowly and need help and encouragement, not criticism. Maria and Cliff are over-intellectual (tsk, tsk) and already too deep in the physical. Their intellectuality must be checked and they must be given more artistic work and made to recopy their main lesson books—several times, if necessary. Their parents must be instructed to keep them off the Internet, away from the TV and the video games and to discourage them from reading the modern novels that fascinate them and doing many other things that an intellectually curious child is apt to do. There is no need for me to make this stuff up; I have heard it so many times that I can say it in my sleep. These are the kinds of stock responses that such cases produce, and while some of the advice is good, the best we can say for the reasons for giving it is that they are not necessarily wrong—perhaps only 60% of the time. The kind of treatment given to Maria and Cliff may be beneficial or it may result in frustration and disaffection. Amy and Jack may be slow in coming down and may be reading, writing and calculating as well as anyone else in a couple of years. Or they may not. Learning difficulties are not easy to diagnose but some teachers manage to do it even when the parents and some of the other teachers do not approve of professional help and testing.

The longer such discoveries are postponed the greater the upheaval for everyone. Parents are justified in their complaint that the teacher ought to have realized what was going on a long time ago, but the fact is that a teaching style that emphasizes imitation and copying masks differences in intellectual development except for those children who are far enough ahead of the curve to make a nuisance of themselves. Modern civilization puts tremendous resources into developing the intellect and caring for the physical body but leaves the life of feeling for the most part to fend for itself when it isn't being exploited as a source of revenue. It is right for the Waldorf Schools to work to restore the balance through an artistic and rhythmical method of teaching, but it is only too easy to overshoot and to produce the kind of anti-intellectual climate that is so often to be encountered among Waldorf teachers and is usually accompanied by a strong bias against generally accepted forms of physical education. Amy and Jack get special consideration and stay in the school. There may be some distress at their inability to do anything without help, but they and their parents are comfortable, and their teachers seem willing to allow things to go on as they are, even into high school. Maria and Cliff are subjected to endless criticism, they are forced to do things that seem absolutely pointless to them, and discouraged from doing the things that they enjoy and are good at. Bill and Jill are as smart as Maria and Cliff, but either they really enjoy making the beautiful notebook or they have figured out what the teacher likes and are willing to give satisfaction.

Again, I am not making this up. Long-suffering students sometimes need to let off steam in later years. For some students, the "shades of the prison house" that had "closed about the growing boy [or girl]" open out a bit when they leave their elementary school class, and by the time they are high school seniors they sometimes feel free enough to talk about their earlier experiences. Bill, Jill, Maria and Cliff would have been much happier, more productive and easier to live with if they had been given something more difficult to get their teeth into. This sometimes happens but too often, through the fear of over-intellectualization and the limitations of the teacher, the children's needs are ignored or they are disparaged for lack of conformity and inappropriate aspirations. By the time the class reaches the eighth grade many of the Bills, Jills, Marias and Cliffs are long gone and some of them have been replaced by more Amys and Jacks. Obviously this situation has a profound effect on what happens in the high school.

(iv)

Tell Me What To Do and I'll Do It…[60]

Children who have acquired the copying mentality in the elementary school often have difficulty in getting rid of it later on. Many ninth grade students have the almost ineradicable idea that getting an A means doing exactly what the teacher tells you and copying exactly what the teacher writes, preferably with the addition of gnomes, elves, unicorns, trees, flowers and crystals. I remember one particularly bright student who said to me after a few weeks, "Oh, I get it. You actually want us to *understand* this stuff!" As a high school teacher, you may encounter students who have been lulled into dullness, or you may have the pleasure of working with students who are actively curious about everything and want to understand processes and do things for themselves. Some students are born dull, some have dullness thrust upon 'em, but I don't believe I have ever met one who achieved dullness through his own efforts.[61]

A child whose enormously productive capacity for imitation has not been transformed to some extent into the ability to understand and the will to take initiative, develops a strong tendency to demand to be told exactly what to do in every detail in order to come up with a product that will satisfy the teacher. I'm not talking about the need for a clearly specified assignment. I'm talking about the essay, the lab report or the charcoal drawing, which the student takes to the teacher with the question, "Is this right?" In other words, "Have I done it exactly the way you want it, and if I haven't, show me where it's wrong and I'll change it, fair copy it and get an A." It's hard to explain to a student that a piece of work that is even slightly dependent on imagination or insight can be less than ideal without being "wrong", and that it is possible to examine it carefully and show where it needs improvement, but that the improvements have to be made by the student. Otherwise it's the teacher who's getting the A, not the student.

I don't wish to assert that this is a situation for which there is only one cause, but the connection with the style of the class teacher is inescapable. In classes heavily biased towards the "tell me what to do and I'll do it" mentality the children who are not there—those who think independently and enjoy complexity—are just as conspicuous as those who are. For reasons that I have already discussed most of them have disappeared along the way. What makes these correlations so clear is that every so often the high school receives a class of students who are bursting with enthusiasm for new discoveries and intellectual challenges. Such classes are sometimes able to do something that most classes can't do—to reach the academic levels expected by Rudolf Steiner. Things like this do not happen by chance but I'm sorry to say that the teacher who has presented the high school with such a gift is apt to be told by the other class teachers that he or she was really *lucky* to have had the opportunity to work with such a wonderful group of children. Anthroposophists are very keen on biography and there is a lot to learn from the biography of a class. This biography is often given by the class teacher and there is as much enlightenment to be had from studying the teacher as there is from hearing the historical survey.

(v)

Oh, Those Intellectuals

"Boethius…distinguishes *intelligentia* from *ratio*; the former being enjoyed in its perfection by angels. *Intellectus* is that in man which approximates most nearly to angelic *intelligentia*; it is in fact *obumbrata intelligentia*, clouded intelligence, or a shadow of intelligence. Its relation to reason is thus described by Aquinas: 'Intellect is the simple (i.e., indivisible, uncompounded) grasp of an intelligible truth, whereas reasoning is the progression towards an intelligible truth by going from one understood point to another….' We are enjoying *intellectus* when we 'just see' a self-evident truth; we are exercising *ratio* when we proceed step by step to prove a truth which is not self-evident. A cognitive life in which all truth can be simply 'seen' would be the life of an angel. A life of unmitigated *ratio* where nothing was simply 'seen' and all had to be proved would presumably be impossible."
(C.S.Lewis, *The Discarded Image*, C.U.P., 1964)

There is nothing inherently wrong with the step-by-step process that Boethius called *ratio* and to which we still refer as reasoning. It works perfectly well as long as it has somewhere to start and is not being used for grinding axes rather than axioms. Mathematical systems such as Euclid's *Elements* have to start with statements of obvious truth or, in the modern world, with postulates that we agree to accept. Reasoning applied in this way is called logic. Logic is like a system of signals telling a train where to go, but the train won't go anywhere unless it is fueled by some form of prior knowledge—premises to the logician, axioms to the mathematician, preexisting conditions to the HMO. If the premise is an insight—the simple grasp of an intelligible truth—rather than a postulate or an observation, it comes through what Boethius called the intellect. If A = B and B = C, we do not require a proof that A = C. We just see it, and if we tried to prove it we should find that we had to bring in other axioms, perhaps of a more dubious kind. Similarly we can see without the use of logic, and without the help of the Ten Commandments, that it is wrong to steal. For most of recorded history people of many faiths and races have agreed about the major moral insights, but have disagreed about almost everything else. Intellect, being the attribute in which we are closest to the angels, is linked to conscience. My conscience tells me to live according to my moral insights. This doesn't always make it easy to decide what to do in a given situation, but at least I have somewhere to start with my reasoning. If I disobey my conscience my reasoning starts in the wrong place and gets the wrong answer. Garbage in, garbage out, as computer people say. It is also fatally easy to bend the process of reasoning to produce the desired result.

One thing that makes it difficult to discuss these matters is that about 550 years after Aquinas and 1300 years after Boethius, Samuel Taylor Coleridge reversed the usage of the words "intellect" and "reason", associating the latter with quasi-divine insight and the former with logical processes. This has merely caused a certain amount of confusion, but other changes in people's thought patterns have been less benign. By this time mathematicians had begun to wonder whether there is any such thing as a statement of obvious truth—the word "axiom" has largely vanished from modern mathematical textbooks, and when it remains it merely means something that we have agreed to accept, not because it is true but because it is convenient—and philosophers to abandon belief in the existence of moral insights. The power of reasoning, known now as intellect, needs somewhere to start from, and when it lost its points of departure in angelic insight and mathematical axiom it became available for all kinds of excursions, from relatively harmless geometries based on weird postulates to such things as *Das Kapital*, B. F. Skinner's system of child-rearing and Daniel C. Dennet's theories of consciousness. Francis Bacon's strictures on decadent scholasticism apply just as strongly to the efforts of certain modern writers, who, "knowing little history, either of nature or time; did out of no great quantity of [subject] matter, and infinite agitation of wit, spin out unto us those laborious webs of learning which are extant in their books. For the wit and mind of man, if it work upon [subject] matter, which is the contemplation of the creatures of God, worketh according to the stuff, and is limited thereby; but if it worketh upon itself, as the spider worketh his web, then it is endless, and brings forth indeed cobwebs of learning, admirable for the fineness of thread and work, but of no substance or profit." [62]

As a schoolboy I became familiar with the Ancient Mariner and Xanadu but I reached middle age before becoming aware of Coleridge's voluminous prose writings. When I did so it was thanks to Owen Barfield's essay on the subject in *Romanticism Comes of Age*.[63] Coleridge's interpretation is influential in anthroposophical circles, although few anthroposophists are aware of it, but we can't blame Coleridge for the fact that to be described as intellectual is a pretty severe put-down. To be *intelligent* is another matter. It is unfortunate that legitimate misgivings about the uses of the intellect have become part of an amorphous mixture which also contains ingrained prejudices and personal likes and dislikes.

Anthroposophists are not the only people for whom "intellectual" is a dirty word. There have been intellectuals and anti-intellectuals for a long time. To be called "clever" is at best a dubious compliment but no one objects to being regarded as intelligent.

"Intellectuals", we gather, are very logical people. They are very good at figuring things out and they come up with all kinds of new ideas, but they lack feeling and are not good at visualizing the effects of putting their ideas into practice. Thought processes that seem ethically neutral and socially, economically or politically advantageous in the think-tank can have disastrous effects when their fruits ripen in the public domain. "Intelligent" people, too, are good at drawing logical conclusions, so what is the difference? The "intellectual" people are the ones we don't approve of and the "intelligent" people are the ones we do approve of, but how do we come to such judgements? Intelligent people have other good qualities besides being intellectually gifted. (It is bad to be "intellectual" but it is conditionally OK to be "intellectually gifted".) "Intellectuals" are generally not expected to have social or artistic gifts. The areas which arouse their enthusiasm don't appear to have much to do with the process of living—not until a window or a wormhole appears between some recondite universe of intellectual discourse and the ordinary world where John and Jane Doe are pursuing happiness and fighting despair. The situation is described briefly and accurately at the end of C. S. Lewis's *That Hideous Strength*. Referring to the powerful and iniquitous National Institute of Cooperative Experimentation (NICE) and the seminal work of the now obliterated University of Edgestow, Arthur Denniston remarks: "One's sorry for a man like Churchwood [who was obliterated with the University]. I knew him well; he was an old dear. All his lectures were devoted to proving the impossibility of ethics, though in private life he'd have walked ten miles rather than leave a debt unpaid. But all the same…Was there a single doctrine practised at the NICE which hadn't been preached at Edgestow? Oh, of course, they never thought that anyone would *act* on their theories. No one was more astonished than they when what they'd been talking about for years suddenly took on reality." As far as I am aware C. S. Lewis himself did not use "intellectual" as a term of abuse. He did, however, strongly object to the unintelligent use of the intellect, as the first part of *The Abolition of Man* shows.

Turning perfectly good words into terms of blanket disapproval is a very bad habit. Certain bone-headed commentators have done this to the grand old word "liberal". It is much easier to label something than to try to understand it. The next step, either through laziness or with political intent, is to supply a set of imaginary characteristics. "Liberals" love to squander money obtained by excessive taxation. "Conservatives" prefer to spend money that they don't have and leave it to future generations to pay off the consequent debts. Like "liberals" and "conservatives", "intellectuals" are often characterized in pejorative terms, but how many stereotypical intellectuals do we actually know? When someone comes up with some schemes that we don't like we are apt to brand them (the schemes) as "merely intellectual", without, perhaps, enquiring diligently into their origins. The way a proposal is judged depends a great deal on who proposes it. If it's someone we approve of it isn't a "scheme", it's an "initiative".

Unfortunately some teachers get into the habit of labeling children, and "intellectual" is one of the labels. A child who is unusually good at arithmetic or reading is deeply suspect, whereas one who is far ahead of everybody else at making hot dish holders is just fine. In my early days at the Rudolf Steiner School I noticed that some of the teachers seemed to believe that excellence in academic subjects was incompatible with artistic ability. As far as I could gather this belief had nothing to do with observation but resulted from a peculiarly distorted group perception of what it means to be intellectually gifted. After a few years people began to notice that the students who achieved the most in artistic work were usually the ones who did well in everything else, but there were some awkward passages along the way, particularly with regard to electives in the eleventh grade. Several students who had no hope of success in the science or language electives were placed in the art elective on the assumption that since they weren't able to do "intellectual" subjects they must be good at art. As a result the art elective was overburdened with students who had no particular interest or ability in art. The one good result was that, having listened to the art teacher and the class adviser speaking their minds on the subject, people realized that they needed to do some actual observing and thinking.

◆ ◆ ◆

It may be that the only way in which human beings and their institutions can move in any direction at all is by ignoring some of their ineradicable contradictions. Before ignoring something, however, we have to acknowledge that it exists, that in the process of doing what we believe to be best for those who seem to us to be most in need we may be neglecting or even harming those with different needs. Intellectually gifted children are often treated like the unfortunate visitor who accidentally strayed into the Country of the Blind in H. G. Wells's story, and whose condition the natives thought they could improve by removing his eyes.

Among the many good things that you can do for a child, one of the most important is to find out what that child is good at and give him or her the opportunity to spend significant time doing it—whether it's making more intricate patterns in a crafts project, playing more difficult music, understanding authors whom the rest of the class and possibly the teacher have never heard of, inventing different ways of solving math problems, or shooting baskets. Children suffer in many ways and there is nothing better for their health and well-being than the sense of being good at something and being appreciated for it.

11

Being a Teacher, Part 2

(i)

High School Teachers Wanted...

Nanette Grimm taught chemistry and biology in the high school for more than twenty years and her retirement left a gap that has never been filled adequately.[64] Nanette was devoted to her work and to the welfare of her students. She was always seeking to widen her knowledge and no teacher was ever better prepared. She was highly organized, demanding and inspiring. The only complaints I ever heard about Nanette were that she made the students work too hard and that they had to learn too much. The reason why I heard these complaints was that they were sometimes given as excuses for unfinished math assignments.

"I had so much biology I just didn't have time to do it", or, as a variation, "I really wanted to do it but it was past midnight and my mom made me go to bed."

Apart from that I remember one incident concerning a certain senior class, back in the days when I was High School Administrator and Senior Adviser. This class included several conscientious radicals so by the time they were seniors they had become used to complaining and were quite good at it. They loved to discuss all kinds of things at great length but they hadn't quite grasped the idea that a discussion is not worth much unless it is based on some knowledge of the thing discussed. After a few days of the chemistry main lesson a deputation arrived in my office. Oddly enough all its members were faculty children, future faculty members or administrators, or both.

"She's making us learn the whole periodic table." I knew this wasn't true, but I let them go on.

"And we're supposed to know how many protons, neutrons and electrons each element has."

"And all that stuff about α-rays, β-rays and γ-rays, and nobody has a clue what it really means."

"Are you sure it isn't just you", I asked, having noted that many of the more intellectually gifted students were not of the radical persuasion.

"Nobody gets it. It's all abstract and none of it's relevant."

If you are over the age of fifty you probably remember about relevance.

"How long have you known Mrs. Grimm?" I asked.

They agreed that they had known Mrs. Grimm for a long time and had had her for six previous main lesson blocks.

"Well", I said, "I know you think she makes you work too hard"—"I don't think that", protested a couple of them—"but didn't you always get the impression that she knew what she was doing?"

They agreed that this was so. They were really a very nice bunch of radicals—for the most part.

"So does anyone have any suggestions?"

Long pause.

"You think we should wait a little while and see how it turns out?"

"Good idea", I said.

So they all trooped out and after that nobody ever referred to our little meeting.

I did hear, however, that once the class had learnt enough about radioactivity to make a discussion worthwhile they had a really good time and wrote some excellent essays on nuclear weapons and the responsibility of the scientist. Some of the radicals got quite worked up about it, so it must have been relevant after all.

(ii)

...Especially in the Sciences

Sir George Thomson, the son of the man who discovered (or invented) the electron, and a great physicist in his own right, gave a talk to a group of Cambridge undergraduates in about 1954 on the question, "What is Physics?" As I remember it, his conclusion was that physics is what people do in places labeled "Physics Lab". Something similar might be said about chemistry, and between these two indefinable disciplines there is no clear dividing line. Rudolf Steiner was of this opinion, declaring that the division was artificial and meaningless. "In physics and chemistry one ought to be able to put into practice the principle that the whole system of physics and chemistry is one organism, a unity and not an aggregate as is seen today."[65]

I did a lot of work on unifying the physical science courses in the eleventh and twelfth grades. A few years before my retirement I was able to put the idea into practice in New York and, as a visiting teacher, at Kimberton. In addition to unifying the courses it is fully in accord with Steiner's ideas that we should make a thorough survey of the atomic theory and its ramifications. I once asked a very experienced high school science teacher[66] at what point the atomic theory was tackled in his school and his reply was, "We put it off as long as possible." For that and many other reasons I did not expect that my ideas would be universally welcomed and swallowed whole. Some of them might well have proved indigestible even after thorough mastication but in the long run very few people had the chance to chew on them at all. It is very hard to get a hearing if you are neither part of the inner circle nor a protégé of someone who is, so I decided to write it all down and circulate it privately among people who might be interested. After struggling with the project for several months, however, I came to my senses. I had decided to circulate my work privately because of the difficulty of getting anything published at all, let alone in the form envisaged by the author. Having seen what happened to books written by some of my fellow anthroposophists I realized that the one thing that is harder than getting your book published is getting anyone to read it. Then I thought of the possible readership for this particular book. Although I was writing about something that concerns the whole Waldorf community, and doing so in a style that I tried to make accessible to non-specialists, I had no realistic expectation that I could convince anyone who was not in the business of teaching high school science that there was anything there of general interest. But Waldorf science teachers are even fewer and farther between than Waldorf high schools, and they already have their own set of gurus. Could I really expect anyone to take the time to investigate a typescript by a maverick who had never bothered to apprentice himself to any of the establishment figures and whose work was based on the idea that it is the teacher's job not so much to teach Goethean science as to teach science, and everything else, Goetheanistically? That is what it means to teach artistically and not merely decoratively. So I transformed my work into something that was even closer to my heart, a history of the evolution of atomic science starting with the pre-Socratic philosophers and linked to Rudolf Steiner's insights into the evolution of human consciousness. I'm not at all convinced that anyone will read that either—or this, for that matter—but it is something that I had a burning desire to do and it is independent of changing fashions in Waldorf Schools. J. R. R. Tolkien remarked that as people didn't write the kind of books that he liked to read, he had to write them himself. That's the way I feel about my book on atomic science. Physics and chemistry, as they were practised and written about from ancient times at least as far as the time of the Bohr atom, are wonderful and fascinating subjects. I love to read about them and I have put as many of the best bits into my book as I possibly could. Since the time of Bohr the going has become much more difficult and, in spite of the inspired work of Richard Feynman, the kind of pictorial representation available to the general reader has become correspondingly less satisfactory. If you read a book about modern science and feel grateful to the author for making things so easy to understand, the chances are that he is deceiving you. As Feynman says in the introduction to his *QED*[67], "Many 'popular' expositions of science achieve apparent simplicity only by describing something different, something considerably distorted from what they claim to be describing." The same thing may be said about popular expositions of anthroposophy.

Apart from the intrinsic interest of the scientists as people, and of the transformations in their thinking, you might expect that anthroposophists who find atomic theories objectionable would like to understand what it is that they are objecting to, but for the most part this is not the case. It takes work and might entail giving up the comfortable garment of disdain that cloaks their lurking insecurity.

(iii)

Patience and Fortitude Required…

At the time when I was working on my unification project I experienced some events that made me feel that it was time to leave the teaching profession. One of the Waldorf schools where I worked as a visiting teacher had built up a high school program which seemed to me to go as far as one could reasonably hope towards the goal of a healthy, balanced education based on Steiner's insights into the nature of the adolescent. While glorying in the artistic nature of Waldorf education, teachers sometimes conveniently forget that Steiner expected academic accomplishments that go beyond—sometimes far beyond—what is usually achieved in Waldorf schools. I was extremely disappointed to find that this particular school had been washed over by a new wave and was busy dismantling a large part of the academic program that it had so painstakingly built up, particularly in the sciences. There was, I was told, too much emphasis on the intellectual development of the students. At the same time I discovered that the eleventh graders had become extremely reluctant to use their brains for more than a few minutes at a time, and if asked to concentrate on something for half an hour or so would complain to their class adviser. Having been asked to visit other teachers' classes I began to get the impression that a new sort of ethos had invaded the school and that the idea of the teacher as the person who takes charge of the classroom and directs the traffic had become extremely unfashionable.

As a teacher you have to be responsive to the soul states of your students and ready to welcome or, at least, to entertain their ideas and initiatives, but you must remember that you are there because you have wisdom, knowledge and skills that your students do not possess. You may learn from them but they *must* learn from you. A useful sidelight on this assertion is given by the anecdote about Nanette Grimm and the senior chemistry class, and by Steiner's remark that the Socratic method is fine but you can't expect it to work if you are teaching something about which the students have no previous knowledge. One symptom of pedagogical anemia was what happened when a small class occupied a large room. In one math lesson that I visited there were ten students in a room with twenty-five desks. They sat all over the place, leaving a large gap in front of the teacher and forcing him to keep his consciousness spread out over the periphery. The lesson was correspondingly diffuse. A few of the students were attentive, while the rest chatted, read magazines or dozed. When I made the obvious suggestion that the teacher would be able to achieve greater concentration by getting the students to sit in a group in front of him, he was very reluctant to take any action. He didn't want to coerce them into anything. Having had to deal with such situations I knew that one's object can usually be achieved without coercion and without having to belabor the obvious.

People sometimes say that if only the students understood why they should or shouldn't do whatever it is there would be no problem in getting them to behave appropriately. As high school administrator and class adviser I reluctantly witnessed quite a number of interviews between affronted teachers and malfeasant students, and often had to sit through long and labored explanations about such things as why a student shouldn't bring cans of beer to school and use the toilet tank as a refrigerator, and why one shouldn't throw clay in a sculpture class or fight in the back of the classroom. Students sit there and squirm, not because they feel guilty, but because they can't stand being lectured about things that they understand perfectly well already, especially when the teacher keeps saying in the kind of tone that might just be acceptable to a seven-year-old, "Now you do understand that, don't you." They *know* that throwing clay interrupts the lesson and leaves marks on the walls. That's why they do it. Throwing clay is fun. If clay is not available you can throw soggies, bunches of paper towel soaked with water and squeezed like snowballs. Soggies stick beautifully to the classroom walls and can be seen adorning the neighboring buildings on warm days when the windows are open. Dried soggies are very hard to remove. Steiner never spoke a truer word than when he said that it is a good idea to meet transgressions with humor and a bad idea to let the students see that they are getting to you. If throwing clay puts the teacher into a tizzy then, obviously, it is a good idea to throw some more.

Having a sense of humor doesn't preclude toughness and, when appropriate, anger. One of the things I agreed with Henry Barnes about is that it is a good thing if students experience the fact that their actions have consequences, including anger. I have heard teachers state, seldom truthfully, that they never raise their voices and never get angry, as if these were almost unmentionable vices from which they were abstaining. Anger coming from a place of weakness is indeed useless, and the hollering and screaming that go with it only emphasize the ineffectuality of the performance. If you remain centred and unfazed, and if your anger is expressed through intensity rather than volume, you have a much better chance of keeping control of the situation. If you have succumbed to the idea that it is not the teacher's business to be in control, there probably isn't anything that anyone can do for you. It is legitimate for an inexperienced teacher to depend on support from a higher authority, such as an administrator or a class adviser, when things are difficult in the classroom, but teachers who are still in this position after five, ten or fifteen years, and expect the class adviser to exercise discipline by remote control, are probably as incurable as the conditions which they are seeking to alleviate.

There are things that are much harder to deal with than soggies. During my stint as a visiting teacher some real nastiness occurred, including obscene messages left in students' lockers and verbal assaults on teachers. The only even dubiously positive result of these events was that they revealed the rift in the school quite clearly. Some teachers showed compassion for the victims, anger towards the culprits and a strong impulse to administer appropriate consequences, not excluding the possibility of expulsion. Others exposed a very familiar, but nonetheless nauseating "holier than thou" attitude, and, with the usual smile of conscious superiority, asked such questions as, "Ah, but have you really *met* the child?" It was noticeable that the former group tended to feel a great deal more concern for the perpetrators than the latter group did for the victims. The theory seemed to be that when children—rather large ones in this case—behave in these despicable ways it must be because certain adults have bruised their little souls by not treating them with sufficient tact. It is certainly true that the souls of children (and adults) are frequently bruised. Most of us don't respond violently, but a few do. Are we going to condone their misbehavior because, for instance, a certain teacher held them to a higher degree of accountability than they or we—with our 20/20 hindsight—thought proper? Perhaps we'll give them long explanations so that they can understand that what they did was wrong…Perhaps next time they'll show up with AK47's. There are students who think that their teachers are very naïve, and in some cases they are right.

I am not in a position to say to what extent this abrogation of the responsibilities that go with age and experience has permeated the Waldorf movement but I have seen and heard enough, in this country and in Germany, to know that the sickness is widespread. It is not a matter of form; it is a matter of will. The dumbing down and loss of discipline in Waldorf education is a reflection of what has been going on in society in general for quite a long time. Society as a whole has shown signs of coming to its senses and it is to be hoped that the same thing will happen in the Waldorf Schools. One thing that tends to get lost in all the shuffling is the fact that many—probably most—students very much prefer teachers who take active control of the classroom situation. There is some analogy to the faculty meeting. Those who are thoughtful and introspective and have a melancholic or a hysteroid tendency do not fare well when the louder, more demanding and self-centred members are allowed to call the shots. If they are not given the kind of nurturing that they need they are apt to retire into their shells or go elsewhere, and this is a pity since they are often the most rewarding to work with.

(iv)

Previous Experience Unnecessary…

I can think of eight teachers who were hired to teach chemistry and biology in the Rudolf Steiner School after Nanette retired. Only one of them had any commitment to anthroposophy and only two had any previous high school teaching experience. Several of them were rather weak in chemistry, including one who had a Ph. D. in the subject. It is worth remarking that spending a few years determining the magnetic moment of an obscure particle or studying the decay of the feudal system in East Anglia is not necessarily a good preparation for teaching high school classes with students varying from those who are smarter and more knowledgeable than most of their teachers to those for whom long division is still one of the deeper mysteries and who have some difficulty in making their subjects agree with their verbs. People do not generally spend several years obtaining their doctorates in order to teach in small private high schools.

As the senior member of a tiny science and math department I had the responsibility of helping the new teachers to settle in. In most cases this involved giving an introduction to Waldorf education, including the basic anthroposophical knowledge of the developing child. What I had not bargained for was the need to give some of them lessons in elementary chemistry and basic lab technique. Even the most experienced mentor cannot, however, be prepared for all eventualities. One teacher who wished to demonstrate the reaction between metallic sodium and water, but who had never previously performed the experiment, thought that it would be more interesting for the students if she used a piece of sodium the size of a walnut instead the usual sliver. The resulting explosion was heard all over the school and it is a matter of luck or angelic intervention that no one was hurt. Such exciting moments are not confined to the high school. A seventh-grade teacher giving a lesson on combustion left a piece of yellow phosphorus lying on the table. When it burst into flame she tried to solve the problem by sweeping it into her waste paper basket. After leaving the school she became very prominent in teacher training. An eighth grade teacher wanting to demonstrate the properties of hydrogen prepared the gas by the usual method of allowing granulated zinc to react with sulphuric acid in a conical flask fitted with a delivery tube. He made three mistakes and the only thing that he did right was to try it out beforehand. He used sulphuric acid of ten times the needed concentration, he heated the flask, which is absolutely unnecessary, and he held a lighted match to the end of the delivery tube in order to see if any hydrogen was coming. The explosion showered hot sulphuric acid and fragments of glass all over the lab, ruining a great deal of new woodwork, but again the angels were on the lookout and our hero not only escaped injury but lived to write a book about how to teach physics in the upper elementary school.

I have no complaint with the people responsible for hiring the new science teachers. I hired one or two of them myself. Given the salary scale, the working conditions and the strange (to them) philosophy of education, one might be surprised that there were any applicants at all.

(v)

Imitation, Discipleship and What?

If you teach in the preschool you are there to be imitated, so you have to be very careful never to do anything, wear anything or even think anything that you wouldn't want to rub off on the children. As an elementary school class teacher you are an authority and the children are your disciples, although it cannot be guaranteed that they will automatically adhere to that relationship. Steiner is very explicit about these things. It is OK for a class teacher not to know everything, but it is not OK to be wishy-washy. If you are a high school teacher it is not quite so clear what you are. Some students like the disciple-authority relationship and will continue it until you find some way of shaking them out of it. Others may challenge you all along the line. Whatever authority you have comes from what you know, what you can do and how well you respond to moments of stress. Franz Schubert was given the nickname Kanevas because of his habit of enquiring, "Kann er was?" on acquiring a new acquaintance. "What's he good at?" is what the students would like to know about you. The way in which they find out is to give you a hard time at the beginning. Once you have shown that there are things that you really are good at, especially your subject, and that you have some sort of instinct for dealing with the smart alecks, things soon settle down. One thing you have to realize is that you can't have it both ways. You want to have a well-ordered classroom and you would like to be treated with respect, but perhaps at the same time you have the desire to get alongside the students and get them to treat you like one of their number. This may be fun and it may fulfill something in you that ought to have been fulfilled in some other way. If you are very young you might actually be able to get away with it for a few years. If you are still doing it as you approach middle age you present an increasingly pathetic spectacle and the students will begin to think that there is something odd about you. What you may not have realized is that you are splashing around in a sea of hyperactive adolescent astrality and that this may be dangerous to your health. The effect of all this astral interaction may be to punch holes in your etheric. Not all the illnesses to which teachers are prone are caused by bacteria or viruses.

It is not really a question of putting some distance between yourself and the students. That distance is there whether you like it or not, even if some of them are only a few years younger than you are. By recognizing it and acting accordingly you will be protecting yourself and them. Excessively friendly relations between teachers and students may give a lot of pleasure for a while but they are very apt to go sour and cause a great deal of distress on both sides. If things are going well you may be welcome as a visitor to the intimate world of the adolescent and you may even be invited to sit down and have a serious chat, but you mustn't outstay your welcome or behave as if you were a permanent resident. You have your own world, a world which needs to remain unmoved by the teeming soul life of your students. You may remember that the more embarrassing episodes in the lives of the ancient Greek deities took place when they got tangled up with mortals. There is a lot to be said for preserving an Olympian serenity, but if you want to be like Zeus you had better show some discrimination about which of his activities you emulate.

(vi)

An Endangered Species

It seems to me that the ideals of the liberal arts education often do not survive the practice. The rewards of a wide range of studies accrue only to those who tackle the work with enough enthusiasm to go some distance beyond the call of duty—the necessity to complete assignments, pass exams and get credit. Failing this enthusiasm there is a strong tendency for the variegated mass of subject matter to pass rapidly through the student's intellectual digestive system, like so many encapsulated nutritional supplements, and leave not much more than a rack behind. People have often deplored the "narrow specialization" of the English educational system that I had the good fortune to grow up in, but it must be said that the specialization imposed on students in their post liberal arts years in the U. S. A. is often far narrower than anything I ever encountered in my student days. To put it as briefly as possible, it could be argued that my education was narrow inasmuch as I started to specialize in science when I was fifteen. But my *scientific* education was broad inasmuch as by the time I went to university I had already completed major studies in mathematics, physics and chemistry. I continued these subjects at Cambridge, added mineralogy and crystallography, symbolic logic and the history and philosophy of science, and rounded off my formal education with an intensive study of atomic and nuclear physics. Biological sciences I had to pursue on my own, but I had the good fortune to know how to study. The point of this personal history is that in trying to unify the teaching of physics and chemistry in the high school I constructed a curriculum in broad outline and assumed—without, I must confess, giving the matter much thought—that there would be teachers who would accept the general idea and have the breadth of knowledge to design and teach their own courses. I was, of course, profoundly mistaken. At one time I used to be surprised whenever I met a physics or biology major who knew hardly any chemistry, or a chemistry major who was largely ignorant of physics. This kind of situation has become par for the course now and I'd be much more surprised to meet someone who is fluent in two of the sciences. However broadly or liberally these good people may have been educated in their earlier undergraduate years their scientific knowledge is usually one-dimensional and occasionally less than one-dimensional.

The requirements for teaching the kind of course I had in mind don't stop with fluency in the sciences. While I believe that what I was suggesting could have been adapted for any kind of school, I was speaking particularly to Waldorf teachers, who need also the anthroposophical knowledge of the nature and evolution of the human being and some understanding of Goethean scientific method. Some of these requirements can be met by taking training courses and working with experienced teachers, but there are no substitutes for intelligence, enthusiasm and self-education. It all takes rather a lot of time. One of the most unpalatable facts about becoming a teacher is that the first generation of students one encounters is apt to suffer through one's growing pains for the benefit of the next. It is true that students, who can be amazingly kind and helpful, learn something from the process; but it is not always what one was trying to teach. I regretfully concluded that a unified science course would probably have to be taught by a team of teachers led by someone with enough experience and knowledge to see it as a whole. One reason for my regret was that, as you know already, I don't have much faith in committees. A horse—pardon me—a *course* designed by a committee is apt to end up resembling a camel. I think you will see what I mean if you bear in mind that a main lesson block is a work of art and try to imagine *The Last Supper* or *The Rite of Spring* as produced by a committee. ("I'll write the string parts, you can do the woodwind, Sally can do the brass and Jim can take care of the percussion." "Yeah, but who's going to conduct?") In the years that have elapsed since I suspended work on the project the suspicion that I was nurturing an impossible dream has become a conviction.

◆ ◆ ◆

"The nineteenth century was the golden age of what I call 'dirty hands chemistry', in which there were still unknown elements in the crust of the earth and new compounds that could be synthesized and investigated without the aid of a large staff and a mega-dollar laboratory. Textbooks remained largely devoted to descriptive chemistry throughout the first half of the twentieth century. Of the nine hundred pages of Mellor's *Modern Inorganic Chemistry*, in its final, 1939 edition, six hundred are devoted to descriptions of the elements and their compounds. Of the eight hundred pages of Philbrick and Holmyard's equally revered *Theoretical and Inorganic Chemistry*, four hundred and sixty take the reader systematically through the chemistry of the elements. A typical textbook of the nineteen nineties can spare less than one tenth of this space to descriptive chemistry. If, for instance, you want to know about industrial processes for fixing nitrogen from the air or producing sulphuric acid, or if you need some information about the synthesis and properties of red copper oxide, looking in a modern chemistry book will not help you. You will, however, find out as much as the authors think that a student is likely to be able to understand about the electronic structures of nitrogen, sulphur and copper and the theory of chemical bonding. Mellor opened the 1932 edition of his book with the following remarks. 'Every teacher now recognizes that it is a sheer waste of time to introduce many abstract ideas into an elementary[68] science course without a previous survey of facts from which the generalizations can be derived. In most cases the historical mode of treatment is correct, because the generalizations have usually developed from contemplation of the facts.' Philbrick and Holmyard began with a fifty-five page historical introduction and their whole book is written in a most engaging and literate manner. How times have changed! Many of today's authors mix linguistic solecisms with scientific howlers and have a rather low opinion of their students' abilities. They write down to them and, once again, what is conveyed is often only the illusion of understanding."[69]

The chemistry of the nineteenth and early twentieth centuries—in other words, the chemistry of Rudolf Steiner's time—is in many ways repugnant to the Goethean scientist. It treats nature violently and is committed to mechanistic theories of phenomena. It did, however, work with actual substances that could be seen, touched, smelt, heard and even tasted. This remained true through the 1950's when I was a student and Mellor's remark about abstract ideas, which now has a pathetic ring, could still be taken seriously. Now the textbooks start, continue and end with theory. "Theory" originally meant something like "pondering" or "contemplation". Contemplation of facts, as Mellor says, leads to generalizations. These days "theory" usually implies the systematic working out of generalizations or principles as in the theory of numbers or the kinetic theory of gases. People often use "theory" in the sense of "hypothesis", implying a tentative explanation based on inadequate evidence. Sometimes the second and third senses get mixed up, as in the case of the theory of evolution, which may be regarded both as a set of hypotheses about the origin of species and as a detailed working out of principles. My complaints about this kind of textbook—apart from the generally low standard of literacy and accuracy—are that there is rarely any attempt to give any experimental evidence for the generalizations and principles on which the body of theory rests and that students get no idea of the chemistry of the actual physical world in which they live.

There are, of course, excuses. Today's high school chemistry texts are already far too long. To include such a great amount of theory, to give an adequate historical, observational background and to add a worthwhile account of the elements and their compounds would require a tome about twice the size of *War and Peace*. If one demanded an excuse for the present way of doing things it would presumably be that what I still regard as having an essentially hypothetical basis is actually accepted fact. You might still think that anyone who is interested in chemistry would want to know how it came about that all the incredibly intimate details of atomic and molecular structures came to be regarded that way, but either the authors do not believe that this is the case or they are bowing to the demands of the curriculum designers and publishers. You might also think that this is not a good way to educate future scientists. The position, at any rate, is that neither the conscientious Goethean nor the conventionally educated scientist is likely to have much knowledge of the kind of chemistry that I think is an essential part of the tenth and eleventh grade curriculum.

You may think that this is an exaggeration, but I can tell you that I have worked with people of both persuasions and have been amazed and appalled at the ignorance I have encountered. I'm not talking about advanced or arcane matters, but things like how to set up a simple voltaic cell, which sugars act as reducing agents, what happens when you heat a carbohydrate, which metals react with dilute acids or how to correct the volume of a gas for temperature and pressure.[70] I sometimes feel that I am experiencing the loneliness of the last representative of a lost species. There must be a few of my fellow dinosaurs scattered about the country but I am not personally acquainted with any of them. Dinosaurs, incidentally, have turned out to be a great deal smarter and more versatile than used to be thought. I should add, lest I be misunderstood, that I believe very strongly in the basic principles of Goethean science as propounded by Rudolf Steiner, which shows that even a conventionally raised dinosaur can have an open mind. The same cannot always be said about unconventionally raised specimens of

Anthroposophisticus occidentalis, in whom a predilection for *scientia Goetheanistica* is often linked to a disdain for *scientia vulgaris.* What all this lamentation is leading to is the observation that it is now next to impossible to find anyone with sufficient knowledge and practical skill to take charge of a free-standing chemistry main lesson, let alone a combined physics and chemistry block.

I am haunted by the fact that I could teach this stuff, but that no one wants to know it. I could put it into a book but that would be useless since no one would read it. Besides, it's already been done. Anyone who really wants to can track down copies of *Mellor* and *Philbrick and Holmyard.* All that is required is half an hour on the Internet. I said at the beginning that what I'm really trying to do is to take care of an irritation. It has turned out to be several irritations and I think I've scratched this one enough.

(vii)

So What about the Main Lesson?

At the time—1995—when I originally made those comments about the liberal arts ideal, I was uncomfortably conscious of the ease with which they could be applied to the main lesson system. Parents who are considering a Waldorf School learn that the system makes it possible to present an extremely rich curriculum in such a way that the students undergo profound experiences of many subjects without having to suffer the overcrowded consciousness that would result from studying several of them at the same time. I believe that this is an important and valid part of the rationale of the main lesson system. To the students, however, the unbroken chain of nine or ten main lesson blocks often seems more like an obstacle course than a sequence of learning experiences. Let me try to explain this from a student's point of view. There is no such thing as a typical student. You won't like the one I've chosen but don't forget the punch lines of Burns's poem about the lady with the louse.

> O wad some Pow'r the giftie gie us
> To see oursels as others see us!
> It wad frae mony a blunder free us,
> And foolish notion.

"Having just returned from summer vacation I am rather tired, but I am one of the naturally gregarious ones (that's one of my SAT words) and it's fun to see people again and get the new schedule. Hmmm, the first block is physiology with Mrs. Andersen. She's very strict and gives lots of notes and diagrams. It takes for ever to make the main lesson book. It has to be perfect and you have to memorize the whole thing for the final. You can still bomb though—she expects you to remember everything she says in the whole block. Then there's Mr. Branch for history. He's very funny sometimes but you have to read hundreds and hundreds of pages of really boring stuff and write essays about stuff that you don't really understand and no matter how much you write you still can't get an A. When you ask him what you have to do for an A he gets upset and won't tell you. The good thing is that a lot of the time you don't really need to listen, specially when he gets off on his conspiracy theories. Let's see. Oh, Miss Boysenberry for History of Poetry. I'm going to be OK on this one. My boyfriend Scott gave me his main lesson book from two years ago and I can mostly copy the same poems that he did. I can also copy his picture of Chaucer. He says it took him several hours but he had to copy it from a small photo. I know I can do it much quicker. What he says is is the main thing is to do exactly what she says and always agree with her opinions. Then there's Mr. Wrangle for algebra. He's nice but he's a bit weird. He's always asking you to think. He doesn't give much homework and you don't have to memorize a lot and then he asks you these questions that you just can't answer. Mostly we just try to follow what he's saying and hope for the best. I can't remember a thing from last year except some of his jokes. Oops—Miss Underwood for geometry. That's the worst. Scott says you have to copy dozens of theorems perfectly and you have to memorize them for the final. Miss U says that you're supposed to understand them not memorize them, but Scott says that's impossible and hardly anyone can do it. Then you get halfway through one and you can't remember which one you're doing." And so on...

Other students would express things differently. The conscientious student who loves learning would be more appreciative and less cynical, and would have a tougher time getting through the year. The intellectually gifted student might well reveal a considerable degree of impatience. The less gifted student who is anxious to please and to get good grades might have a miserable time from start to finish.

Why do I call it an obstacle course? Picture this:
You are not the brassy little number who thought she had Miss Boysenberry figured out. You are conscientious, honest and rather a slow worker. It's the

Thursday evening of the last week of the first block and in spite of the exhortations of your teacher to keep up with things you still have twenty-seven pages of notes to copy and a final to prepare for. Unless your other teachers are unusually thoughtful you may have English, math and French homework to do as well. Maybe you won't get your other assignments finished or maybe you'll be up until 2 a.m. Customs vary from school to school, but in your school the notebook is due first thing on Monday. This means that you spend the whole of Thursday evening studying for the test and the whole weekend catching up with the notebook. Some of the notes no longer mean anything to you but you write as neatly as you can and spend a lot of time on the diagrams. You try not to make any mistakes but when you're not quite sure what a sentence means it's hard to know whether you've got it right. Now it's Sunday and you desperately want your notebook to be good because you're afraid you messed up on some of the test questions. There was just too much stuff to learn. Some of your classmates don't care that much and will be quite happy if they get C's. Others seem to learn everything without any visible effort. You know you're not going to get an A and that your parents will not be satisfied with anything less than a B. You get the notebook finished late on Sunday night and on Monday morning you get your test score—73%. You feel sick and hope that your notebook will be good enough to bring you up to a B–. It's about the best you can expect. Five minutes later you have said the morning verse and you are sitting in the first session of the next block, trying to switch your mind from physiology to history. Three or four Thursdays from now you will be going through the same process again, and three or four Thursdays after that, and after that, and…

It's hard to believe that this is the kind of situation that Rudolf Steiner envisaged or that we wanted when we embraced the main lesson system. No wonder we spend so much time debating the questions of finals and grades.

"Students are far too grade-conscious. They're more interested in getting an A than in understanding the work. They would enjoy the lessons a lot more if they didn't have all this anxiety about grades."

"A lot of them enjoy taking finals and getting good grades. It's a challenge and they like to show what they can do."

"But what about the others? Some of them have a miserable time because they work like hell to do well and they just can't manage it."

"I don't think we ought to be trying to design a system that disguises differences of ability. I think it's important for students to understand their limitations."

"If we didn't have tests and grades some of them wouldn't bother to work at all."

"A single letter grade for a whole course is practically meaningless. We should give detailed written assessments."

"But how are we going to do college applications and transcripts if we don't have grades? You can't expect admissions officers to figure out how to compare our written assessments with other schools' grades."

"And have you thought how much time it's going to take? Even with the present system the reports often don't go out until the middle of July."

"We have to do written reports in any case. It wouldn't take much longer to turn them into assessments. That's what they usually are anyway."

"And how about the colleges?"

"We might have to have letter grades just for the applications."

"And not let the students see them?"

"I don't think that would be right."

"We could tell them what we're doing and individuals could be told their grades if they asked."

"Can you imagine the line outside Kevin's office? Everybody would ask and we'd be exactly back where we started, except that it would have taken us a lot more trouble to get there."

That's just a sample of quotations from actual faculty meetings. The grading system is like a medication that you are supposed to take. It is effective in some ways but it is apt to have nasty side effects. If you think that we should always stick to homeopathic remedies you should bear in mind that even anthroposophical doctors sometimes prescribe conventional medicine. One of the results of the fall is that we often have to choose between worse and not so bad rather than between good and evil. In my experience tests and grades are far more problematical in main lesson courses than they are in skills courses. A main lesson in English literature, for example, goes into a student's soul in a more intimate and personal way than a course in grammar or algebra. There is no shame involved in having a hard time with quadratic equations or the structure of complex sentences. It is, indeed, not always socially acceptable to excel at such things. But if your heart and soul are drawn into the story of Moby Dick and you identify with the characters and write passionately about them and their quandaries, and you end up with a C+, you are apt to feel completely crushed, especially if you have observed that by mechanically following the rules and procedures and taking careful note of the teacher's opinions it is usually possible to get a B. It may or may not be that if there were no grades to worry about students would proceed in a more creative way. In the absence of grades the teacher would have to find ways of encouraging hard work and creativity. The need for some kind of reward seems to be part and parcel of the human condition. When I dig the garden in the fall I have a vision of the cherry tomatoes I'll be munching as I walk between the rows the following summer. It may be harder to convince the students that in two or three weeks' time they will be enjoying the fruits of their preparatory spadework. While grappling with this problem it is as well to remember that even with the grading system all that some students ask is to be allowed to do the minimum and to be left in peace.

Perhaps the most awkward thing about the situation is that all the teachers have to agree to do the same thing and to support whatever has been decided. You may feel that you have to acquiesce in something that you are uncomfortable about, but you are not then at liberty to tell the students that it is a bad idea. Once a decision has been made—about anything—it is your job to do the very best you can to make it work. This may seem obvious, but teachers who do not approve of a decision sometimes feel that it is their duty to prove that it doesn't work. It may be that the Manhattan Rudolf Steiner School is the only Waldorf School in which the same topic has had to be discussed over and over again because some faculty members simply will not abide by a consensus in which they have taken part—but somehow I doubt it.[71]

In spite of all the misgivings the seven Waldorf Schools in which I have taught continue to give grades. Evidently something is wrong but we can't figure out what to do about it. I'd like to go back to a point that I raised in another connection: we try to teach our students too many things.

(viii)

Less is Less—Fortunately

In planning a main lesson block it is usually easy enough to decide what you would like to include. It is much harder to decide what you will have to leave out. It is a bit like trying to perform Bach's Mass in B minor in half an hour. You would like to do the whole piece but even at four times the normal speed you could barely manage it. Perhaps it would be best to perform one complete section. You could do the *Credo*—it certainly would cover a wide range of moods and techniques. Or you could fit in the *Sanctus* and the *Agnus Dei*. Or you could do individual numbers from all five sections. Which way would best represent the composer and his great work? What a decision to have to make! The unfortunate main lesson teacher has to make decisions like this all the time, and the result is supposed to be a work of art. Historically the B-minor Mass is an accretion rather than a conceptually integrated artwork. Nevertheless we experience it as an artistic unity. This is something that we hope to achieve, at whatever level we can manage, when assembling the pieces of a main lesson.

Stockmeyer[72] comments in relation to the physics curriculum that Steiner's indications suggest a breadth of coverage that seems impossible and yet he appeared to expect that everything mentioned actually would be covered. In planning a main lesson we may have to say that it is neither possible nor desirable to do everything that Steiner expected eighty years ago in Stuttgart. The most obvious difference is that we have a great deal less time at our disposal—fewer days in the school week and fewer weeks in the school year. We also have to deal with another eighty years' worth of art, science and history, different sets of expectations with regard to external examinations and preparation for further education, and significant changes in the soul experience of both students and teachers. As with every other question about the running of a Waldorf School we have to ask, "What are we trying to achieve for the students?" and "What are we trying to help them to achieve for themselves?"

I have already referred, somewhat obliquely, to an aspect of the situation that is so obvious that it tends to be overlooked. We should not expect the students to remember much of what they learn in the main lesson. Knowledge and techniques are generally lost unless they are exercised. The physical body seems to do rather better than the mind in this respect. After a lapse of twenty years we can probably still swim and ride our bicycles but in a few weeks we may completely forget the names of the bones in the hand or the sequence of tests in chemical analysis. We certainly have a better shot at remembering things if our emotions are involved and if they are the subjects of repetitive activity—commonly known as drill. Math and language courses run throughout the year with a steady accumulation of knowledge and skills, and are not without their moments of awe and wonder. People keep on doing arithmetic, talking and writing for the rest of their lives—not very well, it must be admitted—but the main lesson course in mechanics, mediaeval history, organic chemistry or transcendentalism may be a student's first and last contact with the subject. Such a course is a waste of time unless you, the student, carry something away with you for life—and what you carry away is not the details, although it may come from the way in which the details are arranged. At some point in the course there needs to be a moment in which your soul says, "Wow!" and you have a great desire to write about it, make a speech about it or do an experiment to see if it's really true, so that the "Wow" is followed up by some action. The outer experience disappears from your consciousness but something in your inner being has been stirred and transformed by it. The lists of names that you memorized for the test, the technique for adjusting the volume of a gas for temperature and pressure, and the symbols for all the sets in the expanding world of numbers vanish, along with the cloud-capped towers and the gorgeous palaces. "We are such stuff as dreams are made on" does not necessarily refer to vague flights of fancy. Imagination becomes a capacity and the man or woman who, like Martin Luther King, says, "I have a dream", can bring the imaginative picture to reality.

Main lessons have their more prosaic uses too. They expose students, who have to take these courses whether they want to or not, to subjects which they otherwise might not experience at all. You may find quite unexpectedly that you enjoy chemistry or mediaeval history and want to continue with it. You may acquire a love of music or literature that lasts a lifetime. You may learn how to do research and how to pick the bones out of a five-hundred-page book in a couple of hours. When you take a course in college you may find that things come back to you that you haven't thought about for several years. It is hard to say that any of these benefits are specific to the main lesson setting. I have no doubt, however, that the depth of immersion and concentration that the main lesson provides allows the experiences to reach further into the soul than they do under the more usual kind of regime. If the main lesson is going well it periodically achieves a meditative quality which might not be attainable or even desirable elsewhere.

In spite of all these good things we still have the spectacle of many students running as fast as they can simply to keep up with the machine—if you will forgive the shocking word. Machines go on grinding away, relentlessly, repetitively, even when a human being gets caught in the works, and to adapt to their unheeding rhythms we sometimes, like workers on an assembly line, have to abandon some of our most precious human qualities. Between the lively and enthusiastic students who find something liberating in the main lesson and the sleepers who prefer to remain uninvolved there is usually a group of young people who are desperately hanging on in the hope of avoiding injury. Is there anything we can do to make the system less of a *system* and more of an adventure?

♦ ♦ ♦

Having for over twenty years been the schedule-maker in New York, the harassed and at times, I fear, hated person responsible for reconciling the irreconcilably conflicting demands of thirty-odd teachers—or do I mean thirty odd teachers?—I know the extent to which main lesson teachers are afflicted with the compulsion to squeeze everything into a course that can possibly be made to go. If all the teachers had their way there would be at least fifteen main lesson blocks in the year and school would have to stay open for sixty weeks.

Let us say that you conceive your course as an artistic whole. If that is the case there is probably an overarching concept or a thread that runs through the whole discourse. Some main lessons are of necessity episodic but you still need that thread which, however adjustable its tension may be, enables you to keep your purpose in mind and to know whether or not you must resist the temptation to stop and look at the flowers by the wayside. Your course may not branch and bloom until it is nearly over, and perhaps not until years later. You know how you want to begin, you know how you want to end, you know that you want to get from the beginning to the end through a series of transitions, and you know that all the time you have to keep an eye on the clock. From the point of view of time and the student's transcript, one four week main lesson block is equivalent to a track course of four periods a week for a quarter of the year. But time flows in a different way in the main lesson. The substance has to sink into the student's unconscious and be metamorphosed. If the process is hurried the result will be spiritual indigestion. If you run short of time it is much better to leave something out and adjust your transitions. Suppose you planned five major stages in your majestic progress from start to finish, and you end up having to leave one or two of them out. Is it really going to matter *sub specie aeternitatis?* Don't forget the Bishop of London.

Here are some practical suggestions. In some schools the year is divided rigidly into twelve three-week periods and Procrustes has a field day (or should it be field night?) with the individual courses. Some privileged subjects get a double dip. After years of trying to allow for teachers' individual needs (or demands) we eventually settled on a four-week rhythm in New York. This meant that there were nine blocks and that certain highly desirable courses were omitted. The fact is that no matter how many blocks there are in the year there will always be valuable things that "the students ought to experience" that have to be left out. In a certain way it doesn't matter so much what we teach as it does that we teach it in a way that is suitable for the students' stage of development, and give them time to work their way through it. Since some ill-disposed person could easily take that remark out of context I must emphasize that I'm talking about main lesson subjects and that no matter what the subject, one of the by-products of every main lesson is the sharpening of academic skills. I'd like to add an idea which has not, to my knowledge been tried. Adopt the four-week rhythm, end every main lesson block on a Wednesday and collect the notebooks on Friday. If students beg to be given until Monday to complete their books tell them that this is not allowed since their weekend assignment is to spend two days not thinking about the course that they have just finished. If the last Thursday and Friday are vacation days the course will have to end on Monday—before, not after. How to use the two main lesson sessions between the end of one block and the start of the next is a question that teachers ought to enjoy thinking about. I simply urge that whatever happens should have nothing to do with the either of the adjacent main lesson courses or any other academic subject. Having been a person with rather a lot of different hats I have often been asked how I managed to do so many things. The first time I was asked this question I said the first thing that came into my head, "By resting a lot." I then realized that this was true. Athletes training for a big race know that rest is just as important as exertion. Some students never exert themselves, so they don't need a rest. We can't, I hope, take this as the norm, and we can't have a sort of Exertion Assessment Board that decides which students actually do need the rest. There are students who need to be protected from themselves, from their parents and, sometimes, from their teachers. There are students who don't need protection but deserve a moment of refreshment. And there are those who don't deserve it but will get it anyway. Even the citizens of Hell get a *refrigerium* from time to time. It probably helps them to recover their capacity for experiencing pain. With the students it might help them to recover the joy of learning something new. There should be teachers available at that hour who can sing, paint, tell stories, discuss politics and do all manner of other things with groups of students drawn from all four high school classes. Remember that an open space in the schedule is like a sleeping antelope in a terrain infested by beasts of prey. Sentences starting with the words, "Well, I could really use that time for..." should be banned from all discussions. I realize that this suggestion will seem wild and impractical—a Quixotically impossible dream—but the need to get out of the lockstep is urgent.

Finally, I should like to point out that there is no rule that says that every main lesson course has to result in a notebook. My experience is that ninth and tenth grade students usually need it as a structural aid to their studies. With older students I frequently did things differently and sometimes found that students who were at first delighted to find that a notebook was not required changed their minds later on. For several reasons I do not consider this to be a good sign. One is that it means that the students have not got out of the habit of thinking that a great deal of careful copying can be regarded as a substitute for understanding. Many of them, if not judiciously chivvied and put on the spot, still behave as though the object of the main lesson were simply to get the notes from the teacher's notebook into their own and that no further participation is required.[73] Another reason is that most of the really interesting and striking things that happen in the lessons are of a nature that defeats encapsulation in note form. Today's spontaneous imaginative flights are apt to have been transformed into something dull, earthbound and unrepresentative, not to mention weary, stale, flat and unprofitable, by the time they appear in tomorrow's notes. People call it moving to the concept, but in many cases the concept is more of a decept.

At the risk of flogging a dead horse let me express my concern in different words. Of all the tasks that face the main lesson teacher the most difficult and the most important is to ensure that the matter of the course, its quiddity, penetrates the inner life of all the students. "All" is a big word and I hesitated a long time before using it, but, if we face up to what we are trying to achieve, this is the only way of saying it. Compared with this, getting all the students to produce decent main lesson books is a breeze. Teaching main lesson is very, very hard work, the hardest I have ever done except for parenting. It is harder than running marathons, digging the garden or solving problems in thermo-aeroelasticity. What makes it so hard is that your consciousness must be doing several different things at the same time, including being focussed at the centre and present at the periphery. You must be doing your own thinking and thinking with the students at the same time. The main object of all the planning and preparation you have done is to enable you to be spontaneous in the classroom. In addition to all this thinking you are alert to what is going on in the classroom at all times. Your eyes, ears and other senses tell you how it is with the individual students—who's with it and who isn't, and what you should do about it. You have used a great deal of imagination in forming a lesson which will appeal to the youthful mind, but by the time the students have reached high school many of them have formed the habit of not listening, no matter how inspiring the lesson would be if only they heard it. In some cases this habit is deeply ingrained and hard to eradicate. You sometimes have the feeling that you are being discourteous when you interrupt their private thoughts, fantasies or slumbers. I was told once by a class teacher twenty years my junior that he kept his lessons so lively and varied the pace so cunningly that such withdrawals never took place. Some time later, having been called upon to visit one of his classes, I found that my enjoyment of his presentation was somewhat lessened by the persistent sound of snoring from the boy sitting next to me.

As I've mentioned before, it's hard to be aware of the things you are not aware of. I have had my share of comeuppances. One came from a particularly polite and charming eighth grade with whom I did a block of mathematics. Their courtesy and attentiveness were such that I was quite taken in. When the students all sit up straight and you can see right into their eyes it is hard not to feel that you are really making contact, and you may be less likely to stop and check things the way you usually do. I was quite startled to find that after a week and a half most of the students seemed to know less than they did when the course started. Looking wide-eyed and attentive while occupying yourself with your own thoughts is a useful art that much older people rarely master. How these youngsters managed to achieve it at such a tender age is an intriguing question.

Somehow you have to get the little blighters[74] involved in the lesson. Compared with that everything else is decoration.

(ix)

It's Not Just Masochism

There are lots of reasons why a person might want to be a Waldorf teacher, and some of them are good ones. First on the list would be a passionate belief in the truth of Steiner's view of the world and the human being, although I have known plenty of people who have worked enthusiastically in Waldorf schools while remaining agnostic about anthroposophy. High on the list would be a sense of vocation, a desire to bring the students the best that you can possibly offer, and the will to communicate your own enthusiasms.

Over the years I gradually came to see that education, if that word means going to school and sitting in classrooms, even at a Waldorf school, is generally bad for children. At some point I'm going to have to explain that, but it's going to be difficult, so I'll put it off for the time being. I do, however, believe that education is usually less harmful at a Waldorf school than it is at other schools, public or private. This is one reason why I persisted. I have tried to explain how and why I got involved in Waldorf education in the first place. I have also mentioned that as a teacher of math and science I was left very much to my own devices and that this was another reason why I stayed so long. (I had been at the school for six years before anyone visited any of my classes.) Practically all the useful advice that I received came from Rudolf Steiner, so I worked out my courses through the interaction of Steiner's insights and my knowledge of the subjects I was teaching.

This was not a static situation. I never stopped reading, haunting the science sections of local bookstores and taking advantage of a flurry of reprints of Steiner's scientific lectures, and my courses were never the same two years running. Among the requirements for a teacher of any subject is flaming enthusiasm. You dig into the subject because you find it fascinating in its own right, not because you can use it to help your students to grow healthy astral bodies, incarnate properly and develop a "correct" outlook on life. Otherwise the whole education tends to become a kind of extended *Aesop's Fables*. When you uncover something that you didn't know before you can't wait to bring it to the students. Practical common sense tells you which students to bring it to and how to go about it. Practical common sense may eventually restrain you from bringing it at all. There are limits. Enthusiasm is infectious as long as you keep it focussed and don't go overboard with it. Once the students catch it their enthusiasm will re-infect you and you'll go back to your sources with renewed energy. This is good for everyone's health and is much harder to achieve if you are teaching a prescribed course out of a poorly written textbook—a description that applies to most of the textbooks I have seen over the past thirty years—and are subject to time constraints such as the necessity of doing one chapter every week. The textbook method requires much less work, but work arising from enthusiasm is almost as good as play. This is one of the great advantages of teaching in a Waldorf school—at least in the one where I spent most of my life—and it's good for the students, too.

◆   ◆   ◆

The students' responses and everyone's enjoyment of the proceedings vary greatly from class to class. Students of the "tell me what to do and I'll do it" persuasion tend to find flaming enthusiasm rather bewildering. Students who have never got into that state of mind, or have been cured of it, can pick up the ball and run with it or pass it to their classmates. There are some of each kind in most classes and it is my opinion that the older the students are, the more fitting it is to give free play to the nimble and athletic minds. Whether the course is *Faust* or Math Topics the glory is in what you take into your thinking, in what changes the configuration of your soul. Some of the best times I ever had were the results of the bequeathal to me, by Amos Franceschelli, of the Math Topics main lesson.

Math Topics was taught in the senior year and it was Amos's baby. On reaching the twelfth grade most students heaved a hearty sigh of relief at the thought that they would never have to take another math course. Amos changed that, but he did it in a humane way. He believed that it was possible to give students an understanding of what kind of a thing the calculus or the mathematics of infinities is, without the necessity of drilling them to the point of fluency, a point which most of them would have been unable to reach no matter how much they practised. He thought that such experiences were of great worth, and I, having a similar opinion about the value of investigating certain scientific topics that lie outside the usual high school curriculum, strongly agreed with him.

When Amos passed the course on to me I continued with some of the topics that he had treated, and also chose some aspects of mathematics which I had pondered for years and which were different from anything that he had done. Two of the topics that I introduced resulted from my having been stuck in Paoli for several hours one day in 1965, while waiting for a train to New York. Paoli used to have an excellent bookstore and it was there that I encountered Eddington's *Philosophy of Physical Science* and *Gödel's Proof* by Ernest Nagel and J. R. Newman. Eddington became very influential in my thinking about the fundamental nature of physical science, one result being the addition, some fifteen years later, of an elementary study of group theory to the math topics course. Later on a fascinating book called *Patterns in Nature* led to a study of organic forms and in 1995 a growing interest in chaos theory, sparked by James Gleick's book on the subject, resulted in my devoting a week of the course to that subject. This, unfortunately, came at the expense of certain other things that I had been doing, but it turned out to be worth it. But of all the books that I read, the one that had the greatest influence on the course, if not on me, was *Gödel's Proof*. Since I don't think it would do anyone any harm to learn something about the work of one of the most creative minds of the twentieth century, I give the following painless introduction. Sufferers from math anxiety may at any point skip to Section (**xi**) without feeling in the slightest degree guilty, but I think that the first two pages of the article are of considerable interest to everyone.

(x)

Gödel, Russell and Emerson

Before encountering *Gödel's Proof* I had only the dimmest knowledge of Gödel, but the title fascinated me and by the time my train pulled into Pennsylvania Station I had read several chapters. Being a physicist who regarded mathematics as a useful servant and who, like Euclid, was unencumbered by any doubts about its internal consistency, I was surprised to read about the problems that had beset the discipline since 1800 or so. I was even more surprised to learn that around 1930 an unknown mathematician—Kurt Gödel—had shown that using only arithmetical relationships it is impossible to prove that arithmetic is consistent. This does not mean that on some days two and two make four and that on other days the answer is different. As Housman says:

> To think that two and two are four,
> And neither five nor three,
> The heart of man has long been sore
> And long 'tis like to be.

No one has yet found an inconsistency or contradiction in any branch of mathematics taught to high school students, and I doubt whether anyone ever will, but it would be comforting to know—*pace* Emerson—that it's never going to happen in any mathematical endeavor whatever, no matter how abstruse.

◆ ◆ ◆

What do "consistency" and "inconsistency" mean in mathematics? What is the point about "using only arithmetical relationships"?

If I tell my wife that I was kept late at the office, and my mother-in-law that I went for a long walk, the two of them will eventually put their heads together and discover the inconsistency or contradiction. This might be called an anecdotal inconsistency. It did not arise from the fundamental nature of language or from my having been in two places at once, but through the inefficiency of my bumbling efforts to cover my tracks. If we add a column of numbers from top to bottom and then from bottom to top, and get two different answers, we do not conclude that the laws of upward addition are different from those of downward addition. If I set out to prove that the sum of the interior angles of any triangle is two right angles and find that it turns out to be three right angles, I do not conclude that there is something radically wrong with plane geometry, only that I made a silly mistake somewhere. Is it possible, however, that somewhere along the line, a mathematician will *legitimately* prove a theorem that contradicts another legitimately proved theorem? The answer to this question depends to some extent on what kind of a thing you think mathematics is.

If you think that numbers are always the result of counting actual objects, and that geometry is about the shapes, sizes and positions of such objects in the physical world—or if you have never thought about such things at all—the idea that two correct pieces of mathematical reasoning might contradict each other will probably never occur to you. The numbers, sizes and shapes of things are perfectly definite and a thing can't be in two places at once. Such statements tend to provoke argument, so it is worth mentioning that serious mathematical work had been going on for several millennia before any such doubts assailed the mathematicians. We always thought that Euclidean geometry was the geometry of the actual world and that we knew about points, straight lines and planes, and could point them out in the physical world. Old-fashioned geometry was based on the idea that these terms could be defined and that there were certain obvious truths about them—axioms—that did not require proof.

If all of this were true it would be hard to see how the system could produce theorems that contradict each other—how could true statements about actual objects produce inconsistencies? But if, as many mathematicians and physicists now believe, the physical world is governed by some other form of geometry, we lose this guarantee of consistency. Now these old notions worry us because of the possibility of confusion between the modern abstract discipline of geometry and the old carefree mapping that had always seemed to describe actual physical space. Mathematicians came to believe that the only way of making mathematics really pure was to start from scratch and create a system that could be guaranteed to contain no unconscious assumptions about the objects in it. Our geometry books still discuss points, lines and planes but refer to them as *undefined terms*. Officially, we have no idea what they are, only that they are related to one another by a set of axioms. We probably don't use the word *axiom* any more, but even if we do we only mean a statement that we have agreed to accept, not something obviously true about the real world. We usually use the word *postulate* instead. "A mathematician", as Bertrand Russell remarked, "is someone who never knows what he is talking about or whether what he is saying is true." Mathematics is a mental construct, so the work of the mathematician is not to explore the arithmetic and geometry of the actual world but, as Russell says, to derive theorems from postulates. On this view of mathematics our arithmetical and geometrical objects are so elusive that they cannot be defined, our postulates are arbitrary, and we have no guarantee that our system will be free from contradictions. If we have done our work properly, however, we know that any contradiction that does show up will be inherent in the system and not the result of unconsciousness, laziness or incompetence. The odd thing is that we still use most of the old vocabulary and continue to apply geometry to the world around us.

It might be argued that if the mathematicians are content to become practitioners of such an abstract discipline, it serves them right if they have to worry about consistency. And if mathematics is not about the real world why should a little bit of inconsistency worry anyone? Perhaps we are just making a big song and dance about the "foolish consistency" which Emerson describes as "the hobgoblin of small minds, adored by little statesmen and philosophers and divines." We gather that the larger statesmen are free from this preoccupation whereas all philosophers and divines are prone to it. "With consistency", continues the sage of Concord, "a great soul has simply nothing to do." This may well be so. As has been observed elsewhere, great souls are apt to grasp the principles of being without having to go through the logical processes needed by lesser mortals; and principles, as everyone knows, often contradict one another. Great souls, if my understanding of what people usually mean by that phrase is correct, are somewhat rare. Most of us, I believe, have a strong predilection for consistency. We favor such things as reliable bus services and equal treatment before the law. And no matter how much the professional mathematicians retreat into a purely abstract world, the fact remains that the scientific and mercantile description of the world we actually live in is overwhelmingly mathematical. For me the question whether mathematics is consistent is of great interest in itself. I think that many people might find it comforting to know that although life as a whole is full of contradictions there is one area of human endeavor which is free from them—if that is indeed the case. What, however, would a mathematical contradiction look like?

◆　　◆　　◆

Most of us have seen "proofs" that 0 = 1. Such things usually depend on trying to conceal the fact that one has divided both sides of an equation by zero or taken the negative square root on one side and the positive on the other. As far as I know, no one has yet come up with a *genuine* contradiction in any branch of mathematics taught to high school students, so we started with one of the many verbal paradoxes that have appeared over the years.

It is perfectly fine for Tom to say that Dick always tells lies and for Dick to dispute this statement. A problem arises, however, if *Dick* says that Dick always tells lies. Since Dick always lies, this statement must be false and therefore Dick doesn't always lie. Well, perhaps we should try it the other way around. Perhaps Dick is telling the truth when he says that he always lies…Oh dear! Note that no paradox arises if Dick always tells the truth, or even sometimes tells the truth. It is when Dick says that *everything* that Dick says is untrue that the problem appears.

It seems that a statement that results in a paradox of this sort has to be both self-referential and negative. Statement (A) asserts that Statement (A) is not true. Gödel created a mathematical formula that says something negative about itself. "Formula G says that Formula G cannot be proved." First it was necessary to find a way of linking verbal statements with number. If you want to find out in some detail how Gödel set about this task, you will either have to read Newman and Nagel or wait for a volume of scientific and mathematical excursions that I expect to publish.[75] If you would just like to get an idea of what kind of activities the students became involved in, you can go on reading.

◆   ◆   ◆

To give the students another example of paradox I invented a verbal version of a numerical paradox used as an illustration by Nagel and Newman. Fifteen years later I discovered that it had already been invented by Kurt Grelling.[76] I asked the students to look at two columns of words written on the blackboard:

Short	Long
Polysyllabic	Monosyllabic
White	Black

After a while—sometimes a long while—the students realized that the words on the left describe themselves. 'Short' is short, 'polysyllabic' is polysyllabic" and 'white' is white, when written on a blackboard. We called such words 'self-descriptive'. Grelling called them 'autological'. Very few words are self-descriptive, and any word that is not self-descriptive is non-self-descriptive. This sounds much more obvious and less imposing than saying that any word that is not autological is heterological, but it means the same thing. I then asked the students if they though that "self-descriptive" is self-descriptive, and on the whole they thought that it wasn't. "How about 'non-self-descriptive'", I enquired. Some of them were fairly confident that that wasn't self-descriptive either, so I pointed out that this caused a problem. To make this clear I wrote the following on the blackboard.

'Short' is short, so 'short' is self-descriptive.
'Non-self-descriptive' is non-self-descriptive, so 'non-self-descriptive' is self-descriptive.

Well, perhaps it would be better the other way round. Suppose that 'non-self-descriptive' is self-descriptive. In that case, however, it doesn't describe itself so it must be non-self-descriptive. Oh dear...

It seemed clear that all words must either be self-descriptive or non-self-descriptive—in Grelling's terminology, autological or heterological—but now we have a word that can't be either without causing a contradiction.

Grelling produced his paradox while working on something known as 'Russell's Antinomy', which I won't describe except to say that the problem arises when you establish a certain class of objects, such as words or numbers, give the class a name, and then enquire whether the class can be a member of itself or whether the name can be a member of the class. All the well known paradoxes have fallacies somewhere in their construction. Gödel's achievement rested on his ability to use *purely arithmetical notation* in the construction of a 'clean' paradox, one which is free from any kind of fallacy.

◆ ◆ ◆

Gödel had to invent some new methods and at first only a handful of mathematicians in the world could understand his proof. It may therefore seem that it was rash to try to introduce this work to seniors most of whom had already lost any appetite for mathematics that they may ever have had. I will also specify that some of the students who took this course would confirm that opinion. There is, however, something fascinating about Gödelian arithmetic. One aspect of it is the invention of a code which enables a whole sentence or formula to be compressed into a single number and ensures that no two sentences have the same number. The following is intended to give an idea of how the code works. You may not be familiar with all the signs, but don't let it worry you.

Gödel started off as if he were making a very simple numerical code, writing down his list of signs and giving each one a number, as follows, starting with signs that always have the same meaning:

Sign	Meaning	Gödel Number
~	not	1
∨	or	2
⊃	If...then	3
∃	There is an...	4

Sign	Meaning	Gödel Number
=	equals	5
0	zero	6
s	The immediate successor of…	7
(	punctuation mark	8
)	punctuation mark	9
,	punctuation mark	10

This is the list of constant signs as given by Nagel and Newman. They tell us that Gödel used only seven but that the use of ten enabled them "to avoid certain complexities in the exposition", a consummation devoutly to be wished. In order to make sure that the students became thoroughly familiar with these signs I put them into a four-part round and we sang it every morning before the lesson.

◆ ◆ ◆

In addition to the constant signs there are numerical variables, x, y and z. x, for example might have the value 2 or, perhaps, 143,672. Gödel wanted to use the minimum number of signs, no matter how complicated this made his formulae. We have an infinite number of different integers but they can all be represented by using two signs, s and 0. s means 'the immediate successor of', so s0 means 1, ss0 means 2, and so on. 143,672 would be represented by a string of 143,672 s's followed by 0. This may seem ridiculous, but you have to admit that it contains only two different symbols. Fortunately the nature of Gödel's work was such that he never had to write this kind of stuff out. For his code, Gödel assigned prime numbers starting with 11 to the variables x, y and z. It should be clear that when we use "11" to represent x, we are not saying $x = 11$; x might represent any integer. "11" is the code number that stands for the sign x, just as "6" stands for 0 and "5" stands for =.[77] Please do not forget that Gödel was not trying to produce a useful system of arithmetic. He was creating a code through which each possible arithmetical formula can be represented by a unique number. So far we have simply seen how he represented the individual signs. We must now go on to see how he combined the Gödel numbers of the signs in a formula. This will probably seem even more abstruse, but remember Good King Wenceslas and his page and don't be faint-hearted.

Let's start with a very simple formula: $x = 0$. We have three symbols to represent and we know the Gödel number of each one: x is represented by 11, = by 5 and 0 by 6. If this were a simple numerical code we should write

$$x = 0$$
$$11 \; 5 \; 6$$

But Gödel wanted to combine the 11, the 5 and the 6 so that x = 0 could be represented by a single number. To do this he wrote down prime numbers in ascending order, one for each sign, starting with 2. For this formula he needed only three prime numbers:

$$2 \; 3 \; 5$$

He then brought in the Gödel numbers for x, = and 0 (11, 5 and 6) by using them as exponents for the prime numbers:

$$2^{11} \; 3^5 \; 5^6$$

and put multiplication signs in the gaps:

$$2^{11} \cdot 3^5 \cdot 5^6$$

Now we have a set of instructions for finding the Gödel number of a formula: write down the formula and under its signs write the prime numbers in order, starting with 2. Give each prime number an exponent corresponding to the Gödel number of the sign above it. Place multiplication signs between the prime numbers. Because of the way in which this number is constructed it contains information telling us which signs the formula includes and in what order they appear.

Gödel did not need to multiply these numbers but we did so in the classroom for the fun and annoyance of it and to make things a little more concrete. It's worth noting that you can always reduce the labor of multiplication by combining the 2's and the 5's. $2^6 \cdot 5^6$ is the same thing as 10^6, so $2^{11} \cdot 3^5 \cdot 5^6 = 2^5 \cdot 3^5 \cdot 10^6$ or $6^5 \cdot 10^6$. This may not seem to be much of an improvement if one is using a calculator, although decreasing the number of operations does save a little time and reduces the chances of making an error. Students soon discover to their horror, however, that the Gödel numbers of even slightly more complicated formulae are much too large for a regular eight-place calculator. The one we're dealing with now comes to a mere 7,776,000,000, but suppose we wanted the Gödel number of the formula $x = 1$.

In Gödel's system 1 is written as s0 (the immediate successor of zero), so the formula is

$$x = s0$$

Now if we follow the same rule as before, writing down the prime numbers in order, starting with 2, we have to write four prime numbers:

$$x \ = \ s \ 0$$
$$2 \ \ 3 \ \ 5 \ \ 7$$

Now we use the Gödel numbers of the symbols in the formula as exponents and multiply the result:

$$2^{11} \cdot 3^5 \cdot 5^7 \cdot 7^6$$

This comes to 4,574,193,120,000,000. It needs nine places and it has to be exact, so an ordinary calculator won't handle it.

The whole point of the code is that the way in which the numbers are formed—by specifying a unique set of prime factors—means that two different formulae cannot possibly have the same Gödel number, any more than two different numbers can have the same set of prime factors.

We also tried doing these calculations in reverse. If you encounter a problem that says, "Retrieve the formula represented by the Gödel number 4,574,193,120,000,000", you have to reduce that number to its prime factors, which, as we already know, are $2^{11} \cdot 3^5 \cdot 5^7 \cdot 7^6$. The exponents 11, 5, 7 and 6 represent the symbols x, =, s and 0 respectively. So the formula is $x = s0$ or $x = 1$. You might like to amuse yourself by trying to figure out how you can tell whether any given number is a Gödel number. Most aren't. Gödel numbers serve no practical purpose and Gödel never needed to evaluate them, but they provided an essential tool in his proof, enabling him to express relationships in a purely arithmetical way, and to judge arithmetic according to its own rules.

We also practised the method by numbering the letters of the alphabet, starting with A as 1. "I am bad" is represented by $2^9 \cdot 3^1 \cdot 5^{13} \cdot 7^2 \cdot 11^1 \cdot 13^4$, which comes to 28,864,460,625,000,000,000. "I am" is represented by $2^9 \cdot 3^1 \cdot 5^{13}$, which comes to a mere 1,875,000,000,000. So we now have a purely arithmetical was of relating "I am bad" to "I am", a factor of $7^2 \cdot 11^1 \cdot 13^4$ or 15,394,379. Let me say quickly, before you throw the book out of the window, that this is pure whimsy, an exercise designed to get students used to how the code works and to make a certain point. The relation that we have found is not between "I am bad" and "I am", but between two encryptions that have nothing to do with the actual meanings of the sentences, but only with the letters from which the sentences are constructed. The exercise emphasizes a vital point about modern mathematics that I have already raised. The symbols that Gödel was manipulating *have no inherent meaning*. Pure mathematics in the twentieth century wasn't *about* anything. Gödel managed to establish *meaningful relationships* between the Gödel numbers of strings of these meaningless symbols, but that's a long and difficult story.

◆ ◆ ◆

The essential thing that Gödel did with his numbers was to produce an arithmetical formula that talked about itself. He then showed that what it said about itself would, in certain circumstances result in a contradiction. The most famous part of his proof had to do with the consequences of avoiding that contradiction. Gödel's work was not only about consistency. He showed that for any system of arithmetic that we care to invent there will always be theorems (statements about the undefined terms) that cannot be proved from the axioms or postulates, but are nevertheless true. Now a computer is a machine that works strictly from a set of arithmetical axioms. It therefore seems that there must always be true statements within the computer's universe of discourse that the computer will not be able to discover without human assistance. Does this mean that the human mind does not work from a set of axioms, or that we can change our axioms at will, or that we can work inductively and computers won't unless someone tells them to? Does it mean that there will always be things that a human being can think of that are beyond the reach of a computer? Since generations of computer experts have worked on such questions, producing at least as many new questions as answers, and are not exactly unanimous, you can't expect a high school course to do more than point to the most basic problems, and to make the students think in different ways about the almighty computer.

I, and some of the students, had a lot of fun with Gödel. Others found him quite incomprehensible but still managed to osmose some interesting ideas. Teaching at the Rudolf Steiner School provided exhilarating opportunities to find ways of being creative which would not have been possible in most schools. Imagine having to put all this through a committee or get it past a school administration!

(xi)

Tailpiece

Earlier in this volume I quoted Francis Bacon on decadent scholasticism:

"For the wit and mind of man, if it work upon [subject] matter, which is the contemplation of the creatures of God, worketh according to the stuff, and is limited thereby; but if it worketh upon itself, as the spider worketh his web, then it is endless, and brings forth indeed cobwebs of learning, admirable for the fineness of thread and work, but of no substance or profit."

"Creatures" means things created by God, whether human, animal, vegetable or mineral. Since the pure mathematicians of the twentieth century specified that their work was not about anything in particular, they come under the same stricture as the decadent scholastics. Self-reference, the mind working back on itself, is the very heart of the matter. Self-reference is also the very heart of *The Philosophy of Freedom*. Everything starts with thinking; thinking is what we have to think about. Modern pure mathematics is certainly "admirable for the fineness of thread and work" but the question of its "substance and profit" would require another whole essay. So would the question of the "substance and profit" of *The Philosophy of Freedom* and all that it leads to. I mention it because the comparison is fascinating. I don't have time to write a book about it, but perhaps someone else will.

12

A Christian School?

An excess of ink is likely to lead to blurring and obfuscation. It is the function of blotting paper to remove the excess and let the word shine out.

(i)

Let Your Light so Shine...

Thirty-five years ago the New York Rudolf Steiner School was blessed with a teacher called Margot Halden. Margot was Jewish and quite willing to share her opinions about things. At that time the school closed for all the major Christian holy days except Ascension Day, but not for the Jewish ones. This became a bone of contention, not primarily because of any religious or moral scruples but because there were so many children absent on the major Jewish festival days that teachers found themselves simply marking time with about two thirds of the usual number of students. It was, as some of them said, a waste of time, and it would be better to close the school on those occasions. In the midst of a discussion which was getting somewhat heated without showing any signs of going anywhere, Margot stood up and said her piece.

"This is a Christian school", she said. "Look in the brochure. It's stated very plainly there. Christianity is right at the centre of Rudolf Steiner's work. If we close for the Jewish holidays it will be like telling a lie about the school, pretending we're something that we aren't, or that we're not something that we are."

The passage mentioned by Margot was written by Henry Barnes and appeared on page one of the brochure under the heading, "Underlying Ideals."

Implicit in the pedagogy is a knowledge of the spiritual nature of man which reckons with the freedom and integrity of the individual. The basic ideals stem from

Christian roots and our aim is to strengthen the individual regardless of race or creed. Which church our children may or may not join as adults is not our concern, but to educate them in such a way that the religious element in their human nature is nourished and supported is important. The teachers seek to foster what is essentially human and to harmonize the mental, emotional and moral development in each child.

What Henry had written did not amount to the statement that we were running a Christian school as that phrase is usually understood. We didn't teach Christian doctrine, hold services and conduct catechisms, but we did celebrate the Christian festivals and in describing the school calendar we spoke of having vacations at Christmas and Easter rather than at Midwinter and in the spring. Christian religious instruction and services were regular features at the original Waldorf School and still are at schools that I have visited in Germany. The so-called "free religion lessons" were free in the sense that they were not restricted to any particular Christian denomination. As far as I know the question of providing for members of other religious bodies never arose.

Because Margot spoke with great conviction from the heart she was heard and heeded, but within a few years the pressure increased and the change was made. I now think that the school took the right action, although I had mixed feelings at the time. It is right for a Christian institution to show respect for the diverse customs of all the people with whom it interacts, as long as it can do so without damage to its own integrity. At that time no one questioned the proposition that the school was a Christian institution. How times have changed!

In view of the quantity and quality of Steiner's lectures and writings on the incarnation, life, death and resurrection of Christ, and the presence of Christ on Earth as the helper and guide of humanity, it is hard to see how anyone could doubt the truth of Margot's assertion of the centrality of Christianity in anthroposophy. Observation shows, however, that stating that a certain position is unarguable merely invites argument. I should have thought at least that it was safe to say that Waldorf education is firmly based on the anthroposophical knowledge of human evolution and developmental cycles and that these things cannot be properly understood except in the context of a wider spiritual scientific picture of the world. Here, unfortunately, is another problem. How can we justify this assertion when we know perfectly well that a great many of the teachers at Waldorf Schools have little or no relationship to anthroposophy? Well, we could say that ideally everything would be based on anthroposophy but in practice that doesn't always happen. The fact that registrars and admissions officers often feel forced to tell parents what ought to happen without mentioning that the reality is sometimes quite different is something for the schools' collective conscience. One thing is certain; fifteen years after Margot made her little speech the relation of Waldorf education to Christianity became a matter for serious debate. On the one hand we have the theorem: Christianity is central to anthroposophy and anthroposophy is central to Waldorf education, so Christianity must be central to Waldorf education. On the other hand we have the observation that some anthroposophists and many Waldorf teachers find the presence of the Christian impulse an embarrassment and wish it would go away. By the late 1970's references to any form of religion had completely disappeared from school brochures. The high school brochure written by Roberto Trostli in the mid-1980's states that the curriculum "helps develop a broad humanistic perspective", addressing "basic questions about the nature of the human being, society and the natural world." Humanism can be understood in several different ways. Most of the people I have asked agree that with or without a capital letter it implies a rejection of or, at least, a lack of interest in religion.

I believe that all the major religions of the world, with the possible exception of certain highly successful twentieth century commercial ventures, are based on spiritual insight and revelation. This is a far cry from saying, as some do, that they are really all the same thing. It is not always clear where the revelations are coming from, and to call something spiritual is not the same as calling it good. Satan, after all, is a spirit. Rudolf Steiner explained in exactly what senses Buddhism and Judaism are part of the spiritual history that leads to the incarnation of Christ. This is fine for most anthroposophists and some Christians but not necessarily for Buddhists and Jews. Steiner was a great deal less enthusiastic about Islam. My feeling about that is that just as after the age of forty you have to stop blaming your parents for the way you turned out, including your physiognomy, when a religion is more than a thousand years old and things don't look good it's time to examine the activities of its more recent exponents, which probably have nothing much to do with the original conception. This is certainly the case as far as concerns many people who call themselves Christians, thereby giving Christianity a bad name. It is all too easy to do the things that you want to do and use the name of your religion as a justification. You may be a Roman Catholic monarch persecuting heretics or a Protestant monarch persecuting Roman Catholics; you may be a Christian or a Moslem killing Moslems or Christians in the Balkans; you may be a member of the Taliban destroying a Buddhist culture; you may be blowing up an abortion clinic or murdering a doctor in the name of Christ. Or you may just be an anthroposophist promoting New England morality. All the good things in the world, including anthroposophy, are subject to corruption and degradation. It didn't take the early Christians or the early anthroposophists long to start squabbling. Islam, like Buddhism and Christianity, is a religion of peace and love, but all the major religions have become the ostensible causes of war, death, famine and misery. Given the frailty of the human being and the strength of the renegade spiritual beings who have their own agenda for the future, we should not be surprised at what has happened and continues to happen. As far as the Christian is concerned it is right to love peace and make war on evil, as long as we remember that the main weapons are prayer, meditation and steadfastness of spirit. Asking what you should do if these don't work is like asking what you should do if Christianity doesn't work. I am not saying that violence is never justifiable, and I know that it is no use leaving the problem to the theologians; when the moment comes you don't always have time to ask an expert or to hold a theological debate with yourself. I *am* saying that some of the efforts people make to use Christian principles to justify violence suggest that there is something seriously amiss in the heart of the person doing the justifying.

I have always felt that the presence of Christianity as a fundamental force in Waldorf education is not something to be diffident or defensive about. Rudolf Steiner once remarked that in view of the way in which names become associated with stereotypes it would be a good idea to change the name of anthroposophy regularly. I must confess that I find it very difficult to imagine a succession of new names for Christianity. At the same time I recognize that acknowledging the Christian basis of an anthroposophical school in which a large proportion of each section of the community—faculty, parents and students—is made up of people who are neither Christians nor anthroposophists has its problematical side. Perhaps when all else fails the best thing to do is to be honest. Honesty used to be the best policy but it now seems to be the policy of last resort. One faculty chairperson at the Rudolf Steiner School insisted that the school's policies should be kept as vague as possible because if they were set out clearly the parents might hold us to them.

The original Waldorf School was established for a community in which most people practised some form of Christianity. The original teachers were chosen and instructed by Rudolf Steiner. There was no doubt about the presence and influence of Christianity in the educational philosophy of the school and in the community of which the school was a part. Now we have many schools and communities in which Christians are in the minority. We don't do everything the way it was done in Stuttgart in the nineteen-twenties but the educational philosophy has not changed in any *fundamental* way. We do our best to staff the school with people who believe in, understand and practise this philosophy but we couldn't be exclusive even if we wanted to. People of all kinds of religions and backgrounds become interested in anthroposophy. We need them and we welcome them as long as they are good teachers. When there is a vacancy for a new teacher we advertise in the usual newspapers as well as in anthroposophical and Waldorf journals. There are applicants from the whole spectrum of religions, including atheism, many of whom find any form of esoteric spirituality repugnant, and most of whom have no knowledge of anthroposophy. We try to find good people who will do a good job in the classroom. That is the situation today, and there is much that is good about it.

And still, at the foundation of it all, there is Christianity. Christianity is an evangelical religion, but a school is no place for evangelism. It is also no place for denial. If the students want to know what your religion is, tell them. If the parents want to know about anthroposophy and Christianity, tell them, even if you don't happen to be a Christian yourself. If you give a December concert of Christmas music, call it the Christmas Concert. If you don't want to do that, perhaps you shouldn't be singing carols. Doing one thing and calling it something else is not honest. Do your best to give honor to the names of Christianity and anthroposophy by what you do as well as by what you say. Let what is at the foundation shine through the whole edifice.

> A city that is set on an hill cannot be hid.
> Neither do men light a candle, and put it under a bushel, but on a candlestick; and it giveth light to all that are in the house.
> Let your light so shine before men, that they may see your good works, and glorify your Father, which is in heaven.[78]

(ii)

Esoteric Christianity and the College of Teachers

You might think that a decade of training in materialistic science and a life spent largely in the company of amiable agnostics would have seriously undermined my capacity to believe in miracles, but I have found that the better (as it seems to me) I understand what Christianity is all about, the easier it is to accept the miraculous. It isn't that I believe that reports of apparently miraculous happenings are generally true. I suspect, although I don't know, that most of the reports are the fruits of wishful thinking. But I do think that for anyone who believes in any kind of spiritual world, in an existence that goes beyond the purely physical, the miraculous is neither inherently impossible nor even improbable.[79]

It is the task of a scientist to discover and work with the laws of nature. Since conventional science excludes all knowledge of the activities of God and His angels it is hard to see how a conventionally educated scientist could have any opinions about miracles. The Goethean scientist works with the idea of a constant stream of spiritual influence flowing into the material world. From that point of view the whole of nature may regarded as one huge miracle. A miracle, however, is generally thought of as something out of the ordinary, something that happens rarely and, when it does happen, startles people so much that they are impelled to go around telling everyone about it.

My idea of Christianity is that a Christian is someone who believes that Jesus Christ was exactly what he said he was. Our primary reason for being Christians is that we think that Christianity is true. When the high priest asks, "Art Thou the Christ, the Son of the Blessed?" and Jesus replies, "I am, and ye shall see the Son of man sitting on the right hand of power, and coming in the clouds of Heaven", we joyfully assent. We also believe that our impulses to tell the truth, feed the hungry and take care of friends and strangers are signs that the risen Christ is speaking in our hearts. We think that if Christianity ever became truly the religion of the people, the world would be a much better place, but we don't think that we could achieve the same result by leaving out all the difficult bits and simply adopting the moral teachings. Either Jesus was telling the truth or he was a madman. Those of us who think that he was telling the truth should have no difficulty in accepting the Immaculate Conception, the Virgin Birth, the miracle at Cana of Galilee and the raising of Lazarus. The intellectual objections that may have discouraged us at one time have been seen to be based on misunderstandings, and to be rather easily disposed of. Once you have accepted the realities of God and Christ you know that you have to tighten your seat belt and hold on to your hat, because you don't know what you are in for. But you also know that wherever the ride takes you, God will be with you.

Then, perhaps, you encounter anthroposophy and discover that Mary may not have been a virgin after all, that there were really two Josephs, two Marys and two Jesus children, that the great light that hovered over Bethlehem was the *Nirmanakaya* of the Buddha, that the miracles occupy an ill-defined region that seems to be reached by something disconcertingly close to nineteenth century rationalism, and that when you thought you were communing with God you were really talking to your angel. Steiner's insights sometimes have the effect of reconciling apparent contradictions between different biblical accounts of the birth, life and death of Jesus, and give vivid meaning to elements of biblical revelation that usually remain obscure or overlooked. They give pictures of the hierarchies and of spiritual currents that barely reach the surface of the gospels. Sometimes, however, they seem to be designed in order to get over non-existent hurdles. You may have worried quite a lot about the enormous differences between the descriptions of the nativity given by St. Matthew and by St. Luke, but the Virgin Birth and the other miracles may not have seemed problematical at all.

While you are wrestling with all this you realize that you also have to come to terms with reincarnation, karma, the details of the life between death and rebirth and the work of the hierarchies in the evolution of the world and the human being. This is not all. Perhaps the most difficult thing is that you get the impression that anthroposophists think of Christ as *a* great spiritual being.[80] That indefinite article on its own may be enough to give you the feeling that anthroposophy is not for you. The continual references to the members of the hierarchies as *Gods* do not help.

Please understand that what I am talking about cannot simply be described as the difficulties of an *orthodox* Christian who encounters anthroposophy. There are many orthodoxies—each movement has its own set, including the anthroposophical movement. ("Orthodoxy is my doxy; heterodoxy is another man's doxy."[81]) Real Christians, who believe in the divinity of Christ and the propriety of miracles, have become rather rare and may well be repelled by anthroposophical Christianity. The decent pagan, the milk-and-water Christian and the spiritual butterfly have different sets of problems. People whose beliefs are matters of social and intellectual convenience are apt to be more disturbed by the real Christians' beliefs than by anything that they find in Steiner, and to tell us that all the major religions are really the same thing. "We all believe in the same God, don't we?" Well, of course, they aren't and we don't. The only possible excuse for saying that all the religions are really the same thing is that many people who call themselves religious don't believe in anything in particular at all. This should not be surprising since, as Steiner said, we are all infected with atheism; *all*, including anthroposophists. The idea of believing something simply because it is true is very difficult for some people to comprehend.

I shall return to the problems of being a committed Christian in the old-fashioned sense but first I have some other fish to fry.

◆　　◆　　◆

Having been present at faculty meetings in which these matters were discussed I know that all of these points of view are represented and that there are significant numbers of teachers who would like to suppress all reference to Christianity in Waldorf literature. How to deal with this situation is a question which the College of Teachers has to face up to, and the make-up of the College is sometimes part of the problem.

It is easy to say that ideally the College should include only those who are active students of anthroposophy. Clearly this would not mean that the members would agree about everything, but it would enable them to work with shared perceptions and intentions. My experience has been that Colleges usually include teachers who have embraced the life of the school without becoming committed to anthroposophy and that this situation has advantages as well as disadvantages. It depends very much on what kind of work the members expect to do. To go into this question thoroughly would require enormous space, so I'll sketch a polarity. The polarity may be a simplification, but it is genuine. The College of Teachers of which I was privileged to be a member for many years had a strong tendency to oscillate between two extremes and I have seen similar tendencies in my travels as a visiting teacher.

One extreme is the position that the College should concern itself with purely spiritual matters and leave the nuts and bolts to other groups or individuals. The other is that the College should take the responsibility for everything, right down to the shape of the bathroom doorknob. Proponents of the first view say that it is the task of the College to maintain the lines of communication with the spiritual beings who hover over the school, and if the College doesn't do it perhaps no one will. The school is a spiritual organism and there must be an organ to receive and cherish what flows in from the spirit. Those who take the second view say that decisions about the nuts and bolts *are* spiritual matters and would probably agree with Ralph Vaughan Williams: "If you hold your head in the air and think great thoughts when you should be doing the obvious chores of life the great thoughts won't come." The real problem is that although both sides are right the result of trying to work from both points of view is often pure frustration. There are simply too many pressing questions and too little time. In my days as College Chair I had the unenviable task of setting agenda priorities and often found that there were thirty or forty items that people wanted to discuss and that at least half of them were considered urgent. This resulted in some questions remaining in limbo for months at a time and others having to be decided by committees which had to go beyond their stated terms of reference in order to do so. Meanwhile teachers, including the chairperson, would plaintively remark that we really ought to find time for study and meditative work. A College study was, in fact, instituted, but it frequently had to be sacrificed before the rush of untoward events. The effort to please everyone had the effect of pleasing no one, and the displeasure was sometimes expressed in very acidulent tones, with the chairperson on the receiving end. As we used to say in the Vietnam era, "Everything is possible for those who don't have to do it." The conclusion that I reached at that time was that the College has to decide to go one way or the other and, whichever course is adopted, to follow it wholeheartedly.

One factor that goes into the decision is the constitution of the College. If the College decides to commit itself to esoteric work it may be that there are members who feel that they cannot participate. This may well be the situation of the mainstream Christian, as well as the pagan, the social Christian and the sipper. Some may decide to leave the College and there is a danger here. In some schools there is already a sense of alienation between the College and the school community as a whole, and this may be exacerbated if the College becomes an esoteric body to which some of its members feel unable to contribute. If this course is adopted and committees are established to make vital decisions previously taken by the College it is still essential to provide some kind of forum for general discussion. I speak out of long and hard experience on this matter. Teachers, whether or not they are College members, need to have a sense of participation in the whole process of the school. In the 1980's the idea of having a committee for everything got entirely out of control. Some schools had more committees than faculty members and the result was chaos. The opposite idea of entrusting the administrative role of the College to a small number of appointed officers is equally dangerous, but for different reasons. In relation to the ideals of the Waldorf Movement it is a great step backwards towards the nineteenth century concept deplored by Rudolf Steiner.

If, however, the College decides that its task is to oversee the operation of the school as a whole, not, perhaps, worrying about doorknobs, but making life-and-death decisions about teachers, students, visitors, curricula, events and so on, the essential lifeline to the spirit of anthroposophy may be lost in a welter of administrative details.

My opinion, for what it's worth, is that it would be a great mistake for the College to withdraw from its general decision-making responsibilities. I also believe that there is no single form that is going to provide a solution to the problem of doing everything that ought to be done in a Waldorf School, no matter how many beautiful and enlightening diagrams are drawn on blackboards by consultants for the edification of teachers. The College needs to make decisions for the school *and* to maintain its ties to the spiritual world, and the members of the College need to remember that they are teachers and have a responsibility to the children they will be greeting again on the day after the meeting. Getting home late at night after an exhausting sequence of meetings, too tired or agitated to think about tomorrow's lesson, is not going to help anyone. Waldorf teachers, even class teachers, usually have lighter teaching loads than teachers in other schools, but the work is undoubtedly harder.

The demands of the situation probably mean that members of the College will have to arrange another meeting, regular but not necessarily every week, in which they do their esoteric and meditative work. Members who do not feel that they can take part in this work will still be able to participate in the work of the College to which they originally committed themselves, and those who attend the second meeting will be free to proceed in whatever way they consider appropriate. Something akin to this system was tried at the Rudolf Steiner School in the 1980's but its success was sadly jeopardized by its having arisen in a politically loaded, *ad hoc* way and not as a consciously considered decision of the College.

It is important to note that if the second meeting is instituted, College members must feel absolutely free to take part or not to take part. If it is simply a matter of study there shouldn't be a problem, but if teachers are asked to bring their meditative lives to the meeting some may legitimately decline. In *The Knowledge of Higher Worlds* Steiner makes it abundantly clear that one's meditative life is a very individual matter. The decision whether or not to bring it in any way into the group is very much a matter of temperament and soul-configuration. The hysteroid is likely to find the process debilitating. Dealing with the inner pain of everyday existence is hard enough already. Consciousness, not only of one's own inner being but also of the radiations of others, can become so intense as to be almost intolerable. This is something that epileptoids often find hard to understand. At a College meeting about ten years ago the position was stated very clearly by a well-known member of the Waldorf community. "I find that the only way I can become really conscious of my inner being is by bumping into someone else's." The hysteroid who has been bumped into often takes days to recover. My impression is that with the exception of *The Knowledge of Higher Worlds* most of Rudolf Steiner's advice was given with epileptoids in mind. This makes sense, since there are far more epileptoids than hysteroids.

◆ ◆ ◆

Finally I'd like to return to the dilemma of the "real" Christian, the one who actually believes that Jesus Christ is the Son of God and experiences the Holy Spirit as a living presence, and for whom the miraculous is not a problem. Experience shows that Rudolf Steiner's insights into child development and the nature of the human organism are valid. We have individual experiences of life, we share the experience of working with the children, and we see that Steiner is right. But some of us have also been affected in deep, lasting and wholly beneficial ways by our experiences in the church, and the church that we know and love is something quite different from the one about which, to the best of my knowledge, Rudolf Steiner never found a good word to say. Evidently Steiner experienced something dogmatic, dead, ossified and impervious to the spirit. Many people have had exactly the opposite experience, finding church communities that are warm-hearted, friendly, undogmatic (in the loose sense of the word) and open to the spirit, and ministers who are people of great wisdom and insight.

To be undogmatic in this sense does not mean to believe that all viewpoints are equally acceptable. In its best sense a dogma is the statement of a perceived truth that you cannot give up without fundamental damage to your whole picture of existence—something like an axiom in Euclidean geometry. So when I say that the church, of which my experience has been almost entirely within the Anglican Communion, is undogmatic, I am using the word in its broader sense. We are not subjected to authoritarian, arrogant assertions of unprovable principles. In the old sense the church *has* to be dogmatic—in other words there are rock-bottom beliefs without which we should merely have a social organization rather than a church. We believe in the Holy Trinity, the incarnation, the crucifixion, the resurrection and the forgiveness of sins. We hold that these things are not just matters of religious preference, but that they are objectively true whether people believe in them or not. As anthroposophists most of us[82] believe in these five items as strongly as Anglicans, Roman Catholics, Methodists and Baptists but the anthroposophical interpretations are very different and almost certainly incompatible with those of mainstream Christians. I do not believe (*pace* Canon Shepherd) that a marriage could possibly be arranged between Anglicanism and anthroposophy, but quite a number of anthroposophists have become members of the Anglican Church, including, notably, Owen Barfield. This indicates, as I have found in my own life, that there is something missing from anthroposophy or, at least, from the way in which anthroposophy has incarnated. Anthroposophy, when thought of as a path of spiritual development which people follow freely, is admirable and irreproachable. Anthroposophy as a body of knowledge is a different matter. As Owen Barfield remarked, Rudolf Steiner did not want us to *believe* the things that he told us, but fundamentalism and dogmatism are as likely to be encountered among anthroposophists as among the members of any of the churches. There are certain things about which I think Steiner was demonstrably mistaken. He said many things which people mistake for anthroposophical knowledge but which merely reflect the general climate of belief in which he grew up. No matter how hard we work there are things that he has told us in which belief would be merely a matter of trust. I don't think that was what he wanted. But I do think that it must be very hard for anyone to work at a Waldorf school without accepting and working with the anthroposophical foundations of the pedagogy. I have to say "must be" rather than "would be" because many people who work at Waldorf schools are actually in that position.

◆ ◆ ◆

The College of Teachers can legitimately decide to concern itself with the esoteric and the life of meditation, but its members may need to remind themselves that there are dangers attendant on such a course in addition to the possible exclusion of some deeply spiritual people. Some of these dangers were clearly identified by Rudolf Steiner. Egoism and feelings of superiority tend to arise insidiously and unconsciously. We mustn't forget that the person who sweeps the floor and spends the evening watching Joe Millionaire may be spiritually healthier than the teacher who spends the evening and much of the night preparing, reading lectures and meditating.

13

Epilogue

(i)

Frankie and Johnny
(She shot her man...)

This story has no moral,
This story has no end;
This story only goes to show...

Like the story of Frankie and Johnny, this loose succession of episodes and editorials has no moral, and although it comes to an end it can never be finished. People don't get shot but they do get fired, and not always with enthusiasm. The Frankies and Johnnys of this world are always with us, and so are the cycles through which Waldorf Schools pass. History repeated itself in many ways during the last dozen years of my stay at the New York Rudolf Steiner School, but always with a new twist. Some very surprising things happened, in fact, but many of those who saw the school through some of its darkest times still work there today and do not need to be additionally burdened by the task of coming to terms with such recent history. I have not yet come to terms with it myself. If I ever do I may write about it, or I may decide that it doesn't really matter, especially since a great deal of what went on had nothing whatever to do with Waldorf education.

When I first decided to hitch my waggon to the star of the Waldorf movement I didn't think much about how the association was likely to end. Now I can't help thinking of the rueful lovers in the well-known song:

> It was just one of those nights,
> Just one of those fabulous flights,
> A trip to the moon on gossamer wings
> Was just one of those things.
> If we'd thought a bit of the end of it
> When we started painting the town,
> We'd have realized that our love affair
> Was too hot not to cool down.

It wasn't "just one of those things", but there is some analogy. Between the golden visions of the neophyte and the sober realities of the old hand falls the shadow. Like romantic passion, the flaming ardor of the recent convert has to suffer the effects of a great deal of cold water. Love, as Ambrose Bierce remarked, is a form of insanity easily curable by marriage. At the end of the song the analogy weakens a little.

> So goodbye then and amen,
> Here's hoping we meet now and then,
> It was great fun, but it was just one
> Of those things.

I certainly did have fun, and a great deal more, in my days as a Waldorf teacher, but I am not by any means the only teacher who has puzzled over the question of why so many colleagues, including many of the movers and shakers whose names appear prominently in the history of the school, have left with difficult feelings not untinged by bitterness. I admit to difficult feelings, although not to bitterness. Anyone who makes a deep commitment to Waldorf education, or to anything else worth the devotion of a lifetime, is well advised to remember Captain Scott's verdict on his polar expedition: "We took risks; we knew that we took them; things have come out against us; therefore we have no cause for complaint." It is not uncommon for people leaving an institution to which they have devoted their lives to feel that the object of their labors is going downhill or progressing rapidly in the wrong direction. We are apt to have the impression that when we were young, people were much more inclined than the present generation "to build and not to count the cost, and to labor and not to seek for any reward." "In my day", we have been overheard saying, "we expected to give a lot more and receive a lot less." Well, in terms of what is recordable as statistics, we certainly did receive a lot less. For the rest I can only say that the discordance between my views of what it means to be a Waldorf School and those of the people in charge at the time of my departure made for considerable discomfort on both sides and accounts, in part, for the fact that neither I nor they have not felt any particular desire to "meet now and then."

◆　　　◆　　　◆

Soon after arriving in this country I went to a conference in Spring Valley. Among the activities was eurythmy with Sabina Nordoff. Two short sentences from those sessions made a deep impression on me. One, from Rudolf Steiner, was, "Becoming aware of the idea in reality is the true communion of man." I resist the temptation to comment on this observation because, in its way, it is the whole of anthroposophy. The other was, "That which is sacrificed must be recognized or it comes back knife in hand", which, I believe, is from Laurens van der Post. At first I thought that the knife mentioned in this statement was destined for the hearts of those who had failed to recognize the sacrifices of others. Later I found it hard to understand how I could have been so obtuse. The dagger is destined for the hearts of those who made the sacrifices.

The contribution of a teacher, whether for a few years or a lifetime, is not measured by words spoken at a farewell party. Words, of a sort, are easy to come by. I am not talking about success or failure, approval or disapproval, but about giving up part, perhaps the largest part, of one's life for an ideal. (When I reread this sentence "ideal" is apt to morph into "ordeal".) For some people work is a job, but for Waldorf teachers it is a calling. You may find that you don't like some of the terms and conditions but you keep slogging away at it, even in the face of cold showers of amorphous disapproval from your colleagues, because you are doing the best you can and what else is there? Recognition is not in the words. It is in the way people treat each other and respond to each other's needs. There is something about anthroposophical endeavors that makes it very hard for people to work together. A Christian Community priest told me forty years ago that where the spirit is revealed there is always turbulence, but what I have seen over the years is something less elevated than turbulence. As Screwtape says in one of his letters to Wormwood, the downward path is made of small steps, not major events. That, I believe, is equally true of the upward path. Associations, conferences, keynote speakers and weekend retreats have their uses and are apt to make people feel really good for a day or two, but their efficacy is very limited. There is no sudden *eclaircissement* that will reverse the field for the Waldorf Movement, only small daily acts of heroism in the trenches.

One thing that I was not too obtuse to recognize long ago—before, in fact, I had ever heard of the Waldorf Movement—is that it is foolish to expect gratitude or recognition. Anything of that nature that comes along is a matter of grace, not of desert. Gratitude, in any case, is a very dubious matter, unless it is spontaneous and not a burdensome expectation. Recognition is a state of mind, and can't be forced. Others have experienced its lack far more seriously than I have, and have left the school with far more difficult feelings. On the whole I would say that Waldorf teachers do not treat each other well. There was a greater spirit of cooperation and camaraderie in the other schools where I have worked. This is not something that can easily be cured, but recognizing that the problem exists would be a start.

(ii)

Prognosis

At one time I had the impression that many anthroposophists thought that Rudolf Steiner's insights would lead to a new temporal world order and that the Waldorf Movement would play an important part in bringing this about. I'm not sure whether I ever believed this but, forty years on, I know that I don't. Anthroposophy resembles theoretical physics in that it is difficult, and differs from that discipline in that the anthroposophical path requires much more deep-seated characterological adjustments. The millions of people whose goodness of heart and simple faith in the Lord Jesus Christ qualifies them for whatever heaven lies in the future of the human race will never become anthroposophists. It may be that most of them remain asleep in the ways in which Steiner wanted us to be awake, but they are under Christ's protection.

There are now fifteen times as many Waldorf schools in North America as there were when I arrived in Manhattan, but the expansion has been attended by a significant degree of dilution. When I joined the movement the proportion of teachers working out of a deeply felt anthroposophical impulse was considerably greater than it is now. The schools do the best they can with the good and well-intentioned people who make themselves available, but something vital has been lost in the transition. Anxieties about enrollment and finance sometimes give rise to a desire to present the school as a smart college prep school and keep the real basis of the pedagogy so far in the background that most of the parents and even some of the teachers are unaware of it. An opposite and equally unfortunate tendency is to loosen the rigorous anthroposophical foundations to the point where the school can appeal to almost anything that can vaguely be described as spiritual.

If we have to admit the fear that the Waldorf Movement is losing its commitment to its anthroposophical foundation, we must at the same time acknowledge a similar anxiety about the Anthroposophical Movement as a whole. We hoped that anthroposophy would change the world, but we begin to see that the world has changed anthroposophy. Anthroposophy asks what we can do for the world and its evolving, and the world asks, "What's in this for me." The world acts according to a principle analogous to that of the increase of entropy, always seeking to degrade the specific and demanding into the generic and comfortable. The path of development indicated by Rudolf Steiner for the individual and for the world as a whole is very specific, very demanding and not at all comfortable, whereas the object of some "spiritual" movements seems to be simply to make their adherents feel good. There is nothing inherently wrong with feeling good unless you regard it as an end in itself.

I said at the beginning that I did not altogether agree with the Bishop of London. Some things *do* matter, and one of them is that there are still Waldorf teachers who know that what they are doing is not only for these particular children on this particular day or even for this particular life, but for the whole future of humanity in whatever cycles of the earth are still to come. Such an attitude may result in an excess of seriousness, so it is as well to let it be combined with large measures of humor and humility.

(iii)

Requiescant

I write this epilogue in the shadow of the catastrophe of September 11, 2001. Having been a child of the blitz, familiar with the sight of stretchers and demolished buildings, and having grown up in the shadow of an impending (as we were told) nuclear cataclysm, these are not the circumstances under which I should have chosen to experience old age. The situation does, however, put things into perspective. What Henry Barnes and Keith Francis said to each other in another age of the world seems of little import at a time when the bodies of three thousand people lie buried under the enormous rubble of the World Trade Center. I have always believed that being killed is not the worst thing that can happen to a human being, but in the face of such an onslaught of death and heartbreak my opinion is another thing that seems of little value.

That war is an image of life is a thought that is as old as war itself. To the Christian, life is a battle against evil, whether we sing *Vexilla regis prodeunt*[83] or Onward Christian Soldiers. We are constantly at war within ourselves. The evil that we fight is both inside and outside. Our highest aspirations are, as Rudolf Steiner said, always in danger of being brought low by egoism, selfishness or hypocrisy, and under the rubble there lies the spark of the human spirit, the desire to know and face the truth.

De mortuis nil nisi bonum[84] is a saying that is honored as much in the breach as in the observance, but it appears to be the watchword of institutions intent on repainting the past. People are often remembered for things that they did not do and qualities that they did not have. Real flesh and blood characters have been described as if, during their life on earth, they were already endowed with harp, wings and halo. I have heard and seen accounts of events through which I lived during my tenure in New York which were in large part fictional. A few days ago I came upon a different slant on the old saying: *De mortuis nil nisi veritatem.*[85] It may be, as Melissus of Samos said twenty-four centuries ago, that nothing is stronger than what is true, but truth is a gentle, introspective giant unless unduly provoked, whereas falsehood circulates and multiplies very easily. "A lie", Winston Churchill is reported to have said, "gets halfway around the world before the truth even has a chance to get its pants on."[86] How much truth do even the most perceptive of us actually know about anyone? It is hard enough to be quite sure of what actually happened, let alone what all the motivations and subplots were. The safest recommendation would undoubtedly be *de mortuis nil*. Unfortunately, as has often been said, burying the past, whether through silence, forgetfulness or falsification, condemns us to repeat it.

I have tried to report what I actually experienced, including what I thought and what other people said. If I were charged with having made a selection of events that presents a negative image of life at a Waldorf school I'd have to point out that there was an educational purpose behind the selection and that there is much, much more. The remarkable thing, which attests to the strength of Rudolf Steiner's insights about the child, is that so much good work is done in the schools over so much background noise. The better the work is, the more likely it is to have been accomplished unobtrusively, without fanfare or historical record. When we are weary of the praises of famous men we can think of those that have no memorial, but are perished as though they had never been. Achievements that no one ever knew about cannot be distorted or spruced up for the public record. Most of what is done by teachers and much of what is done by administrators answers to this description. Unpublicized as it is, however, it does live on in the hearts of the students. "Their bodies are buried in peace, but their name liveth for ever more."

◆ ◆ ◆

Wilfred Owen, one of the poets of the First World War, wrote of the truth untold:

> "Strange friend", I said, "Here is no cause to mourn."
> "None", said that other, "save the undone years,
> The hopelessness. Whatever hope is yours,
> Was my life also: I went hunting wild,
> After the wildest beauty in the world,
> For by my glee might many men have laughed,
> And of my weeping something had been left,
> Which must die now. I mean the truth untold,
> The pity of war, the pity war distilled...
>
> Then, when much blood had stained their chariot wheels,
> I would go up and wash them from deep wells,
> Even with truths that lie too deep for taint.[87]
> I would have poured my spirit without stint...
>
> I am the enemy you killed, my friend...
> Let us sleep now...

Every day we kill each other a little. Every day we play tricks with the truth and some of it is lost or buried. I wanted to do my best to preserve a little of it. In its small way it seemed important. I wanted to do it lightly and lovingly but it was not easy and I could not always succeed. However tangled our motivations, and however imperfect the fruits of our labors, I believe that all of us who appear flickeringly in these pages tried to work for the good.

Endnotes

1. In the sense of being supine, not mendacious.
2. Pronounced with the stress on the second syllable.
3. *More Poems*, VI.
4. Including, of course, the President of the United States of America.
5. I have found that, in the minds of many of my anthroposophical friends, *passion* is almost as bad a word as *intellectual*. In this passage I am using the word in the sense of what the American Heritage Dictionary calls "boundless enthusiasm", which is closely allied to what Steiner called "flaming enthusiasm", the quality of soul that leads people to get straight on with the job without pausing to remove their jackets. "Enthusiasm", however, doesn't quite do the trick. To speak of an "enthusiasm" for truth and justice, eurythmy or cricket doesn't convey the degree of urgency and commitment implied by "passion". People are "enthusiastic" about lite (ugh) beer and the latest style in jeans. The real problem may be that for many people the kind of "passion" uppermost in their minds is the sexual one.
6. The physicists' situation is parallel to that of the late nineteenth century mathematicians who found that they had to treat such things as "point", "line" and "plane" as undefined terms. See p.168.
7. Steiner, *Goethe the Scientist*, Tr. Olin D. Wannamaker, Anthroposophical Press, New York, 1950, p. 205.
8. Rudolf Steiner, *Anthroposophy and Science*, Stuttgart 1921; Mercury Press, Spring Valley, NY, 1991.
9. See, for instance, Steven Weinberg, *Dreams of a Final Theory*, Vintage, New York, 1994, p.174.
10. First, second and third class honors are the equivalents, respectively, of *summa cum laude, magna cum laude* and *cum laude*.

11. Subsequent history suggests that they did. The Britannia was a beautiful and very successful turbo-prop airliner known as "The Whispering Giant."
12. Revised and expanded edition, Norton, New York City, 1996.
13. L-head.
14. Gloucestershire for a miniature, grass-covered hillock.
15. Now published under the do-it-yourself title of *How to Attain Knowledge of the Higher Worlds*.
16. This undoubtedly explains why composers of the baroque and classical periods were so fond of the repeat sign.
17. See *The English Hymnal*, No 489, O.U.P. 1933: Tune, Aurelia.
18. On re-reading this I realize that it may give an incorrect impression: Mrs. Lord was a good and likeable person and she was doing exactly the kind of job that Mrs. Myrin had hired her for.
19. I have no intention of casting a slur on the ancient and honorable status of the guru. I am simply using the word in the mundane, colloquial sense into which it has fallen.
20. University of Chicago Press, 1936.
21. Rudolf Steiner, *The Philosophy of Freedom*, translated by Michael Wilson, Rudolf Steiner Press, London, 1964. This great and fundamental work has recently been tendentiously and inexcusably retitled, *Intuitive Thinking as a Spiritual Path*.
22. Constant, that is, in proportion to the quantity of radioactive substance present.
23. The latest figure (2002), based on radiation thought to be left over from the "Big Bang", is 13.7 billion years.
24. The double truth theory is said to have arisen from contradictions between philosophy and theology, with particular regard to difficulties encountered by medieval philosophers in making the experience of individual thinking and the doctrine of individual immortality philosophically respectable. The figure chiefly—and mistakenly—associated with the double truth heresy is the Arabian-Spanish philosopher Averroes (1126–1198), who, in fact, explicitly stated that truth cannot contradict

truth and that philosophy and revelation must be in accord. (See *Averroes on the Harmony of Religion and Philosophy,* tr. G. F. Hourani, London, 1961.) Whether anyone really thought it possible to believe each of two statements that contradict each other is an open question, but in the thirteenth century suspicions of adherence to the double-truth theory and kindred heresies were apt to result in penances, trials and excommunications. Those suspected of such departures from orthodoxy were lumped together as "Averroists", in spite of the fact that Averroes had explicitly stated that truth cannot contradict truth.

25. This is why I wrote *From Abdera to Copenhagen.* (Available from AWSNA Publications) See p. 150-152.

26. Rudolf Steiner Press, London, 1963. The original German edition was published in 1909 and there have been many subsequent editions, recent ones using the word *Esoteric* instead of *Occult.*

27. "He who is noble and of humour placid, needs no blunt instrument or prussic acid." (Horace's Ode, Wimsey's translation.)

28. I may be mistaken about the name of this periodical. Unfortunately I made the mistake of lending my copy to someone.

29. See p. 183.

30. Owen Barfield, *Romanticism Comes of Age*, Rudolf Steiner Press, London, 1966. Barfield's profession was the same as Lyell's…

31. Quoted in Philbrick and Holmyard: *Theoretical and Inorganic Chemistry*, J. M. Dent, London, 1932.

32. *Sic*: the English persistently use collective nouns as plural subjects.

33. This reminds me of the famous baseball story, supposedly true, of the exasperated manager who bawled out a non-performing player and ended with the question, "Which is it, ignorance or apathy", to which the player replied, "I don't know and I don't care."

34. From an address given by Rudolf Steiner at Stuttgart in 1919.

35. Also known as Puncification.

36. John Mortimer, *Rumpole and the Summer of Discontent*, in *Rumpole à la Carte*, Penguin, 1990.

37. See the discussion on p. 123.

38. I may be wrong about this. The only evidence I have for "Schwabian" is my recollection of a light-hearted conversation in which Swain Pratt, speaking to William, said something like, "You Schwabs are all alike."
39. This was written a few weeks before the terrorist attacks of September 11, 2001 made us all think about such problems with renewed urgency.
40. "The generosity with which [Johnson] pleads the cause of Admiral Byng is highly to the honor of his heart and spirit. Though *Voltaire* affects to be witty upon the fate of that unfortunate officer, observing that he was shot '*pour encourager les autres*', the nation has long been satisfied that his life was sacrificed to the political fervour of the times." James Boswell, *Life of Johnson*, Charles Dilly, London, 1791.
41. A. E. Housman, *Last Poems, IX.*
42. Not "badly"—if you feel badly you have a hard time finding your way around in a dark room.
43. Keith Francis, *Death at the Nave*, Writers Club Press, New York, 2002.
44. See p. 133.
45. i.e. they can be hammered into shape.
46. *Sic*; the relative pronoun gets its case from the clause that follows it. The *whole clause* is the object of the preposition *on*.
47. See, for instance, the *Arabian Nights* story of the young woman and her five lovers.
48. Anyone who suspects me of mixing my metaphors is requested to remember what happened to Lord Nelson.
49. *Timeo Danaos et dona ferentes.*
50. The other Clerihews have been censored.
51. Peter Wimsey's mother, the Dowager Duchess of Denver, pondered the question, "How does one reduce a circumstance?" I feel that a similar problem attends the process of straitening one. Perhaps one gives it a narrow look.
52. This remark is based on observations at Kimberton, Spring Valley and Garden City.
53. Or, as Sir Donald Tovey used to say, *ad vitam aut culpam*—for life and as long as one's indictable offences remained undiscovered.

54. It is worth pointing out that when, a few years later, it was decided to pay the teachers throughout the year, this did not constitute a raise: teachers were—and for all I know till are—paid only for ten months, but the salary was spread over twelve.
55. In 2003 it was 45%, a figure stated in the 2003 Annual Giving Report. Between 1965 and 2003 a nine-fold increase in faculty salary expense was accompanied by a sixteen-fold increase in all other expenses.
56. Business manager, financial secretary, registrar and two receptionists.
57. Pertinacious readers will discover that I change my mind later on.
58. Having been taken to task for not attributing this observation to Mark Twain, I feel impelled to mention the editorial comment in Bartlett's *Familiar Quotations*, ed. Justin Kaplan (Little, Brown and Co., Boston, 1992): "A famously [ugh] moot quotation frequently attributed instead to Charles Dudley Warner (1829–1900)." When I was a boy everybody seemed to regard it as common lore.
59. See Note 46.
60. I owe this phrase to Johnny Root.
61. Except insofar as dullness in this incarnation may be attributed to one's achievements, or lack thereof, in a previous one.
62. *The Advancement of Learning*, Oxford Authors, O. U. P., 1996, p.140.
63. Rudolf Steiner Press, London, 1966.
64. As of 1996
65. Teachers' Conference at the Stuttgart Waldorf School, 4/25/23. At that time physics and chemistry were closer to unification than Steiner realized.
66. Al Tomlinson at the Garden City School. Al was an excellent and very resourceful teacher.
67. Princeton University Press, 1985.
68. Mellor's idea of an "elementary" course corresponds roughly to what the modern American student might meet in an undergraduate chemistry course.
69. Keith Francis, *From Abdera to Copenhagen*, AWSNA Publications, 2003.

70. I didn't choose these items at random. A visiting Goethean scientific expert who came all the way from England to teach the tenth grade chemistry main lesson block was ignorant of the first two, a chemistry Ph. D. was confused about the third, one of the chief American Waldorf chemistry authorities was mistaken about the fourth and a high school chemistry teacher I met at Highland Hall couldn't manage the last. This is just a short selection of the howlers that I have encountered while visiting science main lessons.

71. A few years ago, when I was doing a stint at the Highland Hall School, the question of making a decision and sticking to it produced the finest confusion of metaphors that I have ever heard. Dana Williams, the eurythmist, informed us that we were "skating on thin eggs" and added, "When it hits the fan you have to take it on the chin."

72. E. A. Karl Stockmeyer, *Rudolf Steiner's Curriculum for Waldorf Schools*, translated by R. Everett-Zade; The Steiner Schools Fellowship, London, 1969.

73. A lecture has been defined as a way of getting the notes from the notebook of the teacher into the notebook of the student without going through the mind of either. Fortunately I never used a notebook.

74. I have noticed that Americans are less inclined than their English allies to use a term of mild abuse as a form of endearment.

75. There are, of course, other books on the subject.

76. In 1933 the Nazis forced the distinguished Jewish mathematician, linguist and philosopher, Kurt Grelling, (1886–1942) into retirement. After *Kristallnacht* Grelling worked in Belgium, where he was arrested in 1940 on the first day of the German invasion. For two years he was interned in Vichy France, where he was joined by his wife, Greta, an "Aryan" who had heroically refused to divorce him. Friends in the USA secured a visa and a position for him at the New School in New York City, but by then it was too late. Kurt and Greta Grelling became part of the "final solution" and died in the gas chambers at Auschwitz in September, 1942. (From a biography by A. S. and E. H. Luchins)

77. I have used quotation marks for 11, 6 and 5 in order to emphasize that they are being used as labels. Later in the process they are used as num-

bers. Trying to figure out when to use quotation marks is a confusing business and later in the paragraph I simply gave up on it.
78. Matthew 5: xiv-xv.
79. A great deal of light has been shed on the problem of miracles by Emil Bock (*The Three Years,* 1948) and C. S. Lewis (*Miracles,* 1947)
80. This unwelcome *a* appears in the translation of St. John 1: i used in the Christian Community services. "…and the Word was *a* God."
81. William Warburton (1698–1779), quoted by Joseph Priestley.
82. I have to say "most of us" since it is not unknown for an anthroposophist to reject the centrality of Christ's incarnation and to claim to have received communications from Rudolf Steiner indicating that he now realizes that he was mistaken.
83. "The banners of the king go forth." (Gregorian hymn)
84. Literally, "About the dead nothing if not good."
85. "About the dead nothing if not the truth." Unfortunately I can't remember where I saw this.
86. Quoted in the 2002 *Old Farmer's Almanac.* Presumably Lady Churchill was responsible for the distinctly American diction.
87. If you are familiar with Benjamin Britten's setting of these words in his *War Requiem,* you will notice that the composer made a number of changes, including the substitution of *wells* for *truths* in this line.

0-595-30960-7

Printed in Great Britain
by Amazon.co.uk, Ltd.,
Marston Gate.